Biblical Hermeneutics Rediscovered - 19

An Interpretation of First Corinthians

A Moral and Theological Clarification of Paul to the Ecclesiastical Discrepancies

Jojan Jose

CWI

Christian World Imprints

First Published in 2019 by

Christian World Imprints
Christian Publishing & Books from India
H-12 Bali Nagar, **New Delhi-110015**
info@christianworldimprints.com
www.ChristianWorldImprints.com
Phone: +91 11 25465925

ISBN: 978-93-5148-321-2 (HB)
ISBN: 978-93-5148-322-9 (PB)

Printed in India.

Contents

Foreword-1

I am privileged to have received the opportunity to read the book *An Interpretation of First Corinthians: A Moral and Theological Clarification of Paul to the Ecclesiastical Discrepancies* written by my dear friend and colleague Jojan Jose. Personally, I know Jojan from 2002 and he and his family serve as resident faculty at the Mission India Theological Seminary, Nagpur in the department of New Testament and Mission. Previously, he wrote a book on the *Concept of God in James; Importance and Implications* and this is his second attempt. In this scholarly work, Jojan has tried to take the readers into the deep exegetical exposition of the book in his words without losing its originality. There is no doubt that the author has successfully explicate the sound doctrinal regulations Paul gives to the Body of Christ.

The 1st epistle to the Corinthians is an exemplary letter written by the apostle Paul to resolve the doctrinal and practical issues rising within the church. Paul emphasizes on 10 different problems and gives a clear Godly insight on these issues: a sectarian spirit, lawsuits, marriage and divorce, fornication, incest, eating food offered to idols, wearing of the veil, the Lord's Supper, spiritual gifts, and the resurrection of the body. In the second chapter, the author elucidates the text by bringing out the issues addressed by Paul in the Body of Christ and the solutions to it as a pastor and mentor. In chapters 1-4, he is warning against the divisions in the Church. In chapter 5, he is instructing the church to exercise their authority to drive out sexually immoral people and warns the Body of Christ about the dare consequences of compromising such sins. Paul is warning against lawsuits in chapter 6: 1-11, and thereafter from verse 12 he is warning against fornication. In chapter 7, he gives direction about the principles of marriage, and from verse 25 – 40, he is giving instructions for the unmarried and the widows. Paul exhorted the church in regard to food and idolatry in chapters 8-10, and in chapter 11, he talks about the context of head covering and Lord Supper. In chapters 12 – 14, Paul emphasizes on the equal importance of exercising the spiritual gifts as well as the necessity of mutual understanding and proper order in the Body of Christ. In chapter 13, Paul talks about 'love', which is declared as the cardinal virtue of Christian life that binds everything together in perfect harmony. Chapter 15 is Paul's powerful refutation of the Corinthian's disbelief in regard to the resurrection of the dead, which questions Jesus' resurrection and the gospel preached by Paul and his fellow workers. Paul declares the authenticity of resurrection to its readers by affirming the resurrection of Jesus who is the first fruit of the dead, and gives a hope of a glorious everlasting life. Paul closes his letter by giving his travel plans and thanking people who stood with him in the ministry for the Lord's sake.

Jojan has taken a commendable effort in bringing out the originality of the text and literal exposition; it goes adjacent to the author's intent. He begins this book by giving an abridged introduction to the city of Corinth and then moves on to the analysis of 1 Corinthians and to its author. He has addressed the different matters of concern that Paul stated in his letter which he faced in the church, and has given an extensive and profound elucidation about it. He has been able to capture the heart of Paul in this book by accentuating the importance of the straightforward instructions of Paul for such moral and theological differences, which if not tackled with, could lead to disastrous outcome for the church. This book is insightful and informative for Biblical Students, Pastors, and laypeople that look forward to an in-depth study on 1 Corinthians. I congratulate Jojan for the tireless effort taken by him for this noble cause. This research will be a significant addition to the New Testament scholarship. Blessings!

Rev. P. D. Joseph
Chief Functionary
Mission India
Nagpur, MH.

Foreword-2

The first epistle to the Corinthians is one of the finest artistic compositions of Paul. The complex argumentations of the book, the raw display of the disposition of the church, and the sincere concerns of Paul are explicit in this letter to the Corinthians. Paul, the pastor of the church had addressed many issues of the church in this letter. In chapters 1-4, he tackled the problem of disunity in the church based on leadership issues. In 5:1-13, he exhorted about the incest matter. In 6:1-11, he wrote about the problem of lawsuit while in 6:12-20 he penned about the problem of prostitution. In chapter 7, he exhorted the church believers to remain in the condition that they were called. In chapters 8-10, he encouraged the strong people in the church to consider the weak in the area of eating food offered to the idols. In chapter 11, he discussed about the issues of head-covering and Holy Communion in the communal gathering. Similarly, in 12-14, he addressed the concerns of the proper use of spiritual gifts such as speaking in tongues, and prophesy. In chapter 15, he clarified the misunderstanding about the resurrection. Therefore, in First Corinthians, Paul deals with varied number of issues, which only display the immediate need for the epistle, and the concerns of Pastor Paul in addressing these issues.

The breadth and depth in addressing these issues are also varied that in some instances Paul used extensive materials with exemplifications and self-exemplifications in his exhortation (for example in chapters 8-10) while in some instances he just completed the discussion in just few verses (6:1-11). In some instances, Paul explicitly mentioned the problem (as in 5:1-13) but in some instances, he was more subtle (as in chapters 1-4). In some instances, he expressed his deep emotions (as in 5:1-13 and 11:17-34) while in some places he commended the church for their good behaviors (as in 11:2-16). Therefore, First Corinthians is a complex literature which demands careful reading and intuitive exposition.

Jojan Jose has taken this important task of interpreting this epistle in this book. His insightful comments, serious exegesis, sincere exposition, succinct background information, and perceptive analysis of the arguments are commendable. His elucidation of the text by bringing out the arguments of

Paul is deeply appreciable as well. His writing brings out the role of Pastor Paul in addressing the problems of the Corinthian church and displays his pastoral heart. Jojan makes it clear that Paul in this epistle does not shame the church or insult them but he writes the letter to restore them from the irregularities found in the church. He also bridges the gap from the text to the context by giving suggestions to present churches and their issues sporadically.

I am proud to say that Jojan was my student when he studied M.Th in New Testament in Hindustan Bible Institute and College, Chennai. His sincere attempt in writing an interpretation of First Corinthians is a welcome attempt and I am sure that it will be an important addition to the resources for interpreting First Corinthians for pastors and lay people.

Arren Bennet Lawrence, PhD
Assistant Regional Secretary
Asia Theological Association

Preface

Paul's letters to the Corinthians are the most captivating books in the New Testament and it remains as the supreme guideline to the New Testament churches for all time. Among the two, 1 Corinthians is a striking one for many reasons. The style of its composition, systematic arrangement of the issues and its presentation through the specific arguments that blended with strong words improved with solid correction, sharp sarcasm, and gentle comfort brands the letter a more interesting and attractive one to all the readers.

However, like other books in the New Testament, the socio-political, religious and economic background of the first Corinthians was entirely different from that of the present. Since the book was written to the people lived in an entirely different sitz-im-leben, it is important to know the background of the I Corinthians to understand the currents of the text in a better way. Though the present work is not a verse-by-verse exposition of the text, it offers a pure background exposition that goes very close to the author intended meaning by avoiding any kind of superficial treatment of the text. Though there are both the immediate and extended context, like many, I do strongly believe that there is only one interpretation for any text in the bible. The one interpretation must be the author intended meaning and any preacher and reader of the bible can only bring out the application from the text to the different context of his/her own or the listeners of his/her sermon. Thus, through *An Interpretation of First Corinthians: A Moral and Theological Clarification of Paul to the Ecclesiastical Discrepancies*, I have employed a pure exegetical exposition of the text to bring out the right meaning of the text than eisegesis.

Each section of this book is a result of the careful investigation of the text in its literal background. The specific and the supporting arguments of each unit vividly depicts the corrupted religious life setting of the Corinthian congregation and Paul's indication of the irregularities both in terms of their social and religious life and command for a holy living. Consequently, in its entirety, the work sheds light on the original background and the meaning of the text. A careful reading of the present work offers a better way for everyone to be away from any kind of interpretational misconceptions of the 1 Corinthians and to walk away from the pitfall of spiritualizing the text from its original meaning.

Introduction

Apostle Paul's writing in the New Testament is a unique contribution, as each of his letters addresses different aspects that are closely related to the early Christians with regards to their socio-political and religious life. All these writings are considered to be written for the purpose of reading aloud in the common gatherings of the early Christians. Thus, 1 Corinthians is also written to be read aloud in the congregation.

This book is reckoned under the undisputed letters and the first of the three major epistles (1 & 2 Corinthians, and Romans) of Paul. Though I Corinthians is primarily written to the church at Corinth, the content of the letter such as corrections, exhortations, warnings, guidelines regarding true Christian living, the hope of a Christian etc., are applicable for the 21st century churches all over the world. First Corinthians is known as, *the letter of correction,* which is very much evident from the content of the letter.

After the first Jerusalem council held in A. D. 48 (Acts 15), Paul began his second missionary journey (A.D. 49-52) to visit the churches in Asia Minor. On his way, he reached Corinth and stayed there with Aquila and Priscilla and taught and preached in the synagogues for eighteen months (Acts 18:11). Gradually, many people accepted the truth of the gospel of Christ. Many Corinthians, including the diaspora Jews accepted Jesus as their Lord, and the church was established. Until Jewish opposition became stronger, Paul stayed in Corinth, and then went to Ephesus.

It is believed that before writing 1 Corinthians, Paul had already written another epistle to the believers at Corinth which no longer exists (1 Cor. 5:9). However, after a while, Paul received a letter from Chloe's household addressing certain problems the church was facing [1-6 (1:11)] and also from some other members of the Corinth church asking for clarifications on certain questions [7-16 (7:1a)]. So, as a solution to the problems addressed, and an answer to the questions asked, Paul wrote this epistle to the church at Corinth.

There were **three** major problems the Corinthian church was facing during that time. They are:

Divisions (1:10-4:21): In this section, Paul deals with the problem of division in the church as reported by Chloe. Paul begins by sturdily exhorting them to be in agreement, and not to have any kind of division among themselves. He authenticates that there is no division among the apostles as the leaders of the church (3:9). Furthermore, he requests them to stop boasting about human leadership, and ends this section with a fatherly admonition.

Sexual Immorality (5:1-13; 6:12-20): This was a major issue in the Corinthian church. There are two kinds of sexual immorality which Paul discusses in these chapters, namely, incest and prostitution. Incest is a sexual relationship in the familial relationship such as parent, child, sibling, or grandchild. Concerning the seriousness of this sin Paul says, "the kind of this is not even found among pagans" (5:1). Then in chapter 6:12-20 Paul deals with the issue of prostitution within the church.

Lawsuits (6:1-11): Lawsuit was another serious problem in the Corinthian congregation. They were not serious about the aftermath of taking the issues of the body of Christ to the worldly judges. As in the earlier cases, it also is a result of Corinthian believers who were totally driven by human philosophy and worldly wisdom. Gradually their old ways of thinking and acting reinvaded into their life and the expression of the newness of life was broken. As a result they become like pagans and were envious and critical of their own fellow brethren in their religious and social life. Therefore, in chapter 6:1-11, Paul reminds them about the dare consequences of lawsuits in the body of Christ.

Apart from the above addressed problems, Paul received a letter from the congregation asking for clarifications on certain questions, such as:

Questions related to marriage (chapter 7): In this chapter, Paul gives advice to the married people, mentions some basic principles regarding marriage, and offers instruction to the virgins and widows.

Eating food offered to idols (8:1-11:1): In chapter 8, Paul deals with true Christian conduct where love plays a vital role than the exercise of knowledge. In chapter 9 apostle Paul talks about the proper exercise of Christian freedom and authority. In chapter 10:1-22, he talks about the sinfulness of idolatry and how it leads to self- destruction. In chapter 10:23-11:1 Paul discusses the issue of eating food sold in the marketplace.

Head Covering (11:2-16): This issue is presented in three subsections. Verses 2-6 deals with the argument from the perspective of culture; 7-12 deals with the argument from the point of view of creation, and; 13-16 details about the perspective of practicing correctness in the congregation.

The Lord's Supper (11:17-34): In this segment, Paul begins by discussing the misconduct practiced by Corinthians as part of Lord's Supper (11:17-22). Secondly, Paul discusses the right manners that must be practiced while conducting and participating in the Lord's Supper (11:23-34).

Spiritual Gifts (chapters 12-14): In these chapters, Paul deals with the misunderstanding of the Corinthian believers concerning the gift of speaking in tongues as the most important spiritual gift. Hence, Paul talks about varies kinds of spiritual gifts (12:1-11); the equal importance of those gifts in the church as the body of Christ (12:12-31); the supremacy of love over spiritual gifts (chapter 13); the need of interpretation of tongues in the congregation for the betterment of everybody present; and the need of order in church gathering and his exhortation to exercise the spiritual gifts according to its proper purpose (chapter 14).

The resurrection of the dead (chapter 15): The resurrection of the dead at the coming of Christ is the central aspect of Christian faith. So, to validate the fact of resurrection, Paul, first of all talks about the resurrection of Christ from the dead (15:1-11). Taking Christ's resurrection as an example, from 15:12-34, Paul discusses the certainty of resurrection. Further, in verses 35-49 he explains about the resurrection of the body and the assurance of victory over death (15:50-58).

Collection for the suffering saints in Jerusalem (16:1-12): This section includes procedure for the collection (16:1-4), and the travel plan for Paul's next journey (16:5-12).

This book provides a detailed background study of all the aforementioned aspects. It is an important study, because it offers a better understanding of the problems that were faced by the first century church at Corinth, and the questions asked to Paul by its congregation. Thus, this book is presented with the intention of helping the current readers of 1 Corinthians to read and understand it in its original background, and to draw applications to deal coherently with the present perils of the church.

City of Corinth: A Brief History

The history of Corinth falls back to the Bronze Age, and the information regarding the city is even mentioned in Homer's *Iliad.* The city was situated on the southwest of the Isthmus, the narrow land bridge that connected Northern Greece and Southern Greece, the Peloponnesus. Probably, this might have made Corinth a big commercial center in those days. Because of the distinctive geographical situation with crossroads and intersections between the east and the west and the north and the south, Corinth in the ancient world was a significant place of strategic position for commercial prosperity.

As mentioned above Corinth was situated on the Isthmus which is the master of two harbors. One of this leads straight to Asia and the other to Italy. This makes easy interchange of stocks from both the countries. Subsequently, O'Connor states "Corinth is called wealthy because of its commercial enterprises."[1] Apart from the sea port, in support of the commercial importance, the modern classical and archeological studies confirm that there was a roadway built across the Isthmus around 6th century BC. It was used for the conveyance of cargo ships. Slowly the city became the capital of the province of Achaea, and by 2nd century AD it developed as the largest city in Greece.

By the time Paul reached Corinth, the city had been a Roman colony, though formerly it was a Greek city conquered by King Philip II of Macedon in 338 BC, and subsequently ruled by his successor, Alexander the Great, from 323 BC onwards. Finally, the city was destroyed by Mummius[2] in 146 BC. However, the city was rebuilt after the traditional Roman grid pattern in 44 BC by Julius Caesar. Thus, it became a Roman colony known as *Colonia Lus Julia Corinthiensis* (the Corinthian colony is Julian praise).[3]

The people of Corinth comprised of diverse social stratum. It included a multitude of settlers such as Roman military and civil bureaucrats, ex-soldiers, freedmen, trade dealers, craftsmen, entertainers, logicians, educators, employees etc. Gallio, probably a civil bureaucrat,was one of the significant persons,as mentioned in Acts 18:12. The population of the city included a number of Jews from Israel, native Greeks, displaced persons, slaves, and people from many other countries bordering the Mediterranean Sea. The multifarious population in Corinth increased and strengthened the economy and spread the splendor of Corinth all over the ancient world.

Though Greek was regarded as the common language, Latin became the official language of the city. It is even evident in Paul's mention of some of the Latin names of people who lived Corinth, such as Tertius, Gaius, Quartus (Rom.16:22-23), Titius Justus, Crispus, and Fortunatus (Acts 18:2, 7; ICor.1:14; 16:17) etc.

The city of Corinth is often referred to as the city of fornication and prostitution. In those days, the Greeks used the phrase, *to live a Corinthian life*, to denote the city's immorality. Gordon Fee says, "The term 'Corinthian Girl' was known to be a synonym for a prostitute."[4] The sin of sexual immorality was at its heights, and it became a part of Corinth's culture of that time.

The immorality of Corinth was cultivated by the temples dedicated to Aphrodite, the goddess of love, which was known for its wickedness. Aphrodite was worshiped almost everywhere in the Greek world. It is believed that during the Greek period, the temple of Aphrodite had the presence of a thousand prostitutes. These women would walk the streets of Corinth every night in search of men who were willing to pay for sexual favors. Throughout Acro-corinth, such prostitution in the name of religion was very much prevalent and become an income generating source for the temple of Aphrodite.

Aphrodite was worshiped chiefly as the goddess of human love and was also venerated widely as a nature goddess. It was believed that she came from the sea and sailors prayed to her to calm the wind and the waves. The reputation for sexual opportunity was advertised on city's coinage with sexual coins depicting the cult statue of Aphrodite floating on the Acro-corinth, naked from the waist up, and armed with a shield. Sex service in the temple was a popular service attracting visitors and catering to people engaged in various pursuits in the city.[5]

The religious societies of Corinth were devoted to the worship of popular deities. Apart from Aphrodite, Corinthians venerated Asclepius, Apollo, and Poseidon. They also built altars and temples to the Greek god and goddesses such as Athena, Hera, and Hermes; and the Egyptian gods, Isis and Serapis.[6]Besides these assorted religious groups, the Jews in the city were given freedom by Julius Caesar to practice their religion, with the exception of staying away from the act of rebellion against the Roman government.

Thus the Jews built synagogues in Corinth for their common gathering, where they first invited Paul to preach, and later expelled him since Paul's preaching and teaching was contrary to the Jewish Law (Acts 18:12-13). Though the introduction of Christianity was not accepted by the Jewish community, the Gentile community in Corinth was ready to accept the Christian faith as presented by Paul (Acts18:8). Since Paul taught the Gentile regarding the inessentiality of Jewish Law, the Jews dragged him before Gallio. However, the church continued to preach the gospel without fear of death and the Lord added many to the church.

From Corinth, the gospel spread to its surrounding villages and cities, and also to many parts of the Mediterranean world. Unlike other churches established and visited by Paul, the church at Corinth was given priority by him. According to 2 Cor.13:1, Paul visited the church at Corinth at least three times. As a founding father of the church, Paul rebuked, corrected, and comforted them in difficult situations which they went through.

However, all that Paul had written to the church at Corinth has a never-ending significance to the universal church. The theological message set forth in this book is applicable to the troubled Churches and Christian communities of the present age, and the ages to come. Since the Corinthian church was situated in a city which had immense historical significance, this study is presented in its proper historical background to facilitate the contemporary readers to understand I Corinthians in a better way.

Endnotes

1. J. Murphy-O'Connor, *St Paul's Corinth: Texts and Archaeology* (Wilmington: Glazier, 1983), 53.
2. Mummius was a Roman statesman and general. He later received the agnomen Achaicus after conquering the Achaean League and bringing all of Greece under Roman control. In 154 BC, he was praetor in Hispania Ulterior and was the first Roman commander which dealt with the Lusitanian rebellion of 155-150 BC. In 146 BC, he was appointed to take command of the Achaean War, and having obtained an easy victory over the incapable Diaeus, entered Corinth after a victory over the defending forces. All the men of Corinth were put to the sword, the women and children were sold into slavery, and the statues, paintings, and works of art were seized and shipped to Rome. Corinth was then reduced to ashes. However, two of the ancient authors named Cicero and Dio Cassius gives account that the city was not completely destroyed.
3. Simon J. Kistemaker, Exposition of the First Epistle to the Corinthians, *BNTC* (Grand Rapids: Baker Books, 1993), 5.
4. Gorden D. Fee, *The First Epistle to the Corinthians* (Grand Rapids: Eerdmans, 1993), 27.
5. Davie E. Anue, ed., *The Blackwell Companion to the New Testament* (UK: Oxford, 2010), 420.
6. Kistemaker, *BNTC*, 6.

The Anatomy of 1 Corinthians

Before discussing the anatomy of Pauline epistle, it is important to know the genre of Pauline writings. Deissmann's understanding of 'letters' and 'epistles' made a sizeable argument among scholars regarding Pauline writings.[1] According to him, letters are understood as natural, daily, and situational; and epistles are more of mechanical, artistic, and literary. Therefore the question is whether to consider Paul's writings as "private personal letters" or not.[2] Paul's writings are undoubtedly private letters. But most of his writings were addressed to communities of Christian believers, and intended to be read aloud in their common gatherings. Therefore, they are considered both as letters and epistles.

Paul was very much concerned about the situation of the believers in the first-century churches. Hence, his writings were occasional, contextual, and addressed to the specific circumstances of his recipients. They are letters because it was written to different groups of people according to their troubled situations. On the contrary, these are epistles because Paul used many literary devices and techniques as he addresses the different conditions of the people, both, as individuals and community. However, generally, they are known as, epistles.

The Greek word *epistole*¯ ('epistle'/'letter') originally referred to an oral communication sent by a messenger. In antiquity, the term 'letter' was employed as an expansive description of different types of documents. It included a great variety of commercial, governmental, and legal documents, in addition to political and military reports, along with other sorts of communication. However, investigations of Pauline writings advocate that he borrowed Greco-Roman approach of letter formulae to meet Christian purpose.

To divide the anatomy of Pauline epistle into its relevant sections is still a debated issue in the scholarly field. The major question which arises is, is it composed of three, four, or five parts? Supporters of the tripartite form claim that the letter consists of only an opening, body, and closing.[3] On the other hand, those who hold the view of the letter having four parts suggest that it has an opening, thanksgiving, body, and closing.[4] Proponents who posit that

Pauline letters have five parts argue that there is a section of *parenesis* found between the body and closing.[5] Though the proponents of the second and third category have enough evidence to validate their arguments, the tripartite form (opening, body, closing) is the most accepted and supported method of Pauline method of letter writing. It includes the forms of the other two categories and stands very close to the Greco-Roman way of letter writing method. Therefore, in this book, the tripartite anatomical category to divide and explicate 1 Corinthians is followed.

Endnotes

1. Dictionary of Paul and His Epistles.
2. Dictionary of Paul and His Epistles.
3. John L. White, "Ancient Greek Letters." In David E. Anue ed., *Greco-Roman Literature and the New Testament* (Atlanta: Scholars Press, 1988), 97.
4. Jeffery A.D. Weima, *Neglected Ending: The Significance of the Pauline Letter Closings* (Sheffield: JSOT Press, 1991), 11.
5. Charles B. Puskas, *The Letters of Paul: An Introduction* (Collegeville: Liturgical Press, 1995), 207.

Chapter 1

THE OPENING

Identification of the Author, Co-author/Fellow-worker, Greetings, and Introductory Thanksgiving

1. Opening

1 Corinthians 1:1-9 is viewed as the opening or the introductory unit of the letter. The opening section of Pauline epistles usually includes the identification of the author, co-author/fellow worker, greetings, introductory thanksgiving, and the specific purpose of the epistle. On some occasions, Paul even expresses his relationship with his recipients in the opening. Sean Adams posits that in this course Paul mainly employs two main features. The first feature is the shared experience between him and the recipients to make a better rapport which helps the author to convey his message meaningfully to his audience. Secondly, various titles to increase his epistolary presence and influence to inspire and edify the readers to practice whatever is said to them.

One way or other, these components are well seen in most of Pauline writings and to some extent in 1 Corinthian as well.

1.1 Identification of the Author and Co-author/Fellow-worker (1:1-2)

This section is meant for the identification of the author and co-author. In Pauline writings, the usual epithet Paul employs to address himself is, 'apostle' or 'servant' of Jesus Christ. In 1 Corinthians he identifies himself as, 'an Apostle of Christ Jesus.' The phrase 'an Apostle of Christ Jesus' stands as the key expression which demonstrates the authenticity of his being. The Greek locution ἀπόστολος Χριστοῦ Ἰησοῦ (*apostolos christou* Iēsou), 'apostle of

Christ Jesus' falls under the genitive case which is the case of possession[1] in Greek grammar.

Therefore, his statement, 'Paul, called to be an apostle *of* Christ Jesus' shows the person to whom he belongs. In the beginning of the letter as he introduces himself to the audience he makes it clear that he belongs to Christ, as an *apostle of Jesus*. Further, he mentions that his apostleship came in accordance with 'the call' and 'the will of God' (Gal.1:15-16; 1 Cor. 9:1; 2 Cor. 11:5; Gal.2:6, 9). This bold statement of Paul had dual significance.

Firstly, it validates Paul's apostleship. Though Paul was a great missionary and established many churches in first early century, his apostleship was always questioned. The authenticity of his apostleship was questioned by the leaders of the early churches and by the believers (Acts 9:26; 1 Cor. 9:1-3). The major reason for this being, the absence of his actual accompaniment with Jesus and his original twelve disciples. He was not an eye witness of the life, ministry, and resurrection of Jesus Christ. Apart from this, Paul's inability to speak well was also taken as a reason for questioning his apostleship by his opponents.

Secondly, it validates the teachings, corrections, and warnings of Paul. The authenticity of his apostleship enhances weightage of his message to his audience. Once it is accepted by his audience, then it is imperative for them to accept and practice it. However, Paul never considered himself inferior to any other apostle, but was self-confident in realizing that, like Peter an apostle to Jews, he was called and appointed by Christ as an apostle to the Gentiles.

It is also customary for Paul to include the name of his co-author or fellow-worker in the opening of his letters (1 Cor.1:1; 2 Cor.1:1; Phi. 1:1; Col.1:1; I Thess. 1:1 etc.). Paul always gave his name at the beginning of his letter and frequently gives the name/s of other church leaders who joined him in the writing.

In 1 Corinthians, he includes the name of Sosthenes. Sosthenes is depicted as the co-worker/co-sender of the letter, therefore, he must have been with Paul in Ephesus. However, Paul excludes him from the word order seen in the introductory words, and presents him as 'our brother.' It suggests that Sosthenes is a Christian and a well-known figure to the believers in Corinth. It is also assumed that this Sosthenes was the ruler of the synagogues in Corinth who was beaten at the court of Proconsul Gallio by the opponents of Paul and became a believer and a local church leader (Acts 18:17). It is possible that he became one of Paul's regular 'helpers' or 'scribes', or a source of information about the church at Corinth.

Though there is no firm evidence that this was the same individual Luke mentions in Acts 18:17, the identity of Σωσθένης ὁ ἀδελφὸς (*Sosthenēs hŏ adelphos*), literally, Sosthenes the brother, adds weightage to two factors. First, the definite article before the term 'brother' (ὁ ἀδελφὸς - *hŏ adelphos* - lit. the brother) suggeststhat he is already a well-known personality to the reader as a specific companion of Paul. Second, the transformation of a former synagogue ruler at Corinth to the Christian faith, and as Paul's companion, provides an affecting reminder of the power of the gospel of Christ Jesus at the very beginning of the letter.

Scholars raise many other reasons why Paul includes him in the opening of the letter without connecting him to Acts 18. W. A. Meeks posits that he might be one of Paul's 'staff' or a regular 'co-worker,' like Timothy and Silvanus who assisted Paul in other instances.[2] According to A. C. Thiselton, Paul mentions the name Sosthenes because "from the beginning, the Pauline mission was a collective enterprise with someone as a staff."[3] However, Paul utilized corporate leadership to plant and nurture Christian communities in urban and rural areas throughout his ministry.

Another unique aspect seen in Pauline epistle is his way of addressing his audience. In I Corinthians, after introducing himself and his co-worker, Paul addresses his recipients by employing three phrases such as, 'the church of God,' 'sanctified,' and 'the saints' (1:2).

Firstly, by stating that they are τηε ἐκκλησίᾳ[4] τοῦ θεοῦ (*tē ekklēsia tou theou*), 'the Church of God,' Paul equates the Corinthians with his state of being. In the beginning of the letter Paul authenticates his being by stating that he is an 'apostle of God.' In the same way, by using the Greek locution, Paul here emphasizes who they are, and to whom they belong. By addressing the Corinthians as 'the church *of* God,' Paul highlights that they are 'the Church' and they belong to 'God.'

Secondly, the phrase ἡγιασμένοις ἐν Χριστῷ 'Ιησοῦ (*ēgiasmenois en christō Iēsou*), 'who are sanctified in Christ' falls under the dative case,[5] which indicates the place or the sphere in which the action has taken place. Thus, stating, 'who are sanctified in Christ,' Paul means to explicate where they are sanctified, and that is, ἐν Χριστῷ 'Ιησοῦ (*en christō Iēsou*), 'in Christ Jesus.' Through this declaration, despite their frequent quarrels, factions, and immorality, Paul describes the Corinthians as those who have been sanctified in Christ Jesus.

Finally, Paul, by stating κλητοῖς ἁγίοις (*klētois hagiois*) 'called to be saints' indicate the purpose of their sanctified position in Christ. Here Paul says, you are the church of God, sanctified, and are called to be saints, just as I am called for the apostolic witness. Thus, Paul reminds the Corinthians that it is imperative for them to maintain the lifestyle which reflects their given status in Christ Jesus.

1.2 Greetings (1:3)

Corresponding to the identification of the author, co-author, and recipients; greetings also plays a vital role in Pauline epistles. In I Corinthians Paul greets his recipients by employing the terms, *grace and peace*. The salutation of grace and peace is found in numerous Pauline letters, such as, Rom. 1:7; 2 Cor. 1:2; Gal. 1:3; Eph. 1:2; Phil. 1:2; Col. 1:2; 1 Thess. 1:1; 2 Thess. 1:2; 1 Tim. 1:2; 2 Tim. 1:2; Titus 1:4; and Phil. 1:3, usually with the dual reference to God our Father, and Lord Jesus Christ.

In Hellenistic world, the term χάιρειν (*chairein*), 'greetings,' was commonly used by people to greet each other (Acts 15:23;23:26; James 1:1). This term is derived from χάρις (*charis*), means 'grace.' On the contrary, the Jews greeted each other with the term *shalom*, which means 'peace'. However, the early Christian Church used both the expressions in the epistolary literature by inserting 'grace' first and then 'peace' to maintain the theological consistency in its form. In substantiating this, Lenski says that "grace is always first, peace always second."[6] Further, he explains that grace is the source of peace and without grace there is and can be no peace. So, Paul, who is well aware of this tradition practiced by the early Christian community, links both, grace and peace together in the greeting section of his epistles.

Paul, further, supplements, ἀπὸ θεοῦ πατρὸς ἡμῶν καὶ κυρίου 'Ιησοῦ Χριστοῦ (*apo theou patros emon kai kuriou Yēsou Christou*) 'from God our Father and Lord Jesus Christ (1:3b),' to grace and peace. In this phrase 'God our Father' and 'Lord Jesus Christ' serves as the 'genitive of source,' the ultimate source from where the head nouns 'grace' and 'peace' derives. This gives us the idea that, as a father, God gives grace and peace as a gift to his children through Christ Jesus.

1.3 Introductory Thanksgiving (4-9)

Almost all Pauline letters have a thanksgiving section in the opening, for thanking God on account of his blessings to the recipients. At the same time, it is noted that for Paul, these words are not merely a part of his letter format. It is assumed that Paul really prayed for his congregation and thank God for their life. However, it was fairly typical of ancient letters in the Hellenistic period, to begin with, a thanksgiving to their god and goddesses for the personal benefits received. Paul adopts this Hellenistic epistolary model for Christian purpose. He frequently uses it at the beginning of his letters to express his gratitude to God, the Father of Jesus Christ, for what God had affected in his life, and in the lives of his readers. However, he was not a slavish imitator of this epistolary form, but the structure of his writings was highly developed and sophisticated.

Unlike the Hellenistic thanksgiving section, Paul's thanksgiving section can be categorized into two. First, it begins with thanksgiving and concludes with a ἵνα– clause [or its equivalent] means, 'in order that'/'that,' which spells out the content of apostle's intercession for the reader as seen in Phil 1:3–11; Col 1:3–14; 1 Thess 1:2–3:13; 2 Thess 1:2–12; 2:13–14; Philem 4–7; Eph 1:15–19 etc. Second, this too begins with thanksgiving, but concludes with a ὅτι – clause (*hoti*) such as: 'that,' 'because' and 'since', which notes the reason for the expression of gratitude (Rom. 1:8-10).

The thanksgiving section of I Corinthians falls under the latter category mentioned above. The section commences with a verb of thanksgiving in 1:4a, and concludes with *hoti,* 'that'in 1:5a, whereby the reason for his expression of gratitude begins. The section begins with the verb Εὐχαριστῶ (*Eucharistō*), 'I give thanks.' The expression of this word shows the pastoral heart of Paul towards the Corinthian Church. On the contrary, the ground on which Paul is thanking God must also be noted, since some members of the Corinthian church caused him sorrow with divisions, immorality, and other issues among them.

Kistemaker suggests that Paul's heart is filled with gratitude because God chose to call them out of the immoral and idolatrous atmosphere to be a part of his family.[7] It is remarkable that chapter 1:4b adds weight to Kistemaker's argument, wherein Paul thanks God for 'the grace that has been given to the Corinthian believers through Christ Jesus.' This is the second time Paul mentions the term 'grace' in the opening section of his letter (vv. 3 and 4). This shows the importance Paul gives to the concept 'grace.' Therefore, it illustrates that Paul is amazed at the grace of God that has been given to the Corinthian believers in Christ (location/sphere) in the form of spiritual gifts.

Further, in chapter 1:5a,[8] with the expression *hoti* (that), Paul starts to express specific reasons for his thanksgiving because they have been enriched by God in every aspect of their lives. It is sure that Paul, by saying, 'enriched by every aspect' does not mean about the material possessions of Corinthians. However, as he mentions 'the spiritual gift' in v.7, it is evident that he is talking about the various spiritual gifts (12:4-31) with which the Corinthian church is blessed. Both the adjectives used in the phrase ἐν παντὶλόγῳ καὶ πάσῃ γνώσει (*en **panti** logō kai **pasē**gnō sei*), 'in ***all*** speech and ***all*** knowledge,' adds weight to the abundance of the spiritual blessings they possess *in Christ.*

'Speech' and 'knowledge' had a unique significance in the Hellenistic world. Both these aspects qualify a person in terms of his/her rhetorical skill. Garland quotes B. Peterson's description as he says:

> In Hellenistic society the practice and expectations of rhetorical eloquence were pervasive. Not only were political leaders expected to speak persuasively and eloquently, but so also those who claimed authority in philosophy and religion. Among such people, there was great competition, and success depended upon one's ability to express the power of the divine in his or her performance—not only through miracles but also through rhetorical performances.[9]

However, Paul makes a distinction between rhetorical eloquence and the exercise of the spiritual gifts. Even when he exercised these gifts, he was not led by the wisdom of this world, or by his own abilities (2:1-4, 13; 4:20; 13:1; 14:1-12, 28). As spiritual gifts, supporting Paul, Garland describes 'speech' as spiritual speech which refers to tongues and prophecy seen in I Corinthians 12:10,28; 13:1-2; and 'knowledge' as the spiritual insights referring to the understanding of all mysteries seen in 5:6; 6:2,3,9,15,16,19; 8:1-6; 13:1-2,9,12,16 etc.[10] However, as Paul commends them about the enrichment in their 'speech' and 'wisdom', it is understood that it surpasses the speech and wisdom of the world in every aspect.

Verse 7 explains how the Corinthian believers as a single entity are enriched in their speech and wisdom. Says Paul, "just as the testimony of Christ has been strengthened among you." The verb ἐβεβαιώθη (*ebebaiō the*), means, 'strengthened' or 'confirmed.' Since the verb (strengthened) is in aorist indicative passive, it is sure that it talks about the action done in the past. Further, as Paul employ the term ἐν ὑμῖν (*en humin*) 'in/among you,' he uses it in the plural form. So, it emphasizes that the testimony of Christ was strengthened not among *some of them,* but *among all of them* in the past.

Thus, by adding the term, 'just as' at the beginning of v.6, Paul explicates the way how God blessed all the believers in Corinth with spiritual gifts. Just as they are *all* strengthened by the testimony of Christ Jesus (1:6), [in the same way] they are *all* enriched in their speech and knowledge (1:5). The former one talks about what happened in the past, and the latter talks about its effect. However, as Brown comments, the greatest spiritual gift with which they were enriched has become the greatest strength and liabilities to the Corinthians believers,[11] about which Paul elaborates in this letter.

1.4 Specific Purpose

As stated above, the spiritual gifts which the Church at Corinth received from God were not only a blessing, but it also caused liabilities. Though the Corinthian church was blessed with all kinds of spiritual gifts, they failed to understand the truth that, with more privileged comes more responsibilities. They failed in their responsibility to exercise those gifts in accordance with its purpose and importance. As Carson argues, Paul in the thanksgiving section indirectly signals about these issues, which he deals further in the letter.[12] Though Paul doesn't mention about all the issues he is going to deal with, the specific purpose of the letter is implicit in the Thanksgiving section (4-9).

> 4 I give thanks to my God always for you because of the grace of God that has been given you in Christ Jesus.
>
> 5 for in every way you have been enriched in him, in speech and knowledge of every kind-
>
> 6 just as the testimony of Christ has been strengthened among you-

> 7 so that you are not lacking in any spiritual gift as you wait for the revealing of our Lord Jesus Christ.
>
> 8 He will also strengthen you to the end, so that you may be blameless on the day of our Lord Jesus Christ.
>
> 9 God is faithful; by him, you were called into the fellowship of his Son, Jesus Christ our Lord. (I Cor. 1:5-9)

In vv. 4-7, Paul talks about the blessings the Corinthians possess in Christ Jesus from God. In v. 7, Paul specifically emphasizes that they do not lack any spiritual gifts, however, possessing these gifts they are just waiting for the *parousia*. On the other side, Kistemaker points out that, even in such a context, Paul does not consider them blameless. For in v. 8 Paul mentions, "He *will* strengthen you to the end, *so that* you *may be blameless* on the day of our Lord Jesus [Christ].[13] Paul writes using the future tense, which hints that presently the church is not keeping the code of conduct about which Paul extensively deals in the body of the epistle.

Therefore, despite dealing with the issues and answering their queries, Paul's main purpose in writing this letter was to exhort them to be blameless for the coming of Lord Jesus for which they were eagerly waiting. Although Paul deals with several issues, the unifying theme of the epistle is the practical implication of progressive sanctification in the Christian community, or, corporate holiness.

Endnotes

1. In possessive genitive head noun will always possess by the genitive. Therefore, in 1:1 Paul says, 'he belongs to Christ Jesus.'
2. Meeks, W. A., *The First Urban Christians: The Social World of the Apostle Paul* (New Haven: Yale University Press, 1983), 133–34.
3. Thiselton, A. C. *The First Epistle to the Corinthians: A Commentary on the Greek Text* (Michigan: William B. Eerdmans Publishing Company, 2000), 72.
4. The term *ekklēsia* is an expression used in the Hellenistic world as a technical word to refer to the political or guild meetings. But by the middle of the first century, Christians began to refer this term to denote their own assemblies as the church in Christ with the understanding of the root word (*ekk* – out of, *kaleō* - call) which means, a group of people called out for a particular purpose.
5. In Greek grammar Dative is the case of indirect object. It gives the idea of place/sphere/location [in- eg. I am *In* Christ], the idea of instrument [by- eg. He is sent *by* God], and the idea of true dative [to/for; eg. service *to/for* the saints].
6. R. C. H. Lenski, *The Interpretation of First Corinthians* (Minneapolis: Augsburg Fortress, 2008), 28.
7. Simon J. Kistemaker, Exposition of the First Epistle to the Corinthians, *NTC* (Grand Rapids: Baker Book House, 1993), 31.
8. All the passages in the book are quoted from RSV Bible translation unless otherwise mentioned.

9. David E. Garland, I Corinthians, *Baker Exegetical Commentary on the New Testament*, (Grand Rapids: Baker Publishing, 2003), 34.
10. Garland, I Corinthians, *BECNT*, 34-35.
11. A. R. Brown, *The Cross and Human Transformation: Paul's Apocalyptic Word in I Corinthians*, (Minneapolis: Fortress, 1995), 71.
12. D. A. Carson, I Corinthians, *New Bible Commentary: 21 Century Edition* (USA: InterVarsity Press, 1994), 7.
13. In the original text (Greek), Christ is given in parenthesis.

Chapter 2

THE BODY

Solution to the Problems and Answer to the Queries

2. The Body

The second part of Paul's letters is commonly known as the 'body,' which deals with the main contents of the letter. This part of Pauline letters demonstrates considerable variety according to the purpose and nature of its writing. All Pauline letters were written with different purpose that makes his letters unique from each other. Sometimes, determining the purpose and the beginning of the body of each letter is a difficult task. However, according to P. T. O'Brien, there are four possible ways to find out the opening of the Body of Pauline letters.[1]

They are–the sections/verses begin with the *Parakaleo sentences* ("I urge you, my Brothers," as seen in 1 Cor. 1:10; 1 Thess 4:1; Rom 12:1); the *Disclosure formula* ("I /we want you to know," Rom 1:13; Gal 1:11; Phil 1:12); the *Joy expression* (Philem. 7); and the *Expression of astonishment or Statement of compliance* (Gal 1:6; 1:8-9). While most of the Pauline epistles begin with the disclosure formula, the body of I Corinthians begins with the *parakaleō*.[2] The sentence, "I appeal to you, brothers and sisters," presents Paul's call to the Corinthians to listen to his teaching and return to the right code of conduct of Christian life.

The body of Pauline letters is generally much longer than the typical Greco-Roman letters which are normally limited to one or two sheets. Therefore, while comparing Pauline Body with that of the Greco-Roman letters, it enhances our understanding of the teachings, exhortations, and theology of the early Christian community in terms of their thinking and how it distinguishes them from the surrounding environment.

Mostly, the body of Paul's letters includes two key sections. The first section consists of doctrinal teachings, and the second, his encouragement to live their life based on the teachings. However, unlike other letters of Paul, as mentioned previously, the body of I Corinthians reflects different situations under two main groupings–problems communicated by Chloe's household to Paul (1:10-6:20), and queries asked to Paul by the Corinthians themselves.

2.1 Problems

The problems communicated by Chloe's household mainly include three categories: divisiveness in the church, disorders in the church due to sexual immorality, and, failure in solving their personal dispute among themselves.

2.1.1 Division (1:10-4:21)

Paul, first of all discusses the problem of division in the church that mentioned in 1:10-4:21. It seems that the problem of division emerged in the church because they started to see Christian ministry in the Greek sense. Greek world considered wisdom as an important virtue. Even, Paul in 1 Corinthians 1:22, says "For Jews demand signs and *Greeks seek wisdom*." As we analyze the context, we understand that the problem of division rose among them because of their choice of different leaders, based on their worldly wisdom and speech. In chapter 1:12, Paul mentions four leaders, namely, Paul, Apollos, Cephas [Peter] and Christ.

2.1.1.1 The Fact of Division

Some reasons why believers in the church at Corinth were divided are as follows:

The Pauline group: This group of believers accepted the apostle Paul as their leader, based on the fact that he was their spiritual progenitor. Apostle Paul had established the church at Corinth during his second missionary journey. He stayed in Corinth with Aquila and Priscilla, and taught and preached in the synagogue and to the people outside. Subsequently, many Corinthians, including some among the diaspora Jews, accepted the gospel and became believers of Jesus Christ, and the church was established. Within a few years, the church flourished with many kinds of spiritual gifts and material blessings too and was able to support the suffering saints at Jerusalem, the cradle of Christianity. However, the authenticity of Paul's leadership was questioned few among them on the basis of lack of his physical company with Jesus Christ and his inability to speak eloquently. Because of this reason, the anti-Pauline group claimed Apollos as their leader.

The Apollonian group: This group questioned the authenticity of Paul's leadership on the basis of the major reason that he was not an eloquent speaker. So they chose to follow Apollos, an Alexandrian Jew, an evangelist, and a friend of Apostle Paul, above all a gifted speaker /trained rhetorician.

While Paul was on his third missionary journey, Apollos had reached in Ephesus and started teaching boldly in the synagogues. As per Acts 18:24-28, he was a learned man, an eloquent preacher, and well-versed in the scripture. He taught accurately the things concerning Jesus and powerfully refuted the Jews in public, proving from the scriptures that Jesus is indeed their promised Messiah.

Nevertheless, based on Acts 18:24-28 and Acts 19:1-7 we learn that Apollos' teachings were 'incomplete,' because of which Aquila and Priscilla had to spend some time with Apollos in Ephesus and explain to him the way of God more accurately (Acts 18:26). After this incident, Apollo went to Achaia and continued to proclaim Jesus as the Messiah, powerfully refuting the Jews in public. It could be possible that Apollos had not imparted to his hearers the additional insights he received from Aquila and Priscilla, but departed to Achaia shortly after receiving it. For, while Apollos proceeded to Corinth (Acts 19:1), Paul had reached Ephesus, and found that the believers at Ephesus had not even heard about the Holy Spirit. However, during Paul's absence, Apollos' mission in Corinth was a success, and there emerged a faction who were in favor of Apollos' leadership, based primarily on his rhetoric skill.

The Petrine group: This group claimed Cephas [Peter] as their authentic leader. Peter's original name was "Shimon" or "Simeon", and was later called as "Peter," which means rock. The Aramaic version of this name is *Kêpâ.* He is always listed first among the Twelve Apostles in the gospels and in the Book of Acts. He is also often mentioned in the gospels along with James and John, a special group within the Twelve Apostles. He was an important figure and a well-accepted personality among the early Christian community. Peter was an important spokesperson who spoke in favor of the Gentiles in the first Jerusalem Council.

Be that it may, there is no credible evidence that Peter ever visited Corinth. Though it is difficult to understand what this group represents, the reason could be anti-Paulinism, or the theological tension between Peter and Paul, or the hesitation of the Jewish community to unite with the Gentiles, or because of the physical company he had with Jesus. However, it is this writer's assumption that either one, or the combination of two, or all the above-mentioned reasons, might have caused this group to accept Peter as their leader.

The 'Christ' group: This group of believers within the Corinth church declared loyalty to no human leadership, but boasted of their commitment to Christ, and Christ alone. They appear to regard themselves as the most 'spiritual' group in the church. Theoretically speaking, this group of believers was the leftovers of all the believers who did not wanted to join either the Pauline, Apollonian, or Petrine groups.

In different sections of the main unit, Paul clearly explicates the dire consequences of divisions in the body of Christ [Church], and how a church leader must handle this.

2.1.1.2 Paul's Response

In responding to the problem of divisions in the church, Paul first of all discusses about the actual causes of the division. In this regard, Paul mainly deals with two main aspects. i) Erroneous view of the Christian message (1:18-3:4), and ii) Erroneous view of Christian ministry and ministers (3:5-4:5).

2.1.1.2.1 Against Erroneous view of the Christian Message (1:18-3:4)

In Chapter 1:18-2:5 Paul continues to deal with the problem of divisions in the church, focusing on the message of the cross which was foolishness to human wisdom. So, the main idea of this section is all about Corinthian's emphasis on human wisdom and the division caused against the simple truths of the gospel of Christ. Paul carefully deals with this with effective contrasts, recurrences, and by asking a series of thoughtful questions to the Corinthians. In doing so, he teaches that what is foolishness to the world (the preaching of the cross) is wisdom to God, and what is wisdom to the world (philosophy of man) is foolishness to God.

Paul begins v.18 by explaining his manner of preaching the gospel of Christ. Verse 18 is an explanation of v.17, and the conjunction for used at the beginning of verse 18 serves as a connecting link between verses 17 and 18. In the preceding section, Paul makes it very clear that he never tried to proclaim the gospel with eloquence. The simple reason is that, by using rhetorical skills or eloquent wisdom in preaching the gospel of the cross of Christ, Paul did not want to empty it of its power and glory. In humility, without adopting any kind of human wisdom, Paul preached the gospel of Christ to the Corinthians. Though the message of the cross was foolishness to those who were perishing, to those who believed, it became the power of God.

For the Jews, the message of the cross was a stumbling block because their Messianic expectations were entirely different from that which Paul presented to them. For the Jews, the Messiah meant power, splendor, and triumph. Whereas crucifixion was a symbol of defeat, weakness, and humiliation. Hence, the message of the crucified Messiah was a stumbling block to them.

The Greeks looked for wisdom. The ancient Greeks were attached to philosophy, around which their culture was built. The love of wisdom was an unavoidable aspect of their life. Their culture was surrounded with at least fifty recognizable philosophical movements, and each had its views of man's origin, significance, destiny, and relationship to the gods. At the same time, there were many factions also, each with its own leaders and supporters.

For these people, the redemptive value of Christ's death on the cross was foolishness. They considered Jesus as a criminal, for in those days, only such social deviates were crucified by the Romans. Though many of them, later on, got converted, few of these converts carried their spirit of philosophical factionalism into the church. Some of them still held on to the beliefs of their former pagan philosophy, and just could not get over their love for human wisdom.

For this reason, Paul strongly argues against their wrong understanding of the wisdom of God. To add weight to his argument, in verse 20 he further asks a series of questions to the Corinthians. The first question raised by Paul is, *Where is the one who is wise?* This question presents the first of three classes of learned people who lived in that day. However, a similar question is found in Isaiah 19:12. In the context of Egypt, the wise men were known as the soothsayers, medium, or magicians who promised to give them peace, comfort, and hope, but never produced any good. As Isaiah 19:14 says, without comprehending the ways of God, these wise men ruined the land of Egypt in all that they did, just as a drunkard staggers around in vomit.

Nevertheless, in verse 20, Paul by using the term 'wise men', possibly refers to the thinkers and philosophers of the ancient world who could not give any definitive solution to the problems faced by humanity. The three main questions in ancient philosophy were–*Who am I? Why am I here? Where did I come from?* No thinkers or philosophers could give a proper answer to these questions. However, Paul taught that Jesus through his words and deeds, and by giving his life as a vicarious sacrifice to save the humanity, declared the truth to the world, but the world considered it as, foolishness.

Secondly, Paul asks, *Where is the scribe (the expert in the Law)?* This question was targeted at the Jewish theologians of that day who were trained in explaining the Old Testament scriptures. Though the scribes were well-versed in the Law, they refused to accept the message of the cross as the fulfillment of their teachings. Thus, with all the knowledge they had, yet they perished in their ignorance for failing to recognize Jesus as the true wisdom of God who gives salvation to everyone who believes in Him.

Finally, *Where is the debater of this age?* This question is possibly intended to the Greeks, who were seekers of mystical and metaphysical interpretations. As Thiselton says, the term 'debater' is mentioned only once in the New Testament.[3] This makes it clearer that unlike the other two questions, the third question does not have any counterpart in the Old Testament. So, this question is probably addressed to the Corinthians themselves. The Greek word used for *debater* is συζητητὴς (*suzētētes*). It is often used as a pejorative term, "disputant, debater."[4] However, the term is technically used for 'a true seeker of truth.' It is often used in the Greek philosophical and patristic tradition to denote a Greek philosopher. They were the searchers, students who are constantly involved in serious arguments among themselves to examine the truths and philosophical thoughts of which the Greeks were so fond of.

All the three rhetorical questions asked by Paul vividly emphasize the futility of such learning in view of the message of the cross. Neither the wise men (the philosophers), nor the scribes (Jewish Scholars who are experts in the Law), nor the debaters of this age (the orators/the seekers of truth) actually had true wisdom. However, Paul does not imply that all wise men have left Corinth, but that their attempt to frustrate God's work with the wisdom of this world is futile. So, in asking the above-mentioned questions, Paul elevates the wisdom of God, its permanency, and its effect which is still in action to save all those who believe in Christ Jesus.

In verses 26-31, Paul makes a clear indication about Corinthian believers. Paul begins with a sensitive matter that personally concerns the Corinthian believers. Βλέπετε γὰρ τὴν κλῆσιν ὑμῶν, ἀδελφοί (*blepete gar ten klēsin umon, adelphoi*-Literaly, "for you see the call of you, O! brothers"). The verb Βλέπετε (*blepete*-you see) is considered both as *indicative* and *imperative*. By using this term Paul gives a strong indication of who they are, and a command to rethink about the call they have received from the Lord. He strengthens his argument by using another strong *vocative case,* ἀδελφοι-*adelphoi*, O! Brothers. In those days the term ἀδελφοι was used as an idiom to denote both men and women. In the vocative case (case of addressing), Paul usually employed this term to render his cordial greetings to the recipients. However here, the term is both in the indicative and imperative mood, presenting a strong warning and a call for true repentance.

Further, Paul reminds them about their humble origin. The elite of the first century were described as wise, influential in the political sphere, and well-born. In light of this, Paul mentions three things to remind them about their status at the time of their call. οὐ πολλοὶ σοφοὶ (*ou polloi sophoi*–not many of you were wise), οὐ πολλοὶ δυνατοί (*ou polloi dunatoi* – not many of you were powerful) οὐ πολλοὶ εὐγενεῖς· (*ou polloi eugeneis*-not many of you were of noble birth). Even at the time of Paul's writing, barring a few, such as, Stephanas (v.16; 16:17), Sosthenes and Crispus (synagogue leaders-vv. 1, 14), Gaius, and Erastus (Rom. 16:23), the church at Corinth mainly consisted of ordinary people. However, the powerful act of God, through Christ on the Cross, brought about a reversal of status in their social and spiritual lives. They were made wise, powerful, and noble in Christ and in the wisdom of God. God chose the foolish in contrast to the wise, the weak in contrast to the powerful, and the ordinary in contrast to the elite.

Paul also reminds them of the four-fold blessings which they had received from God, the source of their life. Firstly, the Corinthian believers received

God's *wisdom*. Through Christ Jesus, they became the recipients of this wisdom. Thus, the Corinthians were saved, not because of their intelligence or wisdom, but on the basis of what Christ did on the cross.

Secondly, they received God's *righteousness*. Righteousness is an external act by which a person is declared right with God. In Christ, we are made right with God. God is totally right and he will never vary from his righteousness. When anyone trusts in his Son Jesus, God shares his son's righteousness with them. Any worldly wisdom that a man possesses will never make him righteous before God. There exists no other source of righteousness, but Christ.

Next, they received God's *sanctification*. Sanctification is an internal state attained through the indwelling presence of the Holy Spirit in the believer. Paul makes it clear to the Corinthians that they are set apart and made holy through Christ by God.

Finally, they received God's *redemption*. 'To redeem' means to buy back. The term 'redemption' is drawn from the vocabulary of the slave markets in the Greco-Roman world. During Paul's time, by paying the required price, a slave could be redeemed (bought back) from their present circumstances under their current master, to a new circumstance under a new master. Paul reminds the Corinthian believers that God, in Christ, has purchased them back from the power of sin. Christ Jesus offered himself on the Cross and gave his life as a ransom by the will of God so that no one can boast in the presence of God.

In nutshell, in verses 18-31 Paul makes two main arguments.

1) Worldly wisdom and speech did not save anyone, but 'foolish' preaching which is God's power enabled them to know God (1:18-25).
2) The Corinth believers know God even though they were not mighty in worldly wisdom or speech. Thus, any boasting should be in the Lord only (1: 26-31).

Paul concludes the section by replacing σοφία (*Sophia*- wisdom) as the means of σωτηρία (*sōtēria* - salvation), and reiterates once again that, Christ Jesus is the true wisdom from God, who is also the source of their life (v. 30).

2.1.1.2.1.1 Paul's Illustration of the Insufficiency of Secular Rhetoric and Wisdom (2:1-16)

In chapter two Paul continues to deal with the problem of disunity in terms of their allegiance to human philosophers and leaders. He proves the insufficiency of secular rhetoric and wisdom for their improvement in unity, spiritual growth, and divine insights. Furthermore, Paul explains his own experience and the manner in which he approached them during his first visit.

Verses 1-3 talk about the initial entry of Paul in Corinth. In this section, Paul continuously uses the personal pronoun 'I' to describe his activity and the manner in which it was done. The root word κἀγὼ is employed to describe [*kago*-and I (*kai+egō*)] his activities in Corinth as he first reached there. His entry to Corinth was entirely different from that of the orators and philosophers of those days. In those days the orators and philosophers followed certain well-established *modus operandi*[5] when they enter into a city. They used to give eloquent speeches in praise of the city, its people, and about their own personal achievements. It was done with the intention of establishing their reputation, and to gain financial blessings as political orators, philosophers, and teachers of the rich. However, Paul had not followed these conventional ways of entry. The centrality of Paul's proclamation was about God, Jesus Christ, and Jesus' crucifixion.

Paul openly declares that he did not proclaim the mystery of God in lofty words of wisdom. Neither did he preach the gospel to them as an orator, or a philosopher. The phrase in verse 1, Κἀγὼ ἐλθὼν πρὸς ὑμᾶς (*kagō elthōn pros umas*–and when I came to you) gives us the understanding that he is returning to his own manner of preaching the gospel without persuasive wisdom, with which he began his discussion from 1:17 saying, Christ has sent me to proclaim the gospel not with eloquent wisdom, so that the cross of Christ might not be emptied of its power.

However, the notion in which he starts his discussion in 2:1 substantiate that he used to preach with eloquence and wisdom. Paul came to Corinth from Athens after having his encounter with the Athenian philosophers (Acts 17:16-34). Though he presented the gospel at Athens in an effective way, he did not get a good response from them; rather he was mocked by the Athenians because of their sheer unbelief. Though skillful orators were admired in the Hellenistic setting, Paul brought the message of salvation to the Corinthians in simple terms that everyone in his audience could understand.

For eighteen months Paul stayed in Corinth with Aquila and Priscilla and continued to proclaim the gospel of the cross. Paul along with Aquila and Priscilla formed the nucleus of the church in Corinth. As a result of Paul's preaching to the Jews and Greeks in the local synagogue– Titius, Justus, Crispus, Gaius, and Stephanas with their household believed in Jesus (Acts 18:7ff). By the time it came for Paul to leave Antioch, many Greeks and people of other nationalities got converted and became members of the church in Corinth. Paul credits his success by stating that these things happened, not because of his persuasive and eloquent speech or wisdom, but was a demonstration of the Holy Spirit's power.

2.1.1.2.1.2 Jesus, the True Wisdom Revealed through the Spirit (2:6-16)

In this section, Paul addresses all believers with regards to salvation. He differentiates between spiritual (divine) wisdom and worldly (admired) wisdom of the ruling class. In verse 6-8, Paul states that he not only proclaims the gospel, but also speaks of wisdom (σοφια), but only among the mature. This suggests that Paul categorizes the Corinthians in two, the ordinary Christians and the spiritually 'superior' class. However this should not be taken as a contradiction in Paul's teaching, but it was the rhetoric device (sarcasm) that he employed to mean just the opposite of what he appeared to say.

Professing that he teaches in σοφια to those who are 'mature' in spiritual status, Paul brings them under the category of *infants* who are incapable of understanding divine wisdom. In other words, Paul considers them as people of the flesh, rather than as spiritual people (3:10); and thereby validates his comment of 2:6a by saying, I fed you with milk, not solid food, for you were not ready for solid food (3:2). Though this argument of Paul cannot be considered as pure sarcasm, he cautions the Corinthians about their spiritual status, in light of their quarreling and boasting about different leaders.

Conversely, in verse 6b Paul makes it clear that the wisdom he speaks of is not like that of the orators who do so with the intention of becoming rulers. He then defines it in verse 7 that it is God's secret wisdom which was hidden before for ages, but is now revealed for our glory. Paul says that this wisdom of God is not revealed to the rulers of this age, as, in spite of their sophisticated education, the wise of this world never understood it; for if they knew it they would not have crucified Jesus. Paul continues to promote his distinctive gospel, the message of the cross, which was revealed to him by the Holy Spirit (2:10). Paul further states that the believers have not received the spirit of the world, but the same Holy Spirit, as a result of which they are able to judge all things spiritually.

As a whole, in chapter two, Paul presents two main ideas to the Corinthian believers. He warns them that they should not divide the church by boasting of worldly wisdom, because, i). When Paul came to them, he did not come with worldly wisdom and speech, but with the simple message of Christ crucified (2:1-5). ii) Worldly wisdom and speech are different from spiritual wisdom and speech that God reveals through His Spirit (2:6-16).

2.1.1.2.2 Against Erroneous view of the Christian Ministry and Ministers (3:5-23)

In chapter three, Paul discusses the basic problem of the Corinthian Christians. He contrasts the gospel as against the wisdom of this world and explains the role of Christian preachers. Paul deals with this because the Corinthian Christians misunderstood the role of apostles and their service to them.

2.1.1.2.2.1 Correction of False idea about the Role of Christian Preachers (3:5-17)

The problem of division within the church arose as both, Paul and Apollos had ministered unto them. Apostle Paul and Apollos were merely human instruments used by God in bringing the Corinthians to faith. However, some church members preferred one over the other. They started to pay special allegiance to the leader of their choice by chanting slogans such as, "I belong to Paul," "I belong to Apollos," "I belong to Cephas," and "I belong to Christ" (1:12).

Therefore in this section (3:5-17), Paul clarifies the misunderstanding of Corinthians concerning himself and Apollos, their relationship to the other apostles, to Christ, and to God. To explain it clearly and simplistically, Paul employs three metaphors. 1) A metaphor from the agricultural field (3:6-9); 2) Metaphor of a building (3:9c-15; and 3) Metaphor of the Corinthian community as God's Temple (3:16-17).

2.1.1.2.2.1.1 Metaphor of Field and Laborers (3:6-9b)

This section starts with verse 5. In this pericope, Paul argues that all the apostles are servants of God, and the success of their ministry rests upon their faithful stewardship. Though they are given different tasks, they are all equal. To clarify it Pauluses the metaphor of an agricultural field which was very common in their life-setting.[6]

The agricultural metaphor in 3:5-9 represents Paul and Apollos as co-workers in a common field with a common purpose. Paul preached the gospel in Corinth. He planted seeds where no one had proclaimed Christ. When he left for Ephesus a year and a half later, Corinth had a fledgling church. When Apollos came to the Corinthians, he supplied the water. He helped them by demonstrating from the scriptures that Jesus was the Christ (Acts 18:28).

However, the work of both Paul and Apollos would have been in vain if God had not continued to bless the church spiritually. Though the church was established by Paul, he gives the credit to God for the growth of the church. The emphasis on the last clause in verse 5 "as the Lord assigned to each," distinguishes the respective roles of the servants. To describe the dependence of the servants on God, Paul makes three parallels in this pericope.

- Paul and Apollos are servants – God assigned them to the mission [3:5].
- Paul planted, Apollos watered (they are nothing) – God gave the growth (He is everything), [3:6-7].
- Paul and Apollos are equal – God will reward them for their labor [3:8].

In verse 6, Paul underlines their dependence on God by saying, *I planted, Apollos watered,* ***but God gave the growth***. The verbs used in verse 6 indicate that the work of Paul (ἐφύτευσα – [*ephuteusa*-planted]) and Apollos [ἐπότισεν – (*epotisen*-watered)] was temporary,[7] but that of God is continuous. The verse not only displays the dependence of the apostles on God, but it explains their lower statuses, Paul just as a plower or planter, and Apollos as an irrigator. In portraying them as manual laborers as against the glamorized imagination of the Corinthians, Paul portrays a different picture of the apostles to the Corinthians believers.

Garland makes several other points about the metaphor of the planter and the irrigator in 3:6-9.[8] First, the labor of one without the other is useless. They are inter-dependentand contribute to the same goal of producing a crop. Second, though the role of both is essential to the fulfillment of the task as laborers, the timing of their work is complimentary. The value of the work of one labor, cannot be considered more important than that of the other. They can never expect special recognition or allegiance from others. They must give priority to the work of God. Third, the conflict between a planter and a waterer is illogical. The field should not turn in to a battlefield where the workers fight one another for supremacy. If the farmers do not work co-operatively they cannot have a good harvest. Fourth, God is the ultimate life force who produces the harvest. A Planter only plants the seed supplied to him by God. Waterers only keep the soil moist for growth by using rainwater supplied by God. These four points vividly present the truth that success does not depend on those who preach but on God; who through the Holy Spirit works in the hearts of the hearers.

So, Paul instructs the Corinthians against their boasting by stating that every worker is equally insignificant before God. Against their preference of one leader over another, Paul argues that all leaders are equally essential. Against their self-satisfied contentment, Paul argues that each worker will be accountable to God for their labor. Paul concludes his instructions here by emphasizing their position in Christ once again by saying, *we are God's fellow workers; you are God's field* (3:9).

In speaking of himself and Apollos as 'fellow workers,' Paul uses a specific term to describe those who labor with him in ministry. Paul usually uses the term *companion* to addresses his co-workers. But here he employs a term which is entirely different from that of his earlier usage. As he introduces this term, in the Greek text the emphasis is given more on God. Verse 9 makes it clear. θεοῦ γάρ ἐσμεν συνεργοί, θεοῦ γεώργιον, θεοῦ οἰκοδομή ἐστε, (***theu*** *gar esmen sunergoi, theu geōrgion–* for we are **God's** servants, you are God's field). The phrase *we are God's,* emphasizes their unity as fellow laborers under God. It shows that the Corinthians are under God's ownership, not under Paul's or Apollos'. Thus, the summary of the whole paragraph is that everything is God's-Paul, Apollos, the church, and its ministry. Thus, Paul makes it absolutely clear to the Corinthians that it is foolishness for them to say, 'I belong to Paul, Apollos, Cephas or Christ.'

As Paul approaches the conclusion of his talk in this section, he also shifts his role from that of a farmer to that of a head contractor, by saying, "You are God's building" (3:9c-15); thus presenting a new metaphor.

2.1.1.2.2.1.2 Metaphor of Building and the Testing of Builder's Work (3:9c-15)

In these verses, Paul shifts from the metaphor of an agricultural field to that of a building, in which God is the one who controls the contract and employs the laborers to ensure that the construction is done without any deception. Paul's metaphoric expression of the body of Christ as a 'building' is a common phenomenon seen in his epistles. He repeatedly uses the image of the building trade in his epistles.

In 3:9 and 16 he presents Christians as God's building and notes that Christ is their one foundation (vv. 10–14; Eph. 2:20). He describes the spiritual life of believers as a building process (Eph. 4:29; I Thess. 5:11), and are being built together in Christ (Eph. 2:22; Col. 2:7). The 'building' metaphor was also used in the Hellenistic philosophy and in the mystical theology of Philo to denote personal growth and spiritual enlightenment.[9] As Paul employs this image, he compares himself to a master builder who has laid the foundation through the proclamation of the gospel of Cross.

In verse 10 Paul introduces himself as σοφὸς ἀρχιτέκτων, *Sophos architekton*– "a skilled master builder/wise master builder." Paul's proclamation of the crucified Christ has laid the foundation of the church in Corinth (3:11b). So Paul calls himself an *architekton* – master builder, a title found only here in the New Testament. However, Paul introduces himself as the master builder, not because he completed the work of the building process, but because he was the one who laid the foundation, the one who introduced Christ Jesus to the Corinthians and gave them basic information about Christian life in the initial stage.

On the other hand, Paul's choice of the word σοφὸς ἀρχιτέκτων, directly connects his argument in 2:6-16. As a wise master builder, Paul powerfully preached Christ Jesus and him crucified, without using enticing words of wisdom, and thus laid the foundation of the church at Corinth. This was in contrast to the so-called wise ones in Corinth, who were attempting to build the church by laying another foundation, which Paul compares to, perishable materials.

In verse 10b, Paul gives a strong warning–*Each builder must choose with care how to build on it.* The expanded version of his warning is seen from verses 12-15. The person to whom this warning is intended to is anonymous, as in verse 12, Paul uses the indefinite pronoun τις- (*tis - someone, anyone, somebody*). Since Paul does not mention the name of Apollos in this metaphor, he is probably referring to those who were laying 'another foundation,' which Paul compares to that of 'wood, hay, and straw'.

Moreover, Paul reminds them that the work of each builder will be tested with fire. If the work is not destroyed in the fire, the builder will be rewarded, else the builder will suffer loss. Paul explains it with antithetical parallels from chapter 1:17-3:15; (3:14-15).

Those who preach the gospel along with Paul in its reality	**Those who empty the power of the gospel with worldly wisdom**
Preach the gospel without false motives	Preach the gospel with selfish ambition
Builds with Gold, Silver, Precious Stones	Builds with Wood, Hay, Stones
Will Survive the test of fire	Will be consumed in the fire
Will receive the reward	Will suffer loss

This section vividly portrays that the church which is built on the true foundation of Jesus Christ, will not only survive the present testing, but will come out of the final judgment gloriously, and those responsible for it will be rewarded. On the contrary, the argument here is a direct attack against church division and those responsible for it, and the final judgment and doom that awaits them.

2.1.1.2.2.1.3 Metaphor of Temple and the Indwelling of the Spirit of God (3:16-17)

Though Paul continues the imagery of the building, in 3:16-17 he turns the attention of Corinthian believers to God's holy temple. Through this metaphor, Paul describes the nature of the church and also gives a strong warning to those who take the body of Christ and its function lightly and destroy it by factionalism and worldly wisdom. In this section, Paul tries to help the Corinthians to understand the true nature and significance of the church as the body of Christ, and warns them about judgment on those who destroy its sanctity and regularity.

Verse 16 starts with a question Οὐκ οἴδατε (*Ouk iodate*), Do you not know? The second person plural used here indicates that Paul is not asking this question to some individuals, but to the community of believers as a whole. This is one among the ten such questions Paul asks the Corinthians in this epistle (5:6; 6:2, 3, 9, 15, 16, 19, 9:13, 24). It occurs once in Romans 6:16.

All these ten questions fall under the fourth category[10] of rhetoric question which expects the answer 'yes' from the audience. It is so because these questions start with the word Οὐκ–*Ouk.* In the Greek language, a question which starts with Ouvk always expects a positive answer. Therefore the Corinth believers are left without any option, but to accept that they know *they are the temple of the living God.* The continuous occurrence of the phrase "Do you not know that…" indicates that this is a most serious issue which Paul addresses in this section. The expression of the wording in the later part of the question ο῞τι ναὸς θεοῦἐστε (*hoti naos Theos este*), **that you are the temple of God** indicates the seriousness of their actions as members of the body of Christ.

In Corinth, temples were considered as an integral part of their lifestyle. Temple was a powerful symbol and expression of the identity of the Greco-Roman world and its inhabitants. Apart from the cultic activity, the temple in those days also played an important role in the communal development of the society. It was customary that the Temples were opened for weary travelers to take rest. It was a source of economic growth and prosperity. Most importantly, the temple also played a vital role in their corporate life as social entities, wherein they did not tolerate injustice. So as a community, their ethos, values, status, and boundaries were firmly related to the temple.

In this background, Paul's usage of the temple metaphor is very significant. It is also important because Paul is not advocating a new teaching which the Corinthian are unaware of. Rather, he is reinforcing what they already knew. However, in this section, Paul indicates that the Corinthians themselves are the temple of God, and each one of them are required to practice what they experienced in their former life, but now according to the standards of their new life in Christ Jesus.

Paul clarifies to the Corinthians that the living God can exist only in a temple that is 'alive' which in this case happens to be, themselves. He indicates that the most important thing they must now be aware of is that the Spirit of God lives in them. Thus, Paul presents the Christian church which though a 'building' (3:9), is not one of brick and mortar but constitutes of each member within whom dwells the presence of God (3:16).

Hence, in verse 17 Paul strongly warns, τις τὸν ναὸν τοῦ θεοῦφθείρει ,φθερεῖ τοῦτον ὁ θεός (*ei tis naon tou theou phtheirei, phtherei tooton ho theos* - if *anyone* destroys **God's temple**, **God will** destroy *that person*). Though it is addressed to the church as a whole, in relation to the 'anyone' in 3:12, Pauldirects this specifically to those responsible for factionalism in the congregation. Paul further states that God will destroy that person because ὁ γὰρ ναὸς τοῦθεοῦἅγιός ἑστιν (*ho gar vaos tou Theou hagios estin* – the temple of God is holy). Thus as per this final clause, the main reason behind Paul's dire warning is that God's temple is holy, and God will destroy those who destroy his dwelling place.

Though Paul does not describe how that person/s will be ultimately destroyed, it is clear that in their present church scenario, the body of Christ is divided because of their boastful arrogance, competitive partnership, and eagerness to evaluate others on the basis of worldly wisdom. Therefore Paul educates them that, each church member though different, yet, are members of the one, single body of Christ. As a community of believers, they belong to God and are possessed by God. Thus, if anyone causes division, it is like dividing the body of Christ. Factionalism within the church is a very grave and serious offense in the sight of God, which he will not let go unpunished.

2.1.1.3 Summary of Paul's Argument on Wisdom and Boasting (3:18-23)

In 3:18-23 Paul summarizes his argument presented in 1:10-3:17. Chapter 3:18-23 can be sub-divided into two: summary of his argument on worldly wisdom (18-20), and summary of his argument on false boasting about human leadership (21-23). Both sub-divisions opens with an identical exhortation '*Let no one...,*' and further gives the final warning of self-deception in terms of worldly wisdom and boasting on favored leaders.

As concluding remarks, Paul, firstly, reminds them that the cause of their self-deception is not something or someone from outside; rather the danger is from within. In 18b Paul says, εἴ τις δοκει σοφὸς εἶναι ἐν ὑμῖνἐν τῷ αἰῶνι τούτῳ (*ei tis dokei Sophos einai en humin en tōaiōnai touto* - if anyone thinks he is wise *among you* in this age). The phrase ἐν ὑμῖν makes it clear that the danger of self-deception exists among themselves. By using the identical exhortation '*Let no one...*' in verse 18 and 21, Paul warns each person to guard themselves against such danger, the danger of deceiving themselves by considering themselves as σοφὸς- *wise* in this age. He concludes his final exhortation regarding their fascination of worldly wisdom with a strong imperative. In 18c, he strongly commands those who claim themselves to be wise, need to become as fools in order to become wise in God's sight.

Secondly, based on the preceding passage, Paul exhorts the Corinthians not to boast about human leadership (3:21-23). In this section, Paul shifts his concluding negative remarks on boasting about human leadership by employing a positive assertion, *for all things are yours*. Here Paul indicates the Corinthians to see the involvement of Christ in every creation. However, in verse 21 the expression of πάντα (*panta* - all things) refers to the ministry of those preaching and teaching the gospel to them. So, Paul exhorts the Corinthians that all leaders who ministered among them were servants sent by Christ. In verses 21-23, Paul give two reasons why they should not boast concerning their preferred leaders. First, irrespective of the different calling and gifts the leaders have, all leaders belong to them (v. 22). Secondly, all believers belong to Christ.

As a whole, in chapter 3:5-23 Paul gives five reasons why the Corinthian believers should not divide the church by boasting about the worldly wisdom and speech of their respective leaders. Firstly, the leaders are not the cause of the growth of the church but they are only laborers in the field (3:5-9). Secondly, Christ is the foundation of the church and the leaders are mere builders who build upon Christ the foundation (3:10-15). Thirdly, God is the ultimate authority. He will destroy anyone who causes division in the body of Christ (3:16-17). Fourthly, as far as God is concerned, worldly wisdom and speech is foolishness (3:18-20). Finally, all those who ministered among them were mere servants of God (3:21-23).

2.1.1.4 Interpretation of the Ministry of Apostles (4:1-21)

In chapter 4 Paul focuses on the marks and nature of true apostles. It is considered as Paul's canon, which includes basic guidelines and standards on which apostles need to minister and be evaluated upon. As Paul communicates this, he also addresses Corinthian's theological misunderstanding of the gospel, Christian leadership, the role of teachers etc. To help the Corinthians understand the ministry of true apostles, Paul gives three characteristics of true ministers which are related to their identity (1-7), circumstances they face in the ministry (8-13), and their role in leading and caring for the believers (14-21).

At the same time, since the chapter concerns with divisions over different leaders/ministers, Paul also discusses the importance of leaders bringing unity among the followers. Some reasons for the same are presented below.

2.1.1.4.1 Leaders are Servants of Christ and Stewards of God's Mysteries (4:1-7)

In the first segment of chapter 4, Paul makes an application of the servant model leadership and explains how it relates to their treatment of him. In other words, it is his affirmation about how a minister should conduct himself before his congregation and the congregation's response to the leaders.

Chapter 4 starts with the word οὕτως (*ohutos* – thus). In Greek, the word *ohutos* refers to *things happened before/previously.* Concise Oxford Dictionary gives the meaning of *thus* as, "a result or consequence of this." Therefore the word *thus* refers to previous chapters wherein Paul warns the Corinthians not to boast about human leadership, either in his name for planting the church or in Apollos' name who watered it. Instead, they need to look to Christ in whom they possess all things. Furthermore, they need to regard them as ὑπηρέτας Χριστοῦ (***hupēretas*** *Christou* - ***servants*** of Christ) and οἰκονόμους μυστηρίων θεοῦ (***oikonomous*** *mustēriōn Theou* - ***stewards*** of God's mysteries). By using the plural form *us* Paul describes not only his own ministry but of his co-workers as well.

After introducing them as servants and stewards of Christ and God respectively, in verses 3-5, he shares his real concerns to validate his own ministry in the context of the ministerial struggle he is facing among them.

Firstly, in verse 1, Paul introduces ministers/apostles as the ***hupēretas, servants*** of Christ. The word used in verse 1 for servant is ὑπηρέτας (*hupeēretas*- a servant, or assistant). In the context of current text, the meaning of *hupēretas* is a subordinate servant/an assistant functioning as a free man rather than a διακονος (*diakonos* – servant). Originally, the term *hupēretas* was used to describe the slaves who rowed below a ship's deck. However, during the first century, *hupēretas* was used to include even a domestic worker.

Thus, Paul asserts that he and other apostles are the free *servants of Christ,* responsible only to Christ and not to the Corinthians. Therefore, it is his affirmation to the Corinthians that they should understand the relationship between the apostles and the church, and the church and Christ. Paul also conveys the message that though the apostles render their service to the church, the church is not their master, for they are the servants of Christ Jesus who alone is their master.

Secondly, in verse 1 itself, Paul gives another description of himself and his fellow-workers, namely, ***oikonomous***-*stewards* of God's mysteries. This word is commonly used to emphasize the nature of a servant's task under the supervision of God. It also refers to a servant to whom his master has entrusted the oversight of his household. Thus, a steward is responsible for his master's possessions and is required to give an account to his master from time to time.

However, in this verse, the term *stewards* do not refer to the stewardship of a servant over a household but is closely connected to the noun μυστήριον (*mustērion* – Mystery), which shows that they are stewards of God's revelation in Jesus Christ. In Bassler's words, "Paul and his fellow workers were underlings of Christ and overseers for God."[11]

Another striking factor seen in this verse is that, as Paul uses the term servants and stewards to describe their God-given position, he links it with the genitive of possession. By using the possessive genitive along with both expressions, Paul validates the fact that they are possessed by/belong to/under the ownership of Christ and God. From verse 3-5 Paul switches from the plural form *us* to *I*. It denotes that here Paul mainly deals with the problem between Corinthians and himself. On the basis of 2:15 and 4:3-5 we understand that the Corinthians were continuously examining/judging Paul. So from verse 3ff Paul says, as a servant of Christ and stewards of God he is neither responsible to the Corinthians, nor is to be judged by them for the quality of his service.

At the same time, Paul was not afraid of being examined by the Corinthian believers because he was willing to suffer everything for the sake of the gospel of Christ. If the Corinthians wished to interrogate him, he would count this procedure as a minor matter. Or if they intended to call him before a human court, he would regard that too as something very small in comparison to appearing before God's judgment seat. However, the main fact Paul brings in this segment is that he is not responsible to the Corinthians, but to Christ alone. Also, since Christ is his judge, the Corinthians should refrain from judging his faithfulness.

In v. 5, Paul instructs them not to judge anything, but to wait until the end-time of the Lord when each one will receive commendation from God. The clear meaning of this remark is to remind the Corinthians that they too will face judgment. Therefore for Paul, there is no value of human judgment in his life. In the last part of verse 3, he also says that even his own judgment/ evaluation about himself is unreliable before God who appointed him for the specific task.

Though it seems that the second part of this segment is Paul's self-clarification, in its totality it can be considered as Paul's instruction to the Corinthians in terms of their dealing with all servants of God. For, in verse 6 Paul once again mentions the name of Apollos and himself (6a) and the plural personal pronoun us (3c). By clarifying the above-mentioned realities which Paul faced in Corinth, he describes who the true servants of God are, what their duty is, and how they must be treated by the congregation. Thus, Paul as a faithful servant of Christ Jesus tries to bring unity among the divided body of Christ.

2.1.1.4.2 Leaders are Better/Superior than the Followers (4:8-13)

Some believers in the church at Corinth were proud and boastful. They were proud of their human wisdom and human leaders, and the spiritual status they achieved through the wisdom they possessed. So, in 4:8-13 Paul mocks their spiritual achievement with sharp sarcasm. In verses 8-10, Paul lists out the characterization of the exalted spiritual rank they have gained through worldly wisdom.

These arrogant believers were thinking that they are better than Paul and other apostles. However, in this section, Paul presents that he and other apostles are in fact superior to them in everything. Furthermore, by explicating it under four divisions, Paul validates the authenticity of their superiority against Corinthian's spiritual duplicity.

2.1.1.4.2.1 Paul's use of Sarcasm (v.8)

Sarcasm/irony is a common factor seen in the Pauline epistles. At times his rhetoric is characterized by such indirect elements to address negative issues in a positive way. Though Paul mainly uses such kind of approach in Galatians, it is seen in other epistles as well. Here inv. 8, Paul uses sarcasm to remind the Corinthians who they really are, and what their precise spiritual status is before Christ.

Verse 8 is characterized by sharp sarcasm. Through the usage of three exclamatory remarks, Paul deals with the heart of the matter. The first is, *Already you have all you want!* By this Paul sarcastically remarks that they think they have already received everything from God in terms of spiritual life and material needs. It reflects their false self-assurance that they are in need of nothing more, which according to Paul, was a striking contrast to their reality.

The second sarcastic remark is, Already you have become rich! This was a reference to their arrogant nature. The third remark is, You have become kings! Here Paul uses a common phrase which was often used by the Stoic philosophers of those days who thought themselves to be *kings* and hence, self-sufficient. Thus Paul portrays the Corinthians as influenced by Stoic teachings, for they were considering themselves as rulers, rather than as citizens of the kingdom of God.

Finally, Paul comes to the heart of sarcasm saying, *Indeed, I wish that you had become kings, so that we might be kings with you!* Though they thought they had all the blessings, they were not benefited by these, for if they really were kings, then Paul and Apollos would gladly have taken a seat next to them. But since it is not a reality at present, Paul through sarcasm bitterly criticizes their foolish illusions.

2.1.1.4.2.2 Contrasts between Paul / Apostles and Corinthians (v.10)

The contrast between the life of apostles and the Corinthians specified in verse 10 is also a hard sarcasm used by Paul. However, here it is used with three antitheses, similar to that of in 1:26.

Paul and other Apostles	Corinthians
ἡμεῖς μωροὶ διὰ Χριστόν (*hēmeis moroi dia Christon* - we are fools for Christ) v.10a	φρόνιμοι ἐν Χριστῷ (*phronimoi en Christo* - you are wise in Christ)
ἡμεῖς ἀσθενεῖς (*hēmeis antheneis* - we are weak) v.10b	ὑμεῖς ἰσχυροί (*humeis ischuroi* - you are strong)
ἡμεῖς ἄτιμοι (*hēmeis atimoi* - we are dishonored) v.10c	μεῖς ἔνδοξοι (*humeis endoxoi* - you are honored)

The contrast made by Paul in verse 10 can be categorized under three major domains of human life such as wisdom, power, and dignity.

Firstly, in terms of wisdom, Paul labels himself and other apostles as fools for the sake of Christ. To degrade oneself by labeling as a fool is a severe damage to one's own self-esteem. Nevertheless, Paul introduces himself along with other apostles as 'fools' for a noble reason, that is, to add more weight to the irony he employs in the second part of the same sentence.

Paul's use of the phrase, we are fools for the sake of Christ is also understood in another way that they reflect the truth of the gospel of the cross which was foolish in the eyes of the wise of this world. Inversely, Corinthians are identified as wise in Christ. The inclusion evn Cristw (en Christo–in Christ) in this clause is considered as Paul's special use to balance the dia. Cristo,n (dia Christon – for Christ) in the previous clause.

So, 'wise in Christ' is not a positive commendation, but it accelerates the degree of irony in light of 1:26-28. Paul uses this harsh irony to tell the Corinthians that they are not really intelligent and discerning followers of Christ, rather their so-called wisdom is purely human, which has nothing to do with divine wisdom. By this contrast, Paul shames those who claim themselves as 'wise' in Corinth.

Next, in terms of power, Paul labels himself and other apostles as *weak*. This might be one reason the Corinthians turned against Paul and questioned his apostleship. For in 2:3, Paul himself says, *I came to you in weakness*. However, like in the previous contrast, here too it is understood in a different manner. Paul's usage of the term *weak* does not refer to the physical condition of Paul and other apostles, but it reflects them as carriers of God's 'weakness' which was displayed on the cross. They presented themselves 'weak' as they preached the gospel so that the cross of Christ might not be emptied of its power (1:17).

On the contrary, the Corinthians are presented as *strong*. In light of Paul's argument in 1:26-28, this is yet another sharp irony Paul uses in the second clause of verse 10b. Most of the Corinthians believers were neither wise, nor powerful, nor of noble birth, but they considered themselves as being all these. However, through this contrast, Paul shames those who claim themselves as 'powerful' in the Corinthian church.

Lastly, in terms of dignity, Paul labels himself and other apostles as *dishonored.* Paul visualizes themselves as those placed at the end of the procession, like those condemned to die (4:9), which is an ultimate degree of humiliation and dishonor. Conversely, the Corinthians are 'honored,' for they are like those in the first row of the procession. Nonetheless, even in this case, they seek to fuse the things of Christ with the things of the world. Therefore they gain nothing but bring shame on themselves. On the contrary, though the apostles are mocked and dishonored by the Corinthians, they will be honored by God. Through this contrast, Paul shames those who claim themselves as 'honored' in Corinth.

2.1.1.4.2.3 Paul's Difficulties in the Ministry (vv.11-12a)

As against the self-sufficient nature of Corinthians portrayed in 4:8, here Paul lists the present difficulties that he and other apostles are facing in their ministerial life. Such lists were commonly used as rhetoric and paranetic devices in Jewish apocalyptic literatures, and also in Greek historical writings. It was even used by Hellenistic philosophers like Stoics and Cynics as a device of pedagogical paradigm to portray their life struggle as a manifestation of the very nature of being away from the dominant cultural values.[12]

The phrase, *to the present hour* in verse 11a demonstrates Paul and the situation of his fellow-ministers against the high status already attained by Corinthians (4:8). All the difficulties Paul lists are in contrast to Corinthians approbation, such as, *hungry and thirsty* against *filled; poorly clothed and homeless* against *rich and reigning*.

2.1.14.2.4 Contrasting Action of Apostles towards the Difficulties (vv.12b-13)

Three contrasting actions of the apostles are listed in vv.12b-13. Mainly three antitheses are given in this segment. a) Abused by others, but in return, they blessed (12b); b) Persecuted, but they endured (12c); c) Defamed, but they responded kindly (13a). These three antitheses display the ways how they imitated Christ in midst of the difficulties they faced.

After exposing the boastful nature of Corinthians by employing a series of irony, Paul clarifies what makes the apostles better/superior to the Corinthians. Though Paul and others were facing hunger, thirst, lack of clothing, rough treatment, and homelessness; yet *they toiled with their own hands* (v.12). Though being an apostle Paul had all the right to be supported by the Corinthian church, yet having no desire to be a burden to them, he labored for his own upkeep.

Paul's trade of tent making though was considered menial, he himself was not ashamed of it. For Corinthians such kind of physical labor was assigned only to the slaves. However, without considering his status as an apostle, Paul lowered himself, so that he won't be a burden to his own people. Even when the Corinthians were living in a world of illusion in contrast to their position in Christ, Paul and other apostles served them faithfully in midst of their troubled situations, thus proving that they were in no way inferior to them.

2.1.1.4.3 Leaders are the Spiritual Progenitors and Guardians of their Followers (4:14-21)

Though Paul is done with his argument in 4:13 (which he began in 1:10), the heart of his argument regarding the authenticity of his leadership is explicated further in 4:14-21. Unlike other sections discussed so far, the current segment starts with aunique statement of comfort, *I am not writing this to make you ashamed, but to admonish you as my beloved children.* Even as he admonishes, his main concern was to re-establish the authenticity of his authority as leader to the Corinthian believers. So, like in the previous section, to make the process easier, he brings in another change of metaphor. By employing the characteristics of a father-son relationship he *admonishes* (v.14), *urges* (16-17), and ends with the *consequences* of not valuing his exhortations.

Under admonition, Paul differentiates between the role of a guardian and father in the life of the Corinth believers. In verse 15a Paul says, *though you might have ten thousand guardians in Christ, you do not have many fathers.* Two words used in verse 15 are distinct in all aspects. The word used for guardian in its original text is παιδαγωγός, *paidagogos***.** The English word 'pedagogue' is derived out of this word. In the Greek culture, a pedagogue is either a household slave or a freedman who accompanies the children of wealthy parents to and from school, helps them to do their homework, takes care of them when they are sick, and provides all assistance till they reach teenage. Apart from this, a pedagogue is appointed to instruct the child in proper behavior, chastise, protect from danger, give interest in correct speech, syntax, and expression etc. This denotes that guardians are charged with specific duties by the parents.

However, the role of a father is more authoritative than that of the guardians. It is not limited to any kind of charged tasks. So with an overemphasis, Paul calls the attention of Corinthian believers to the concept of *a father*. Further, Paul makes the appeal that *you do not have many fathers. Indeed, in Christ Jesus I become your father through the gospel.* Since Paul is the one who brought them to Christ he can truthfully say that, in Christ Jesus, he is the spiritual progenitor of the Corinthian believers.

In Jewish culture, a teacher who teaches Torah to the students is considered as a father. In this regard, like Paul, even Timothy, Silas, Apollos, and Titus also are considered as spiritual fathers, for they all taught and contributed towards the edification of the Corinthian church. However, it was Paul who exercised a lasting authority over them. Thus, Paul declares the authenticity of his leadership and apostolic authority over the believers at Corinth against their wrong understanding of himself. Additionally, by reminding them about the way he lived in Christ (v.17b), Paul appeals them to imitate (v.16) him.

In culmination, he resumes with a hard tone of argument with two questions, *What do you prefer? Am I to come to you with a stick, or with love in a spirit of gentleness?* that postures two alternatives. Paul does not make this statement with the intention to shame them during his next visit, but by projecting himself as a good father, Paul admonishes them and tries to bring unity among the church members.

Summary of Chapters 1-4

The discussion above demonstrates Paul's response to the division caused by Corinth believers' misplaced preference of one leader over another. Even before addressing the problem, Paul had begun his letter by addressing the church members as *sanctified* in Christ Jesus, and who are called to be *saints*. In addition, he also expresses thanks to God for the grace they had already received in Christ Jesus, the confirmation of Christ's testimony, and the faithfulness of God.

However, from 1:10-4:21, Paul employed strong arguments to nullify the insufficiency of the secular rhetoric and worldly wisdom on which they were evaluating Paul and other apostles. Apart from this, these chapters also dealt with different contrasts Paul makes between them and himself/other apostles and uses a series of irony to shame the Corinthians for living as if they had everything they needed; which was nothing but their misguided notions.

Against their concept of apostles and their service to the people of God, in chapter 4, Paul talked about himself and other apostles as being mere servants and stewards of God's mystery. Therefore, Paul appeals to them not to cause any fraction among themselves, by choosing one over the other, but to live in unity. He rebuked them by asking whether Christ is divided, or whether their preferred leaders were crucified for them.

Paul further argues that he was commissioned by Christ to preach the gospel of the cross and he has proclaimed it without worldly wisdom so that the message of the cross might not be emptied of its divine power. Since God has displayed his divine wisdom to them through His son Jesus, he urges them not to fool themselves by following the wisdom of this world that causes division in the body of Christ. Finally, by using the metaphor of a father–son relationship, Paul admonishes them to imitate him in all the aspects of their Christian life.

2.1.2 Sexual Immorality (5:1-13)

From chapters 1-4, Paul was mainly dealing with the philosophical and psychological sin of the Corinthians, because they were boasting about their worldly wisdom and self-sufficiency. In chapter 5, he deals with a new problem, the problem of *sexual immorality* (incestuous relationship) in the church which was frowned upon even by the Gentiles. Such kind of sin was punishable by death in the Old Testament (Lev. 18:7, 8, 29; Deut. 22:30). It was illegal even under the Roman law, and the person who involved in such immoral activities were banished from Roman colonies.

Paradoxically, the church was arrogant. Without taking any corrective measures, the church rationalized it on the basis of their philosophical orientation and the love of human wisdom. Therefore, though the sin of fornication was committed by a single man, without addressing him, Paul addresses the rest of the church who refused to act against this extreme wickedness. In chapter 5 Paul focuses on moral stigma and the serious consequences of having such a sinful man in the congregation.

2.1.2.1 Paul's Instruction: "Drive out the Wicked Person from among You"

Against the laxity of the Corinthians towards the extreme wickedness that was happening in the church, Paul instructs them to, "Drive out the sexually immoral person, who has his father's wife..." (v.13). By underscoring his spiritual presence, Paul sets forth *four reasons for expelling the immoral person from the congregation.*

2.1.2.1.1 Such Kind of Immorality is not Found Even among Pagans (vv.1-2)

Corinthian believers had been carefully taught by Paul and other apostles regarding the moral standards they need to maintain in their socio-political and religious life. Even after leaving Corinth, in his first letter (which was lost), Paul had already told them not to associate with sexually immoral persons (v.9). It denotes that this extreme wickedness had not taken place just prior to the writing of this epistle, but was been tolerated by them for a long time. Therefore in vv.1-2, Paul reminds them about the seriousness of this sin which they were allowing in the church.

To address the sexual immorality inside the church, Paul uses the term πορνεία, *porneia*. This term refers to various kind of unlawful sexual intercourse. *Porneia* in chapter 5 refers to incest because it deals with a man living with his father's wife. The expression *father's wife* indicates that the woman was not his natural mother. In Judaism, the expression *father's wife* referred to a step-mother. Therefore in this case, most probably the man concerned was having such an illicit relationship with his step-mother. However, Old Testament portrays such kind of relationships in the same category as relations between a son and his natural mother (Lev.18:7-8).

To show the repulsiveness of this act, in verse 1b, Paul remarks about this as *not found even among pagans*. In order to encourage the church to exercise its authority in implementing disciplinary action against the immoral person, Paul refers to the moral standard of gentiles, as this kind of immorality was strictly prohibited even under the Roman law, and the guilty party was ex-communicated from their colonies. By employing the term *pagans*, Paul indicates the severity of sin which the church member had committed. Under Jewish Law, such kind of act invited capital punishment and anyone found guilty of such an act was stoned to death.

However, the church in Corinth did not view it as a serious issue. Their complacent attitude towards this wickedness reflected their low moral standard, even after being reminded of it by Paul through his presently lost letter. For this reason, the testimony of the church was severely hindered in Corinth. Hence Paul denounces them, *you are arrogant,* for when this issue happened, instead of mourning and chastising the fornicator, they took it very lightly.

The verb ἐπενθήσατε (*epenthēsate*- to mourn) refer to, sorrow for sin that has been committed either by oneself or by others. Paul exhorts the believers to mourn before God, for, as a community, they have committed this sin. Though the act was committed by a single person, the church's failure in disciplining the immoral brother made them equally sinners before God. Hence, Paul calls the church to repentance, to mourn before God for their sins, and to ex-communicate the immoral man from among them.

2.1.2.1.2 Paul already Passed Judgment to Deliver Such Man to Satan (vv.3-5)

Though Paul is away from the Corinthians, in this section he emphasizes his spiritual presence and sets forth the second reason for eliminating the wicked person from among them. Paul exhorts the church to ex-communicate the immoral brother, for he has already judged him, and decided to deliver such a man to Satan.

In contrast to the response of the Corinthians, who are *puffed up* and done nothing, not even grieved about the immoral man's behavior, Paul takes a crucial stand in verse 3. He begins his second argument by remarking that though he is not physically present, he is present *in spirit.* In verse 4, once again he stresses his presence among them with the emphatic usage of *my spirit* which is present, with the power of the Lord Jesus. In contrast to the thinking of some in the Corinthian Church (4:18), repeatedly Paul accentuates that he is already present among them, *in spirit.* Thus he says, I have already passed judgment against the one who has committed such an immoral act. However as Paul does not want to implement disciplinary action by himself, he instructs them to meet as a church and to execute his judgment as if he is present among them.

As per Paul, the ultimate judgment was to *hand him over to Satan*, which signified, excommunication. For in Paul's time, the word *hand over/deliver* was a strong term used in judicial sentencing which was equivalent to removing the person from his community. Thus in the Corinthian church context, handing over the person to Satan, was to put that person out of the Christian community and thrust him into Satan's realm. The result of this disciplinary action was two-fold. First, it protected the church from future immoral acts, and second, the spirit of the man may be saved in the day of the Lord. The destruction of the flesh refers to divine chastening, which could be illness or even death. However, his spirit would be saved on the day of the Lord.

2.1.2.1.3 The Presence of Single Immoral Person will Corrupt the Entire Congregation (vv.6-8)

The third reason for Paul's argument on ex-communicating the immoral person was because the presence of a single immoral person would corrupt the whole congregation. Paul exhorts them to take such a severe disciplinary action because the consequences of not taking such a bold step would cause much more severe damage than removing the single individual from the church. For if that person is not removed, such sin would spread among others, and spoil the spiritual life of the entire congregation. To clarify it better, Paul uses the illustration of, a little yeast that leavens the whole batch of dough.

The pride and boastful nature of the Corinthian believers caused them to be arrogant and neglectful towards the apostles and their teachings. So Paul asks them a rhetorical question, *don't you know that a little yeast leavens the whole batch of dough?* Going after human wisdom and recognition had caused them spiritual blindness. Through the illustration of yeast and dough, Paul exhorts them not to keep the immoral man anymore among them, for as a little yeast leavens the whole dough, the presence of a single immoral man would corrupt the entire church and adversely affect the proper functioning of the body of Christ.

Paul uses the illustration of yeast because it was a very familiar object to the Corinthians. In those days, before baking bread, a small portion of dough would be removed and kept aside to leaven the new batch of dough. It would be fermented in water and later mixed with the new batch of dough in order to make it rise. A *little yeast* in this verse refers to the presence of a *single immoral man* in the church, and the *whole batch of dough* refers to the *entire congregation.* So Paul says, if you allow the immoral man to continue in the church, his presence will permeate the church as a whole and influence others to commit the same sin.

In verses 7 and 8, Paul shifts to another metaphor, the metaphor of unleavened bread, which symbolized how the Israelites were freed from Egypt by the Passover. Through this metaphor, Paul reminds them that the church must be unleavened since it has been separated from sin and death by the perfect Passover Lamb, Jesus Christ.

As he reminds them about it, he employs the verb imperative ἐκκαθάρατε (*ekkatharate*), which means, to cleanse themselves thoroughly (v.7a). In order to be separated from their old way of life, they must remove everything sinful, including the church member who lives in sin. Therefore Paul exhorts them to get rid of the *old leaven, the incestuous man,* so that they can become what they really are, *a new batch of dough.*

By presenting the crucified Christ as the ground for their ethical behavior, Paul tries to correct the moral standards of the Corinthians. Through the death of Christ, the Corinthians were now a new creation in Christ. Ἀζύμοις (*en azumois* - the unleavened) in verse 8 expresses their new existence in Christ, i.e. with *sincerity* and *truth*. These two words express the authentic behavior of a true Christian. Paul calls the Corinthians to such a life of sincerity and truth which will enable them to become what really they are-the holy temple of a holy God.

2.1.2.1.4 Paul in his Previous letter Already Remind them not to Associate with Immoral Persons (vv. 9-13)

In verses 9-13, Paul gives his fourth and final reason for removing the immoral person from the congregation. In this section Paul posits the argument that the church must remove the immoral person from among them because he had already reminded them not to associate with such people (v.9). By this he reiterates that sexual immorality must be judged by the members of the church.

The phrase at the beginning of verse 9 Ἔγραψα ὑμῖν ἐν τῇ ἐπιστολῇ (*egrapsa humin en epistole* - I wrote to you in the/my letter), appears strange because we do not have a canonical letter of Paul to the Corinthians, prior to I Corinthians. However, it is understood that Paul had previously written a letter which is lost. Since it is lost, the content of the letter is not known to us, other than the exhortation mentioned in I Corinthians, *not to associate with sexually immoral persons* (v.9). In this section, however, he is resolving an issue from his former letter which was neglected by the Corinthian believers. It denotes that Paul is still dealing with the boastful attitude of the Corinthians.

This section can be divided into three sub-sections. Firstly, in verse 9-10, Paul clarifies what he meant by do not associate with sexually immoral persons. Secondly, in verse 11 he simplifies what he really meant by such an assertion in verse 9. Thirdly, from verses 12-13, he gives further explanations for his first two points.

2.1.2.1.4.1 Paul's Response to the Misinterpretation of his Previous Letter (vv.9-10)

In his previous letter, Paul had informed the church at Corinth not to associate with the sexually immoral person. But the church had misunderstood and misinterpreted his advice and had stopped having all contact with the 'unbeliever'. So Paul states, *not at all, meaning the immoral of this world, or the greedy and robbers, or idolaters, since you then need to go out of this world* (v.10).

Paul clarifies that he never meant that they should not have any contact with the people of this world. Because if that would be the case then, *you need to go out of this world.* As the main responsibility of the church is to be witnesses of the gospel to this world, we have to continue living in this world and be in contact with sinners; else we could never be able to bring them to the salvific knowledge of Christ Jesus.

2.1.2.1.4.2 Paul Clarifies what he Meant by his Argument in Verse 9 (v.11)

In verse 11 Paul elucidates what he really meant by saying, *not to associate with immoral persons*. Paul starts this verse by saying νῦν δὲ ἔγραψα ὑμῖν (*nun de egrapsa humin* - but now I am saying). The antithetical word *but* at the beginning refers back to verse 10. It itself gives us the knowledge that Paul is further explaining what he had already mentioned in verse 10. Furthermore, by employing the adverb νῦν (*nun*-now), he directs their attention towards the present condition of the church, that is, they are still continuing to tolerate the immoral brother among them.

Paul then specifically mentions that they should not associate with anyone *who bears the name of a brother or sister*. Here, Paul clarifies his intention in the earlier letter. He had expected them to disassociate with all who says they are brothers, but continue in the sinful nature. It is to be understood that it is not Paul's description of such a man, rather the immoral person calls himself a brother. However, he cannot belong to the Christian community because his way of life contradicts the label he bears.

Therefore Paul says, not only to not associate but not even to eat with such persons. Paul does not mean that Christians have to avoid social customs, or not to eat with non-Christians, but only with the immoral member of the church. For, in those days, sharing a meal or having fellowship with one another signified reconciliation and acceptance. Hence, Paul emphatically says to the church that they should never make any compromise, settlement, or acceptance with such person/s; rather, disassociate themselves completely.

2.1.2.1.4.3 Further Explanation of verses 9-11 (vv.12-13)

In this sub-section, Paul gives reasons for the two points given above and concludes the present section and the entire argument on, Ex-communication. In verse 12, Paul asks two questions. Firstly Paul asks, *for what have I to do with judging those outside?* This question reflects Paul's motive in verses 9 and 10. It is about their misunderstanding about Paul's previous letter. Though Paul uses the first person singular *I* in verse 12, it denotes that it is neither he nor the Corinthians, who are to pass judgment on the people of this world, the reason being–*God will judge those who are outside* (v. 13a).

As opposed to the above, Paul asks his second question, *is it not those who are inside that you need to judge?* This is the main argument of Paul in this entire chapter. By this Paul re-emphasizes, that it is the duty of the church to make any corrections that call for decisive separation between the church and the world. If any member of the church refuses to repent and continue in sin, then the church must exercise its authority in disciplining them, for it is the responsibility of the believers to judge him. Hence Paul says, *drive out the wicked person from among you* (v. 13b).

Summary

Paul had heard about immorality within the church, and he rebuked them for not taking any disciplinary action against the person who has sexual relationship with his step-mother. Paul admonishes them to mourn before God and to drive out the sinful man from among them. Paul, through various reasons and an illustration of yeast and leaven made them aware about the seriousness of the issue at hand and its repercussions if they continued to tolerate the immoral brother among them. Hence, the church has to excommunicate him from the community of saints.

2.1.3 Lawsuits among Believers (6:1-11)

As stated earlier, some members of the Corinth church were driven by human philosophy and were doing what they wanted to do. Gradually their old ways of thinking and acting re-entered their life and the expression of the newness of life in Christ was damaged. As a result, they behaved like unbelievers and were envious and critical of their own fellow brethren in their religious and social life. It made them haul even the smallest issues among them to the secular courts where pagan judges presided over the cases.

This was totally against Paul's argument with which he had concluded the previous chapter. In chapter 5 he had stated that the church is not to judge *those outside,* but *those inside*. However, in the Corinthian church, everything was happening inversely. So, in chapter 6:1-11 Paul, through a serious of rhetorical questions, continuous using the hard language consisting of touches of sarcasm, criticisms, and warnings.

2.1.3.1 Paul's Instruction: "Church Must Abstain from Lawsuits"

Paul gives various reasons for the church to abstain from lawsuits. For Paul, the Christians who take their cases to pagan judges cause the church to become ignominious in the gentile world. It was a usual practice in the Greek cities to take cases to the court which was held at the marketplace, and listen to the lawyers debating about it. Though it was a usual practice, it became a form of challenge and entertainment. Thus, it was considered disgraceful.

However, the Jews had their own court to settle issues among themselves. It was totally forbidden for them to take any matter to the outside court. Both Greek and Roman rulers allowed the Jews to continue their practice wherever they are. Similarly, even the Corinthian believers were allowed by the Romans to practice the same, because in those days the Romans considered the

Christians as a Jewish sect.[13] But the Corinthian believers instead of solving disputes among themselves were arrogantly taking it to the outside court. In order to correct this evil, Paul reminds them of three things: 1) Who they really are in relation to this world, i.e., they are the future judges of this world and angels; 2) What should be their attitude toward one another, i.e., they should not do anything wrong to their fellow brethren; 3) How they should maintain their character in relation to the standard of God, i.e., they are the citizens of the kingdom of God.

2.1.3.1.1 The Saints are the Future Judges of the World and Angels (vv.1-6)

Though Paul talks about lawsuits in this section, the kind of lawsuit is not specified. However, Paul describes how lawsuits must be dealt with in the Christian community. Paul's first argument in this section is, the Christians should abstain from the lawsuits because they are the future judges of the world and angels. To validate his argument he asks a serious of question to the Corinthians.

The first question Paul asks is *if anyone has a grievance against another,* ***do you dare*** *to take it to court before* **the unrighteous**, *instead of taking it before the saints?* The word To λμᾷ (*tolma*-dare, have the courage) in the question shows the depth of Paul's feelings provoked by the action of some Corinthian believer/s. Suing a believer in a secular court is a daring act of disobedience to the golden law of Jesus Christ, namely, to seek the good of one's fellowmen even if he is an enemy (Lk. 6:27). To take one brother before τῶν ἀδίκων (*tōn adikōn* - the unrighteous), refers to the unsaved spiritual condition of the judge. So, if the church allows one brother to take another brother before an unsaved judge, it is like giving the world an opportunity to dishonor Christ, for each member in the church is a member of the body of Christ.

In verse 2 Paul asks his second question, *do you not know that the saints will judge the world?* Paul uses the phrase οὐκ οἴδατε (*ouk iodate*-do you not know) six times in this chapter (6:2,3,8, 15,16,19). It denotes that they practiced these not because of their ignorance, but out of arrogance. Because the phrase *do you not know*, shows that Paul had already taught these things when he was with them and had also reminded them in his earlier letter. At the same time, these six questions are asked in such a way that the Corinthians had to respond to it in a positive way,[14] which also denotes they already knew about it. Of course, they knew about it but did not give any serious thought about their life in the *eschaton*.

So once again Paul reminds them about their status in the kingdom of God, that *the saints will judge the world.* Paul considered the Corinthians as, saints (1:2). As saints their role as judges in the *eschaton* is already reserved, for they will judge this sinful world and the earthly judges. They will be both, judges and rulers of this earth. Not only they, but all the faithful children of God will assist Christ to judge this world in the millennial kingdom (Rev. 2:26-27; 3:21).

In the same verse (v.2b) Paul asks his third question (a supplementary question) *if the world is to be judged by you, are you incompetent to try trivial cases*? This question is considered as a literary device of moving from the greatest to the smallest.[15] Paul reminds them of the greatest position they have in the kingdom of God. Now, on the basis of his previous question, he asks another question, if you are the future judges of this world, why are you not able to settle small issues among yourselves, instead of taking it to the pagan judges? Through this question, Paul passes the message that being the future judges of the world the Church should be able to mediate and settle the matters in the congregation itself.

In his fourth question, Paul once again uses the same literary device that he had used above (v.3). Paul includes one greatest thing and one smallest thing in this question to remind them of the need for solving any issues in the church itself. Paul even includes himself as he asks the question – *Do you not know that **we** are to judge angels?* This signifies that like other issues discussed above, Paul had already told them about the fall of the angels and the judgment awaiting them. These angels were spirit beings around God's throne, but because of their pride, they were cut down from their position (Jude 6). Paul stresses that in the *eschaton* the saints will judge not only the world but also the angels. Hence, they must be able to find solutions to ordinary matters also.

Paul's fourth rhetorical question is found in verse 4. He asks, *if you have ordinary cases, then, do you appoint as judges those who have no standing in the church?* The literal meaning of the phrase *who have no standing in the church* is, those who have been counted as nothing. Paul had already mentioned about the law status of the Corinthian believers in 1:28. In that case ἐξουθενημένους (*exouthenēmevous* – despised/disdain/who have no standing in the Church) can be related to 6:4.

However, when we connect it with Paul's entire argument in chapter 6, it does not suit the context, for chapter 6 is all about Corinthian believers taking their problems to the outside court. Even Paul's questions from verses 1-3 vividly portray that the Corinthians appointed outsiders as judges to settle issues inside the church. Therefore, the phrase *exouthenēmevous,* refers not to the believers in the church who are low in status or counted as nothing, rather, it is Paul's sharp accusation to the believers who appoint pagan judges against their fellow brothers.

Though the proconsul or a Roman judge is a well-qualified person in terms of Roman law and other civil affairs, Paul considers them as *having no standing in the church of God*. For Paul, even though the believers are not legally trained, by virtue of being the children of God, and knowing the word of God, they are far more competent to settle disagreements among themselves rather than the experienced, unbelieving judge.

In his fifth question (v. 5) Paul reminds them of their negligence in exercising their authority rightly. He strongly rebukes them with the phrase, *I say this to your shame*. It is a contradicting statement because in 4:14 Paul already said to them *I am not writing this to make you ashamed*...but now Paul clearly says that his words are meant to shame them. To accelerate the austerity of his shaming, he further asks them, *is there no one among you wise enough to decide between one believer and another?*

Though in a sarcastic manner Paul had already told them, you have *all you want*! you have *become rich*! you have *become kings*! (4:8). To such a community where wisdom was so important he now asks, is there no one among you *wise enough* to decide between one believer and another? By asking this question, Paul is not suggesting them to appoint a judge to issue a verdict between brothers who are having the problem among them. Rather, by employing the word σοφός (*sophos*) Paul exhorts them to appoint a *skillful or experienced* person to play the role of a mediator who will be able to bring mutual understanding and agreement among the brothers.

In verse 6 Paul asks his sixth question, *but a believer goes to court against a believer-and before unbelievers at that?* Though the Corinthians are fond of wisdom and speech they were not able to adapt it in their day to day life in a spirit-filled, godly manner. Rather they thought that they would get justice more easily from a pagan court than from their own community.

Through these six questions mentioned in verses 1-6, Paul vividly portrays how the Corinthians were losing their credibility in terms of their future status. Forgetting their status in the eschaton, they were dragging one another in into the unbelieving judges. Hence Paul's question to them was, if you are unable to settle problems among yourselves now, how will you be able to judge the world and the angels in the eschaton?

2.1.3.1.2 It will make the Saints Wrongdoer/Defrauder (vv.7-8)

Paul's second argument against the church taking its issues to the court outside is because it makes them a wrongdoer or a defrauder. For Paul, even if one church member wins his case against another church member, *it is still a defeat* for them, since they were not willing to settle among themselves, though being brothers and sisters in Christ. So, even if a brother wins, he still loses, as he was not magnanimous enough to endure the injury; and the church as a whole loses its credibility forgoing before a gentile court. It is a *defeat* also because they claimed to be wise, and were addressed as *wise* (6:5); but a truly wise person cannot be harmed or be defrauded by any kind of insult. However, the

Corinthians being arrogant and morally weak, dishonored God and harmed the testimony of the church by their self-centered behavior.

In verse 7b, Paul asks two pertinent questions to the Corinthians. He asks, why not rather be wronged? Why not rather be defrauded? Paul asks these questions because taking a fellow brother to a secular court shows the lack of love and unity among them. Hence through these questions, he requests them to exercise Christian love and self-restraint.

In the first question the verb used is ἀδικεῖσθε, *adikeisthe*–means doing contrary to what is right. This is the middle voice of the verb used in the second question which is ἀποστερεῖσθε, *apostereisthe* (steal, rob, defraud). The meaning of the second verb is often connected with the theft of money or property of another.[16] However in both the cases, taking a fellow brother to a court outside is strictly prohibited for the Christian community.

Going a step further, Paul also indicates the seriousness of the effect on the Corinthian community. He states that by doing so, *you yourselves become a wrongdoer and defrauder* (v.8). It is true that the Corinthian Christians were dragging one another to the pagan courts for the wrong done unto them. However, through this action of theirs, they themselves (that is, the righteous party who drags the guilty party to the court) become a wrongdoer/defrauder. In other words, Paul is implying that those who drag a fellow Christian to court, is guilty of the same misconduct which they are charging to rectify.

2.1.3.1.3 The Wrongdoer will not Inherit the Kingdom of God (vv.9-11)

Finally, Paul mentions the dire consequence of having lawsuits among believers. His argument in verses 9-11 divulges that believers should not go to court because it will result in them losing the kingdom of God. The last rhetorical question of Paul in chapter 6 is seen in verse 9a-*Do you not know that the wrongdoers will not inherit the kingdom of God?*

In verse 8 Paul intimates that they are in danger of being in the same situation as the people of this world. In verses 9b-10, Paul lists the worldly people as fornicators, idolaters, adulterers, male prostitutes, sodomites, thieves, greedy, drunkards, revilers, robbers etc. Paul's argument here is that, when they sue their brothers for any wrongdoing, they are no better than the worldly people. Hence, Paul labels them as *wrongdoers* (v.9), and like the worldly people, they too will not inherit the kingdom of God.

In verse 11a Paul reminds them that *this is what some of you used to be*. When Paul reached Corinth the first time, some of them lived in sexual and social sins, but through the light of the gospel Paul brought them to salvation and they were washed, sanctified, and justified in the name of the Lord Jesus and in the Spirit of God (v.11). Hence, they should not revert back to their previous sinful life by taking their fellow brother to court. It not only makes them a wrongdoer but would also prevent them from inheriting the kingdom of God, as no wrongdoers would inherit God's kingdom.

Summary

The discussion above clearly demonstrates Paul's reasons, why the church should keep itself away from court cases. Paul indicated three main aspects as he discusses this particular concern with regards to Corinthian Christians. First of all, Paul reminds them about who they are at present, and what their status is going to be in the eschaton. In verses 1-5, Paul reminds them that they are saints and that they would be judging both, the people of this world and fallen angels. Paul prompts them that they are no longer ordinary people like others in this world, but rather are called by God to be saints and to sit with Christ as judges in the kingdom of God at Christ's return.

In verses 6-11, Paul discloses the dire consequences of taking a fellow brother to court, consequences which has its effects not only in this age but also in the age to come. In verses 6-8 Paul had argued that their involvement in court cases, whether as an accused or a defendant is a defeat for them for, either way, they would have dishonored God and the Christian community.

In verses 9-11, Paul presented his third reason. Paul reminds them that they are now washed, sanctified, and justified in the name of the Lord Jesus Christ and in the Spirit of God, and are set apart. Hence, he warns them not to practice the patterns of this world, by taking their fellow brothers to court, and thus become a wrongdoer once again. Rather, they ought to solve their disputes and differences through mediation, promote the welfare of the Christian community, and bear a clear witness to the world.

2.1.4 Christian Liberty and Fornication/Harlotry (6:12-20)

After admonishing the Corinthians about litigation, Paul now returns to the subject of immorality which was discussed earlier in chapter 5. However, in chapter 6 he talks about it in the broader context of Christian freedom. His discussion about this concern starts with their famous slogan Πάντα μοι ἔξεστιν (*Panta moi exestin* – "all things are lawful for me"), which once again points toward their nature of boasting on worldly wisdom and self-sufficiency. Though not specifically mentioned anywhere in I Corinthians that this was reported to Paul either by Chloe or somebody else, as it was a famous proverb then; it is this author's educated guess that it may have been reported to Paul. Therefore, Paul now attempts to educate them how their freedom in Christ must be exercised in their religious and social life.

Harlotry was a serious issue in the Corinthian church. It is assumed that some of the men in the congregation were still practicing their pre-conversion life. During those days prostitution was a legalized act and was freely accepted as part of their socio-religious life. The City of Corinth was well known for the practice of prostitution. The temple of Aphrodite, who was considered as the goddess of beauty and love, was the center of this practice wherein 1000 prostitutes supposedly worked around the clock.

Though the temple itself had fallen into ruins during Paul's time, these temple prostitutes continued to ply their profession in the city. Having sex with a temple prostitute was not considered as adultery, but was a part and practice of their religious life. For them having sex with one of Aphrodite's servants would lead them to experience a mystical union with the goddess herself. In this way the city of Corinth had become known for its immorality; and the name 'Corinth' itself became for, immorality.

As Paul deals with this issue, along with a few rhetorical questions, he uses diatribe as the main tool to communicate his message to the Corinthian Christians. Some believers in the church at Corinth were misusing their freedom in Christ for worldly pleasures thinking that they were free from the constraints of conventional morality. According to Garland, Corinthian Christians were carried away due to their wrong understanding of freedom from the Law of Moses in Christ Jesus. They assumed that now as Christians because they are free from the Law of Moses, they can sin and still have remission of their sins. Garland also mentions that the Corinthian's problem of immorality began with their wrong notion that the body is just a material substance which has no place in the glorious destiny of the believer.[17]

Therefore, Paul writes that the Corinthian Christians may reflect on the purpose of the human body and its constrained sexual freedom, especially in light of their freedom as Christians. It is debated whether this section is an extension of Paul's discussion in chapter 5 or an introduction of chapter 7, wherein he deals with marriage and celibacy. Though it has the common topic of sexual immorality, in this section he specifically discusses about fornication/harlotry, whether permissible for Christians or not.

Paul emphasizes that Christian freedom does not mean licentiousness, hence it has nothing to do with prostitution or harlotry. The freedom Christians have in Christ is not a license to sin. Everything that is permissible or lawful has to contribute for the good of others. Thus in this section, Paul educates them about the importance of keeping away from prostitution or harlotry, as it is a sin against one's own body.

2.1.4.1 Paul's Response: "Do not Indulge Your Body in Sexual Immorality with a Harlot"

Paul validates his argument in this section with few reasons blended with several parallels (vv.12-17) and strong imperatives (vv.18-20).

2.1.4.1.1 It is Not Beneficial and Will Make Your Body a Slave (v.12)

Paul validates his first argument by responding to the Corinthians saying, fornication is not beneficial as it makes our body a slave. The first phrase in the verse, *all things are lawful for me* (12a), is seemingly Paul's own words. Similar kind of phrasing is seen in many occasions throughout Pauline corpus as part of his hortatory statements. But here Paul doesn't use 1st person singular to make a hortatory statement. Rather he cites a famous slogan from Corinthians' background without mentioning that he is citing it from their own context.

He uses many other proverbs in his writings where he clearly indicates that it is cited from the works of others (e.g., Titus 1:12). Fitzmyr suggests 32 occurrences of such kind are found in Pauline letters.[18] Whereas nothing similar is found here as Paul employs this slogan. Though Paul mainly uses 1st person singular in hortatory statements, in this instance the context is totally different from that of the other. Thus it makes the statement a proverb, rather than a hortatory statement.

This proverb was widely used by the free thinkers among the Corinthian believers. They used this maxim to cover up all their immoral behaviors. They were of the opinion that they are free to do whatever they want. Consequently, they exceeded the limits of acceptable Christian behavior. Therefore Paul uses this particular slogan four times (twice in 6:12 and twice in 10:23) in this epistle to condemn Corinthians' wrong thinking and practice of Christian freedom in their life.

The word ἔξεστιν (*exestin*) in English is translated as lawful/permissible from its root word ἔξειμι (*exeimi,* ἔξ [out of] + ειμι [I am]) which literally means, *I am out of/away from me*. Therefore the word seems to reflect a sense of individual empowerment and authority the Corinthians professed in terms of anything that bound them with restrictions. Bruce rightly connects it with the gnostic group in the congregation who also followed Philo's philosophy, namely, 'One who act rightly will have the power to do anything and to live as he wishes.'[19] In their self-sufficient nature, they thought whatever they do is right, therefore they have the right to do anything. Thus, they were trying to justify sexual immorality in their life. But with sufficient reasons for verse 12b and d, Paul disproves the wrong practices of the Corinthian Christians.

The first reason Paul posits is, ἀλλ' οὐ πάντα συμφέρει (*all ou panta sumpherei* - not *all things are beneficial/profitable* (v.12a). Here Paul limits Corinthian's application of *all things* to immoral sexual acts with the conjunction *but.* Paul's understanding of 'beneficial' was totally different from that of the Corinthians. According to him, what is beneficial predominantly relates to what benefits others. Throughout I Corinthians Paul stresses this ideain his exhortations (7:35; 10:33; 12:7). Therefore Paul says, as not everything contributes to the good of others, or is profitable for others, consequently, we do not have the right to do *all things,* without considering its harmful effects on others.

The second reason Paul posits is ἀλλ' οὐκ ἐγὼ ἐξουσιασθήσομαι ὑπό τινος (*all ouk egōexousiasthēsomai hupo tinos* – but I will not be mastered by anything). Paul's reaction to the second slogan expresses the message that, though everything is lawful, he has to exercise his control over it,so that it does not have mastery/control over him. Paul makes this statement beautifully with a wordplay between ἔξεστιν (*exestin* – permissible) and ἐξουσιασθήσομαι (*exousiasthēsomai* – be mastered/authority over).[20] It can also be rephrased as, though all things are permissible or within my power, yet I will not be mastered or overpowered by anything.

Sexual sins, through one's body, controls the whole being. Therefore, believers must never allow sexual sins to control them but must control it in the Lord's strength. By this Paul exposes sexual sins and its effect on the life of believers. Paul firmly rejects their ungodly concept that freedom in Christ has given them the license to sin. Thus, Paul exhorts the Corinthian Christians to detach themselves from all kinds of earthly things which will enslave them.

2.1.4.1.2 Your Body is not Meant for Immorality, but for the Lord and Members of Christ (vv.13-17)

Moving from a general slogan to a specific saying, Paul now presents his second reason as to why Christians should not contaminate their body in sexual immorality. Paul's second reason to the main argument, *do not participate our body in sexual immorality with a harlot*, is because our bodies are not meant for sexual immorality, but for the Lord and are members of Christ's body, the church (vv. 13-17).

"Food is meant for the stomach and the stomach for food." It is often argued that Paul here introduces another slogan/proverb because it resembles the slogan mentioned in v. 12. However, the sentence, "and God will destroy both one and the other" is most probably included by Paul himself, and could be understood as part of Paul's reaction to the slogan expressed in the first two clauses. Obviously, the slogan would include all bodily functions, particularly sex. Yet, Paul may just be stating a basic and widely accepted truth - food for the stomach and stomach for the food, and both will be destroyed.

After stating this, Paul contrasts this fact with theological truths that the body is for the Lord and the Lord for the body, and God will raise it by his power. Paul brings in this argument because the Corinthians were thinking that the body had nothing to do with one's morality.[21] Perhaps, because of some worldly, philosophical influence, they thought that sex is purely biological, like eating. So, the Corinthians like many of their pagan friends probably used this analogy to justify their sexual immorality. Therefore by emphasizing the temporal nature of body and food, Paul rejects their analogical justification and proceeds to reveal his real concern behind using the slogan of, food and stomach.

Paul's real concern in this argument is given in verse 13c-17. Verse 13c says τὸ δὲ σῶμα οὐ τῇ πορνείᾳ ἀλλὰ τῷ κυρίῳ, καὶ ὁ κύριος τῷ σώματι (*to de sōma ou tē porneia alla tō kuriō, kai ho kurios tō sōmati* – the body is not meant for fornication but for the Lord and the Lord for the body). It is true that the physical body of a human being is indeed involved in, and even intended for sexuality, but not for fornication. For, such kind of sexual acts is contrary to the destiny of human beings, as the human body is τῷ κυρίω, (*tō kuriō*-for the Lord). Here τῷ κυρίω is in dative case (dative of interest).[22]

It is a clear indication that one should use his or her body to serve the Lord. God created the human body not for sinful pleasures, but for his glory. Therefore Paul reminds them that their use of the body for fornication is absolutely against the purpose of God. Hence Paul says, as food and the stomach is meant for each other, the physical body and the Lord are meant for each other. Though food and stomach are temporal, body and soul are eternal. During Paul's time, the Greek philosophers considered the human body as having no value, but the soul was considered very important. Therefore Paul categorically states that, as God raised Jesus physically from the dead, he will raise us bodily also (v.14).

Using a rhetorical question Paul brings his next important argument in this section. With this question, Paul tries to refresh the memory of Corinthians believers and demands a positive answer. Paul asks, *do you not know that your bodies are members of Christ?* (v.15a). Through this question, Paul continues the thought of verse 13, wherein he had stated that the body is for the Lord and the Lord is for the body. Now in this verse, he reveals one more dimension, and that is, the physical body of each believer is a member of the body of Christ, which is the Church.

Paul continuous with another question, *should I therefore take the members of Christ and make them members of a prostitute?* (v.15b) Paul answers himself with a resounding, No! Never! (μὴ γένοιτο (*mē genoito*), literally, not to become!). As mentioned before, fornication and sexual immorality were lawful activities in Corinth, practiced even by some believers. Now Paul teaches them that if they are the members of the body of Christ, then they cannot be sexually united with a prostitute.

Paul gives his reason in verse 16 with another question, *do you not know that whoever is united to a prostitute becomes one body with her?* Here Paul clarifies that sexual union between a man and a woman produces a 'one flesh' union. So, to have a sexual union with a prostitute is akin to uniting Christ with that prostitute. Therefore Paul exhorts the Corinthians not to use their body for sexual immorality as it is meant for the Lord and is members of Christ's body.

2.1.4.1.3 You will be a Sinner against Your own Body (v.18)

Paul's third argument is that fornication is a sin against one's own body. Therefore Paul says, Φεύγετε τὴν πορνείαν (*pheugete tēn porneian* - flee from fornication). This phrase serves as the heart of Paul's argument in this verse. The word Φεύγετε, introduces an emphatic command that summarizes the entire argument of Paul about sexual immorality. Fitzmyer posits that the imperative Φεύγετε (*pheugete* [2nd person plural], lit. you flee) refer to Joseph's escape from Potiphar's wife in Genesis 39:12.[23] Even though this was a well-known incident in ancient Judaism, Paul does not make an explicit use of it. But by employing the verb *flee*, which is in the present tense, Paul highlights sexual immorality that was practiced continuously by some of the Corinthian believers. So, Paul instructs the Corinthians that they must be away from sexual immorality in their *daily life* as they live in the sexually deteriorated context of Corinth.

Another notable phrase Paul uses in this verse isὁ δὲ πορνεύων εἰς τὸ ἴδιον σῶμα ἁμαρτάνει (*ho de poneuon eis to oidion sōma hamartanei* – but the fornicator sins against one's own body). The expression prior to the above-stated phrase adds more weight to the argument of Paul in this verse. It says *every sin that a person commits is outside the body* (18a). It is debated whether it is a Corinthian slogan or Paul's own statement. Some scholars suggest that since the word *other* is not in Greek, it is a Corinthian slogan Paul employs to accelerate the significance of his argument. However, NRSV does not use the word *other* (RSV, NIV) but *every sin.*

Paul continuous his argument in 18b saying sexual immorality, in particular, is a sin against one's own body. By employing the word σῶμα he does not refer it to the corporate body of Christ. But his concern is with the final clause, that in sexual immorality a man sins against *his own body.* All other sins such as greed, idolatry etc. happen outside one's body, but in fornication one sins against his own body and pollutes that which is destined to be the instruments for worshipping God. Sexual sins destroy a person like no other sins, for it is so intimate and entangling, corrupting on the deepest human level. Therefore Paul warns the Corinthian believers to be away from all kinds of sexual immorality.

2.1.4.1.4 Your Body is Purchased with a Price to be the Temple of the Holy Spirit (vv.19-20)

Finally Paul exhorts the Corinthians to avoid sexual immorality because their bodies are purchased with a price to be the temple of the Holy Spirit. In these verses, Paul provides the theological explanation of his entire argument from 6:12-18.In this process he provides two imagery, imagery of a *temple,* and a *slave market.*

Presenting temple as imagery, Paul asks the Corinthians, *do you not know that your body is a temple of the Holy Spirit within you?* The phrase ναὸς τοῦ ἐν ὑμῖν ἁγίου πνεύματός (*naos tou en humin agiou pneumatos* – temple of the Holy Spirit) was known to the Corinthians because the universal presence of the images of Greco-Roman deities in temples were very familiar to them. The images of deities in Corinth usually dominated the temples either by size or by number.[24] So by announcing *your body is a* ***temple of the Holy*** *Spirit* (τοῦ…πνεύματός, is in the case of genitive of possession, therefore it means, "a temple which belongs to the Holy Spirit") Paul clarifies that their bodies in its totality belong completely to God.

In verse 20 we see a shift in the metaphor which again reveals the total ownership of God over believers' body. Paul says *for you were bought with a price*. Though not rightly mentioned, the word used *you were bought* brings to mind the picture of a slave market. Once a slave is purchased by a master, he or she becomes the property of that particular master. The slave does not have any authority over his own body but the master, therefore he is obliged to live according to his master's will. Paul presents the same idea here.

By using the phrase *you were bought with a price*, Paul reminds the Corinth believers about their redemption through the death of Christ on the cross of Calvary. Christ had brought them with a price i.e., his life therefore now they are owned by Christ. Hence they have no authority over their body and should not enslave themselves to be mastered by any kind of sexual immorality. Paul concludes his lengthy discussion on sexual immorality with a verb imperative *glorify*. This signifies that the supreme purpose of our body is to glorify God.

Summary

The concern discussed in 6:12-20 implies that some Corinthians considered the physical body irrelevant for salvation, and the spirit as a superior entity. They felt free to have sexual relations with prostitutes since in their view it did not affect the redemption of the spirit. There are also possibilities that libertarianism prevailed in the Corinthian church. Therefore, Paul attempted to show the foolishness of their logic and tries to convince them that the body is morally significant.

In the course of discussion, Paul cited few Corinthian slogans (vv. 12-17) which emphasized the independence that the free thinkers in the church professed to have. Their attitude pointed to the idea that the body is morally insignificant. The slogan in verse 12 reveals that they boasted about their unlimited freedom. "All things are lawful to me" (v. 12a). In verse 13 Paul mentions the next slogan which demonstrated their reflection on the body as a transient entity. "Food is for the stomach and the stomach for food but God will ultimately destroy both of them."[25] In each case, Paul answers with a negative, which shows that these sayings are illogical and foolish. Indeed, according to

Paul, this so-called freedom was not beneficial to the person (v. 12a) because it actually leads a believer to bondage (v. 12b).

Therefore in verses 18-20, Paul urges the Corinthians to flee from πόρνεια (v. 18) and to honor God with their σώμα (v. 20). By this Paul asserts that the person who engages in sexual immorality, in fact, performs an act which affects one's spiritual condition, because the σώμα denotes more than just the physical frame; it referred to the entire personality of an individual (v. 18b). This is also the implication in verses 15-17. Finally, Paul emphasized the significance of the human body through the metaphor of a temple (v. 19a). Then, using the slave market metaphor also reiterates that a believer's body no longer belongs to them, but to the Lord who purchased them with his own blood (vv. 19b-20a).

In short, the Corinthian dissenters deprecated the physical body and regarded it as inferior because they apparently dichotomized the body and the spirit. As per their compartmentalization, this made the body irrelevant for salvation and thus gave them license to have sexual relations with prostitutes. Therefore Paul strongly warns them not to use their bodies in sexual immorality rather, flee from fornication, and glorify God in and through their body (v. 20b).

2.2 Paul's Response to the Queries

In chapter 7 and following we have apostle Paul's response to questions asked through a letter carried most probably by Stephanas, Fortunatus, and Achaicus (16:17). The sections in these chapters consist of several sub-sections, which start with the phrase Περὶ δὲ (*Peri de*), now concerning. The word *now* is the translation of δὲ from the original text, which means *but/and*. However, here the word takes the meaning *now* indicating a smooth transition from one topic to another.

Starting with the phrase, *now concerning*, Paul responds to the queries one by one (7:1; 25; 8:1; 11:17; 12:1; 16:1, 12). The main topics Paul deals in these sections are as follows. Matters related to marriage and sex (7), idolatry/eating food offered to idols (8-10), abuse of Lord's Supper (11), proper use of Spiritual Gifts (12-14), the resurrection of the dead (15), and collection for the poor saints in Jerusalem (16).

2.2.1 Marriage and Related Matters (7:1-40)

In the preceding section, Paul had already discussed concerning sexual immorality that was prevalent among Corinthian believers. On this issue, Paul bitterly condemned and urged them to live according to their call in glorifying God. However, he didn't discuss anything about marriage, divorce, and celibacy. Now as he responds to the questions asked, he begins by dealing with the issues concerning marriage and other related matters.

From chapter 7, it is evident that the issues related to marriage and related matters were also a serious issue among the Corinthian believers. Like other problems, though Paul had already reminded them regarding this, they adopted the pagan system of the corrupted Corinth in their marital and other areas of life. Therefore Paul was asked to give advice on marital problems in the church. Hence, he deals with the issues like proper conduct of marriage partners, faithfulness in marital relationship, celibacy, and virginity. But Paul's response to these issues was misunderstood by many and they labeled Paul as a misogamist (one who hates marriage). Therefore it is imperative that we look not into the particular text (ch.7) as Paul's ultimate marriage manual but as his response to specific difficulties such as marriage relationship, celibacy, and divorce among Corinthian believers.

Due to pagan influence, many in the Corinthian congregation did not take their marital life seriously. There were believers who had multiple marriages and divorces. Some among them had the notion that being single will help them to be more spiritual, which could also be a reason for divorce in the congregation. Therefore, Paul corrects their wrong understanding about marriage, sex, status, and celibacy, so that believers can pursue their piety in the lord by remaining in the same status at the time of their conversion.

2.2.1.1 Paul's Response: "Believers Can Pursue Persistent Piety in the Lord by Remaining in the Same Status at the Time of their Call"

Paul's main argument in this chapter which is addressed to the married, unmarried, single, circumcised, uncircumcised, and slaves, is that they can continue to live a holy life in the Lord by remaining in the same status as when converted. Paul clarifies this giving different reasons to the believers who were worried that they need to make some social or relational changes in order to be truly committed to the Lord.

Husbands and wives (vv.1-7) were hesitant to touch their spouses thinking that it will make them impure. The believing partners were worried about their purity because of their union with unbelieving partners (vv.12-16). Paul also exhorts the unmarried to remain single so that they can have an undistracted relationship with the Lord (v.35). Therefore, the main message of Paul in chapter 7 is that they can live a pious life without changing their marital status.

2.2.1.1.1 To the Married

2.2.1.1.1.1 Husbands and Wives Must Remain Same by Fulfilling their Conjugal Rights to Each Other (vv.1-5, 10-11)

Though it is difficult to understand the correct meaning of verse 1b, it is essential to identify it because it determines the crux of the entire chapter.

What the phrase really means is a debated issue in scholarly circles. If it is Paul's advice to practice celibacy he would be contradicting Genesis 2:18, *it is not good for the man to be alone*. Therefore, to know the background of this text is very important.

It is assumed that a group of believers was abstaining themselves from immorality which was prevalent in the Corinthian city. Some of them even advocated celibacy and declared it as a norm for rest of the believers in order to have an undistracted devotion to God. But a close reading of the text gives us the understanding that Paul is not saying, it is good for a man not to marry a woman. In Greek, the word ἄνθρωπος (*anthrōpos*) generally refers to human being/man than the *husband* (ἀνήρ - *anēr*). Therefore, it is to be understood in its literal sense *a man not to touch a woman*.

Now the question is, what does Paul really mean by the expression, *not to touch*. In the Jewish context (Gen.20:6; Prov. 6:29) and Greek antiquity,[26] the expression μὴ ἅπτεσθαι (*mē aptesthai*–not to touch) refers to an unpleasant sexual relationship between a man and a woman. So it is clear that Paul is not talking about sexual intercourse between husband and wife, but in light of his prior prohibition of sexual immorality mentioned in 6:12-20, and reiterated in verse 2.

Verse 2a provides a clear explanation of verse 1b – *but because of the case of sexual immorality, each man should have his own wife and each woman her own husband*. The Greek word used for sexual immorality is πορνείας (*porneias*) literally means, fornication. The plural form of *porneia* refers to the regular occurrences of sexual relations with prostitutes. Yet it does not expresses a positive reason for marriage since διὰ (*dia* – but) at the beginning of verse 2 express the notion of opposition or antithesis.

It was a great temptation to live in the ancient city of Corinth where sexual immorality was rampant. However, through the above expression, Paul reminds them about the danger of fornication not only to those who were single, but also to those who were married, yet were leading an unsatisfied sexual life within marriage (v.5). To the unmarried Paul says, *each man should have his own wife and each woman her own husband* (v.2b); and to the married couples Paul commands – *The husband should give to his wife her conjugal rights, and likewise the wife to her husband* (v.3).

In verse 3, Paul emphasizes the equality of man and woman in their marital life. He clarifies that physical relationship within marriage is not just a privilege, but also a responsibility. It is to be considered sacred and obligatory. It is obligatory because, neither husband nor wife has any authority over their own body, but over each other's. Fitzmyer comments that there were quarrels among spouses due to abstinence from sexual intercourse.[27] This must be the reason for Paul's command to spouses to submit themselves sexually to each other's authority (vv.4-5). The word ἐξουσιάζει (*exousiazei* – to have authority over someone), is in the present active tense, which signifies that spouses' mutual authority over each other is continuous and lasts throughout their marital life.

Paul starts verse 5 with a negative imperative, μὴ ἀποστερεῖτε ἀλλήλους (*mē apostereite allēlous* – do not deprive one another). Some of the married couples in the church were depriving each other of their marital rights. So Paul says, do not deprive/do not defraud your spouse with regards to conjugal rights, because God intended marriage to be permanent, so sexual relationship within marriage should also be permanent. Whether the spouse is a believer or an unbeliever, complete sexual abstinence is not allowed in their marital life. When abstaining from sex, it has to be with mutual consent and that too only for a limited period.

Through the clause ἐκ συμφώνου (*ek sumphēnou* – by agreement [lit. out of harmonious agreement]) in 5a, Paul once again emphasis equality of gender in intimate relationships. A significant number of church members were concerned only with their spiritual intimacy with God, and not physical intimacy with their life partner.[28] It was mostly practiced by the prophets in the congregation who thought it is all about their status, freedom, and rights, than fulfilling the conjugal rights of a husband to his spouse andvice versa. Therefore Paul says, they can be away from physical intimacy with an agreement for a set time ἵνα σχολάσητε τῇ προσευχῇ (*hina scholasēte tē proseuchē - to devote yourselves to prayer*) literally, in order to devote/give the spouse time for prayer.

Paul further tells them to resume their normal functions as husband and wife so that they may not be tempted by Satan because of their lack of self-control. Satan is always at work to exploit human weaknesses by tempting either the husband or wife into committing adultery. So to permanently restrain from sexual relationship within marriage, in order to pursue a holy life, is contrary to God's gracious provision of marriage and the gift of sexuality; and can lead the weaker person into sexual immorality.

In verses 10-11, Paul moves on to the issue of divorce. Paul advises the married couple by saying, *the wife should not separate from her husband and that the husband should not divorcehis wife.* By employing the clause οὐκ ἐγὼ ἀλλὰ ὁ κύριος (*ouk egō alla ho kurios* – not I but the Lord), Paul alludes to an early Christian tradition. The prohibition undoubtedly stems from Jesus' tradition (Mk. 10; Lk. 16:18; Matt. 5:31-32; 19:3-9).

The Greek word χωρισθῆναι, *chōristhēnai* means separate/depart/or to leave. In classical and Hellenistic Greek, as well as in Greek marriage contracts, this word commonly meant *divorce.*[29] So Paul not only says that wives should not leave or separate from their husbands but also should not divorce them.

In verse 11a, Paul recommends two imperative options for women who are separated from their husbands–*let her remain unmarried or else be reconciled to her husband.* It is not sure that Paul is addressing an existing issue, or forming a principle as a hypothetical case that can happen in the future. The point to observe is that Paul does not offer a third option to the separated women, of getting married to another man in order to avoid sexual immorality. The only two options Paul gives are, either remain unmarried or be reconciled to their husbands.

Paul advocates the same prohibition to the husbands that they should not divorce their wives (v.11b). In Jewish and Greco-Roman societies only husbands had the privilege to divorce his wife to enjoy freedom in life. However, Paul commands Christian husbands not to divorce their wives, either for personal or for spiritual freedom. By this Paul reminds the married couples that they can continue to live a holy life by remaining in their marital status and fulfilling their conjugal rights to each other.

2.2.1.1.2 To the Widows

2.2.1.1.2.1 It is Good for Widows to Remain Single Who have Self-Control, However Free to Get Married in the Lord (vv. 8-9, 32-35, 39-40)

In the sections preceding and following, Paul's word to the specified group is to remain as they were at the time of their call. On the contrary in this section, Paul speaks to the unmarried and widows to remain in their same status, with the exception mentioned in verse 9. Before going to its details it is imperative to know whether Paul is referring to the unmarried and widows or to widowers and widows. For, the word used for unmarried in Greek is τοῖς ἀγάμοις (*tois agamois*) which is in the dative masculine plural, which literally means, to the unmarried men. Since Paul's special instructions to the virgins are given in verse 25ff, it adds more weight to the aforementioned meaning.

There is also a difficulty in interpreting the verse in connection to the meaning of the word, *unmarried*. The term unmarried is mentioned four times in this epistle (7:8, 11, 32, and 34). These verses make sure that the unmarried and widows are not the same. Further, verse11 tells the divorcees to remain unmarried, which distinguishes them from widows (single from death-vv. 39-40) and virgins (not yet married-vv. 25,28). Therefore the term *unmarried* here refers to those who are married, but now are separated/divorced; and not to widower or widows.

However, the major question here is, how then can Paul allow the divorced to get married again as mentioned in verse 9b. Therefore, the former gives a better meaning to the text in its context. Even Paul alludes himself to the context of the text. He says *it is well for them to remain unmarried as I am* (v.8). Being a widower, Paul affirms his former marriage identifying with the unmarried and the widows. He suggests them so because their status as unmarried gives them the freedom to serve the Lord (vv.32-34).

However Paul makes an exception-if the widowers and widows are unable to control their sexual desires, then they should get married again. Paul is not commanding them to remain single in order to serve the Lord (vv.39). Without marrying, or even remarrying, they can still pursue persistent piety to the Lord, as long as they are don't give in to sexual immorality.

2.2.1.1.3 To the Believing Husband and Unbelieving Wife and Vice Versa

2.2.1.1.3.1 Believers Should Live With their Unbelieving Partners Because the Unbelieving Partners are Made Holy through the Believing Partners (vv.12-16)

In this section, Paul deals with the worry of those who were married to unbelievers and concerned about the purity of their spiritual life in light of Paul's teaching regarding their body as being members of Christ and temple of the Holy Spirit. Some of them thought that the physical union with their unbelieving spouses is equal to blending Christ with Satan. It was a justifiable concern asked by the Corinthians to Paul.

Stating his apostolic authority λέγω ἐγὼ (*legō egō* -I say), Paul gives a categorical answer to the question of mixed marriages, about which Jesus did not give any instructions during his earthly ministry. It is to be presumed that at the time of marriage both the individuals were unbelievers. So the present question arises from the context when one, later on, becomes a believer, and the other, not. Therefore this section cannot be considered as a rule for believers who knowingly marry an unbeliever.

Paul's answer to the believers in this matter is that they should not divorce their unbelieving partners (vv.12-13). Paul advises the believing spouse to continue in their marriage vow if the unbelieving spouse is content to live with them. The reason is being unbelieving husbands and wives are made holy through the believing partners (v.14). In this verse, Paul uses the verb ἡγίασται, *hēgiastai - to make holy, consecrate, or sanctify* to refer to both, the unbelieving husbands and wives. As mentioned in verse 14c, *holy* is always contrasted with *unclean*. Consequently, some of the Corinthian believers feared that their union with the unbelieving spouse will make them unclean. However, Paul exhorts them not to divorce their unbelieving spouses, as such marriages are still legitimate in sight of God, and their union with each other may result in God's blessing to the entire family.

However, there remains a question about the word *made holy* employed in verse 14 since it has many connotations in the Bible. The word is used to denote things set aside for cultic activities (Ex. 29:37, 44); to consecrate people either by baptism (1Cor. 6:11), marriage (1Cor.7:14), or atonement for sin (Heb.9:13); to admire peoples, names, or things (1Peter 3:15); and to purify someone from evil.[30] In this instant, Paul uses the word ἡγίασται, *hēgiastai* (to sanctify), to denote the present status of Corinthian couples, and how their unbelieving partners are made holy through their life.

This seems contradictory to what Paul had instructed them earlier– *a little yeast leavens the whole batch of dough* (5:6b). Nevertheless, the chief idea Paul tries to convey is that the unbelieving partner, by remaining married to the believing spouse, is kept separate from the sinful world and is within the new community of Christ, therefore is made holy/sanctified; just as a *temple* sanctifies *the things* in it, or the *altar* sanctifies *the gift* laid upon it. In both the cases, the object is not holy by itself, but its association with the subject which being holy, makes them holy. In this sense, *the holy* (believing partners) are more powerful than the unholy (unbelieving partners).

In 14b Paul gives another reason to substantiate his argument in verses 12-13. The word ἐπεὶ (*epei* – since/otherwise) in 14b reflects the idea that Paul gives it as another reason for those are not convinced with the first reason mentioned above. Through this Paul tries to convince the believing spouses that they need not separate from their unbelieving spouses, fearing that their children will be defiled by their unbelieving spouse. Paul clarifies that they would be unclean (ἀκάθαρτά, *akatharta* – unclean) if both parents are unsaved, but the children share the believing partners' holiness since they are part of the Christian community. Because of these reasons, Paul strongly commands the believing partners not to divorce their unbelieving partners.

However, it is with the exception of verse 15 where Paul posits, *but if the unbelieving partners separates, let it be so; in such a case the brother* (the believing husband) *or sister* (believing wife*) is not bound.* The words used to describe *unbelieving partners* in Greek is ὁ ἄπιστος (*ho apistos*) which is in masculine, nominative, singular form, which literally means, *the unbelieving husband.* But in this case, the grammatical gender adds more weight to the meaning of the text in its background than the biological gender. Therefore the meaning of the word is mostly considered as an unbelieving partner.

Paul allows divorce only when an unbelieving partner (either male or female) seeks dissolution. Fee rightly calls this as "Pauline privilege."[31] For, in this case, the believing brother or sister is not under bondage or compulsion to retain the marital status. Paul employs the term δεδούλωται (*dedoulōtai* - to bring under subjection, or to enslave), to denote that they are exempted from his command in verse 12 and 13. The bond of marriage is broken only by death (Rom. 7:2), adultery (Matt. 19:9) or an unbeliever leaving his or her partner. In this case, the believing partner is not bound since it is the unbelieving partner who chooses to leave.

Hence, the way Paul handles the issue here is entirely different from that of verses 12-14. Paul doesn't even use words such as remain or reconcile, as mentioned in verses 11a. Paul says so because in that instant both the spouses are believers. However, in this instant, the divorce is initiated by the unbelieving partner. So Paul says *ou dedoulōtai*-literally, has not been enslaved. In light of the meaning of the word *ou dedoulōtai*. Fitzmyer considers verse 15 as an exception for believing spouses to remarry. Even Paul's conclusion in verse 15c-it is to peace that God has called you, seems like his concession to the isolated partner.

But to finalize it in this way is so complicated without knowing whether verse 15c goes with the preceding or following sentence. If it is a continuation of the preceding verse, it gives the idea of Paul's exception for a second marriage; if not, divorce is not permissible even if it is initiated by the unbelieving spouse. The interpretation of this text lies in how we look into it. If it is all about the unbelieving partners leaving their believing partners, then Paul probably allows them to divorce. For Paul is not advocating them to convince or demand their unbelieving spouses to live with them as it may probably worsen their situation, hence separate peacefully, as it is for peace that God has called us.

Linking of verse 15c with the following will give the meaning that the believing partner peacefully struggles with the issue for they might save their unbelieving partners. But the question is, how is it possible in the context of an unbelieving partner leaving the believing one. Moreover, in this section, Paul does not specifically speak anything about remarriage. Therefore, without giving much emphasis on Pauline privilege mentioned in verse 15, one can come to a safe conclusion by concentrating on Paul's main argument given in verses12-14 and 16, which is also the main theme that flows throughout this chapter, and that is, Paul's main teaching in this section is that they can pursue persistent piety to the Lord even if their partners are unbelievers.

2.2.1.1.4 To the Circumcised and Uncircumcised

2.2.1.1.4.1 Believers Should Remain Circumcised or Uncircumcised According to the Status at the Time of their Call Because Neither Circumcision Nor Uncircumcision Matters but Keeping the Commandment of God is Everything (vv.18-20)

The main theme Paul highlights in the entire chapter is about *not changing one's existing status* for the sake of attaining high spiritual standards. Corinthian believers thought that their social status had great religious significance and they were thinking of changing their present status to achieve higher spiritual paradigms. However, Paul clarifies their understanding of *spirituality* by bringing about a radical difference in their perception about it in light of their call from God (1:9).

To make this point more evident, Paul takes one of the elements of social status from his Jewish background which is περιτομὴ (*perotomē* -Circumcision). The Corinthian congregation was a mixture of both Jews and Gentiles. By employing circumcision as an example, Paul reinforces his argument to the Corinthians with a strong command that they must remain in the same status in which they were called. In this section, Paul gives two strong commands (v.18b and d) interjected by two questions.

Paul's first question is given in verse 18a. He asks, Περιτετμημένος τις ἐκλήθη; (*Peritetmēmenos tis eklēthē-* was anyone at the time of his call already circumcised?). If they were already circumcised, Paul commands them Μὴ ἐπισπάσθω (*Mē epispasthō* -let him not become uncircumcised/seek to remove the marks of circumcision). Paul uses the word ἐπισπάσθω because of the unlawful practice that existed among Jewish Christians in the Corinthian church. It was apparently the same unlawful act some of the Palestinian Jews were practicing it in order to achieve a place in the social hierarchy.

Though circumcision was considered as a part of Law obedience by most of the Jews, many young Jews attempted to remove the mark of circumcision for the purpose of progressing in the field of education and sports. They did so because the mark of circumcision was a dishonor for them while they bathed in public and exercised in the gymnasiums.

This practice was very common in the first century. This is mentioned in the rabbinic writings such as Aboth 3:11, Jerushalmi Peah 1 and 16b, Lamentations Rabbah 1:20 etc. Josephus, the Jewish historian also records that during the Greek rule many Jews went through this surgical performance to be accepted by the Greek society.[32] Philo mentioned in his book *De Specialibus Legibus* that circumcision was an act ridiculed by many in his days.[33] A detailed description of such kind of surgical procedure is also mentioned by Celsus the Roman encyclopedist of first century A.D.[34]

As mentioned above the word used here to denote the practice of removing the mark of circumcision is ἐπισπάσθω. The word originates from another word ἐπισπάομαι which literally means, *Let him not pull over the foreskin to conceal circumcision*. This is the only instance where this word is used in the entire New Testament in a medical sense.[35] The Jews who underwent such surgical performance were called as *epispatics*, which also originates from the term *epispaomai*, meaning, *to draw over/to pull towards*.[36] This is the same word Paul uses here to denote the unlawful act of the Jewish Christians. Since the mark of circumcision was a humiliation in the Roman world during Paul's and even before Jesus' time, many Jews tempted to hide their mark of ethnicity to gain higher social status.

Against this unlawful act of Jewish Christians Paul says, Let them not seek to remove the mark of their circumcision. Either to achieve higher social status or spiritual significance, no Jews were encouraged to undo the mark of circumcision. Paul uses this example to show that it makes no difference when one comes to Christianity from Judaism. Denying one's ethnic background or physical condition will not add anything to the grace he/she received at the time of their call. So, Paul strongly commands them to refrain from removing the mark of circumcision.

Paul's second question is given in verse 18c. He asks, Ἐν ἀκροβυστίᾳ τις ἐκλήθη; (*En akrobustia tis eklēthē*-was anyone at the time of his call uncircumcised?). This question is addressed to the Gentile Christians. Paul's command to them is, *let* them *not seek circumcision*. The Gentile Christians did not desire to circumcise themselves, as it was considered a barbaric act by the Romans, and also because of its insignificance which Paul had already clarified. However, the Judaizers made it a prominent norm in order to become a member of their community. This was also a serious issue in the church at Galatia. Therefore, few Gentile Christians wanted to undergo the process of circumcision in order to be accepted by the new faith community. This change of social status was not to gain any social standards, but so that they may be considered as the legitimate sons of Abraham. Though this was vehemently condemned by Paul and other apostles in the Jerusalem council (Acts 15), the Judaizers continued to value circumcision as prime criteria for anyone who wanted to become a child of God. Paul deals with this issue here in order to validate the reasons for Jewish and Gentile believers to stay in the same status as they were at the time of their conversion.

Further, to highlight the inconsequentiality of circumcision, in verse 19 Paul declares that *circumcision is nothing, and uncircumcision is nothing; but obeying the commandments of God* [is everything]. This is a remarkable statement Paul has made in his writings. Simultaneously, it gives the impression of contradiction, since he quashes the practice of circumcision on one side and on the other side encourages to keep the commandments of God which also included *circumcision* (Gen.17:10ff; Exo. 4:24-26).

However, a thorough reading of the Pauline corpus will help us to know that this is a frame where Paul highlights his Christology. Paul nullifies circumcision because Christ will be of no advantage to those who receive circumcision (Gal. 5:2). If so, the issue is, what did Paul mean by saying, *obey the commandments of God* (v.19b). 'Obey the commandments of God' is a technical expression of Jews to specifically denote the boundaries of the Jewish religion. Paul uses this to confirm the decisions which were taken at the council at Jerusalem. Because for Paul, to be a Christian is a new way of life, *a new creation*.

A person is made new in Christ not through any physical or racial status change, but through the change of heart by faith in Jesus Christ. The New Covenant of Christ made by His blood is more than sufficient for anyone to have salvation. However, apart from observing the boundaries of Jewish religion, the other commands are still valid for every Christian. Paul reminds the Corinthians that they are part of God's new creation in Christ Jesus and makes a clear extrication of Christian life from the external observances of the Law with the internal change to obey the will of God that surpasses all kinds of social status.

Thus, Paul does not make any contradiction in this section but conveys the message that the Lord wants both, the Jewish and Gentile Christians to fulfill the moral law in obedience to the will of God, than the erroneous concept of changing their present status to attain persistent piety in the newness of life in Christ Jesus. Thus, concludes the section by accentuating the need of remaining in the same status saying, *Let each of you remain in the condition in which you were called* (v.20).

2.2.1.1.5 To the Slaves

2.2.1.1.5.1 Slaves Who are In Faith Need Not Worry about their Status at the Time of their Call Because they are Free in Christ (vv.21-24)

Paul here continues his discussion on the need of remaining in the same status in the God-given order of one's race and circumstances with a concrete example taken from his own social setting, δουλεία (*douleia*-slavery).

Like in the previous section, Paul in verse 21 starts his discussion with a question Δοῦλος ἐκλήθης; (*Doulos eklēthēs* – Were you a slave when called?). His further expression to the question is, do not be concerned about it. The literal meaning of the word μή σοι μελέτω (*mē soi meletō* - never mind). Though slavery was a legally accepted reality during Paul's time, here he is not approving slavery, but teaches that a person who is a slave is still able to obey and honor Christ without changing his current social status.

Furthermore, Paul says, *even if you can gain your freedom, make use of your present condition now more than ever* (v.21b). There exist various arguments on the phrase in v.21 c-*make use of your present condition.* Kist maker looks into this clause in three ways, such as negative, positive, and contextual.[37] In its negative sense, he connects the clause to slavery. In this case, the verse must be understood as, even if a slave has the chance to become free, he should prefer to be in the same condition as a slave. Positively it refers to freedom. In this case, it is understood as, if there is a chance for him to be free, let him make use of it, i.e., be free from the status of a slave and become a free man. Contextually, it means vocation. In this case, it is understood as, as he is already free from slavery, by all means, therefore live according to the call of God.

The negative and contextual understanding of the phrase *make use of your present condition,* seems almost same. Among these, most of the translators prefer to read the verse in its positive undertone since they perceive that a freedman is in a better position to spread the gospel, than the slave who is hindered by various limitations.

Though the negative and contextual meanings are almost the same, this author prefers the negative connotation of the clause without viewing it as Kistemaker does. That is, though the slaves may have an opportunity to become free, they can still serve Christ being in the same status. Status change in terms of cast, color, or position doesn't qualify someone as a follower of Christ. Thus, this author thinks that it connects better with the main thrust of Paul's discussion in chapter 7, i.e., *remain in the same status as at the time of your call.*

In verse 22, Paul arrays the theological reasons for it by contrasting the Christian status of a slave and a freedman. Verse 22a states, *for whoever called in the Lord as a slave is a freed person belonging to the Lord.* Paul tells the Christian slaves in Corinth that they should not worry about their social status, but rejoice, because in Christ they are free from sin and guilt. Therefore though they are slaves to the earthly masters, they can still serve them with renewed Christian inspiration to serve others with the mind of Christ.

At the same time, Paul also talks about the other side of their freedom in Christ. In verse 22b he says, *just as whoever was free when called is a slave of Christ.* Here Paul clarifies that whoever enjoys the freedom of life in social and political status, however, in responding to the call of God becomes δοῦλος Χριστοῦ 'Ιησοῦ (*doulos Christou Yēsou* – a servant/slave of Christ Jesus), a designation that Paul often uses for himself in his epistles. However, this is not a physical status change that happens in the life of a person at the time of his call, but spiritual, and is applicable to both, slaves and freemen.

Thus in verse 24, Paul says since you are bought with a price; *do not become slaves to human masters.* As some think it does not mean that the Christian slaves cannot continue as slaves since they are freed by Christ and have become a spiritual slave to him. By employing the phrase δούλοι ανθρώπων (*douloi anthrōpōn* – slaves of men), Paul means to say that since they are freed from the slavery of sin and guilt, they should not live like the pagans or like mere mortals. So, he encourages the Corinthians not to entangle themselves again with a yoke of bondage to the standards of this world. Thus Paul in this section exhorts the Corinthians that for a better social and religious status no one should change their present status quo. Consequently, Paul validates once again, that Christians can pursue persistence piety to the Lord by remaining in the same status as at the time of their conversion.

2.2.1.1.6 To the Unmarried/Virgins

2.2.1.1.6.1 It Is Good for the Unmarried Who Have Self-Control to Remain Single Because of the Present Distress (vv.8-9, 25-38)

This section is considered as Paul's longest discussion on marriage and related issues which contains essential information not touched elsewhere in all of his writings. After answering the questions related to conjugal rights, celibacy, and divorce, in verses 25-38 Paul provides counsel on the intimate and strictly personal matters such as virginity, marriage, and service to the Lord, extent of wedding vows, proper conduct towards a virgin etc. Thus as Fee comments, to come to a conclusion of Paul's discussion in this section is a difficult task.

The first reason is, it is not sure what Paul really mean by using the term παρθένος (*parthenos*-virgin). The second concern is about the structure of the argument. The question is, whether verses 36-38 is a conclusion of the entire section or a special case Paul brings to the scene. Thirdly, what was really the problem in Corinth which is used as a background for the matter discussed here?[38] MacArthur considers the entire unit as an answer for remaining single.[39] However, a close reading of the text enables us to divide this section into three sub-divisions. Verses 25-28 provide Paul's advice to the virgins; 29-35 provides the theological and practical orientation, and 36-38 Paul's further advice to those betrothed.

2.2.1.1.6.1.1 Paul's Advice to the Virgins (vv. 25-28)

Until now Paul has not discussed about virgins in chapter 7. Thus he starts this section with the expression, Περὶ δὲ τῶν παρθένων (*Peri de tōn parthenōn* – Now concerning the virgins). The use of Περὶ δὲ shows that Paul here begins his discussion about a new topic. The term παρθένος, basically means *a virgin*. The noun denotes a girl απειρος ανδρος (*apeiros andros* – "without the experience of a man") in the antiquity. LXX gives the meaning, ἡ μὴ εκδεδομενὴ ανδρι (*hē mē ekdedomenē andri* – "who has not been given to a man").

In the New Testament, it denotes a chaste marriageable girl, except in Revelation 14:4 where it figuratively means, those who have not defiled themselves with idolatry.[40] However, the term in its immediate context can be interpreted either as masculine or feminine, since the term ἀνθρώπῳ (*anthrōpō*) in verse 28 refers literally to human being/person in general. For this reason, different translations give varied meanings to this term. For example, RSV and REB translate it as *the unmarried,* which can either mean, a man or woman. Hurley and Elliott comment that the expression *betrothed* explicitly gives it a one-sided meaning. In ESV it is tendentious and wrong as Ford considered it as widow(er)s married only once.[41]

However, as in verse 12, here too Paul comments that he does not have any specific command from the Lord in this regard. By this Paul asserts that Jesus had given no teaching on this topic, although we have just one remark in Matthew 19:12. Yet we cannot think that the teaching of Paul is not authoritative, because the source of all his writings is divine inspiration, not human insights (Gal. 1:12; II Peter 1:20-21). Hence, Paul might be meaning that he does not have any direct command from the Lord concerning the question whether celibacy is good or bad since God himself instituted marriage.

Therefore upon the given apostolic authority, Paul gives this γνώμην (*gnōmēn*) *opinion* to the church in Corinth. Though the expression of the word *gnōmēn*, primarily gives the meaning *opinion*, in its context it has the meaning of *judgment*. Therefore it cannot be considered just as Paul's opinion, but important pastoral and spiritual guidelines with wide theological and practical guidelines to the believers at Corinth.

In verse 26, Paul posits the reason for his advice to the unmarried to remain in the same status. By qualifying his advice with the introductory phrase Νομίζω (*Nomizō*-I think, believe, suppose, consider) states the reason, διὰ τὴν ἐνεστῶσαν ἀνάγκην (*dia tēn enestōsan anagkēn*–because of the impending crisis), it is well for you to remain as you are. The literal meaning of the phrase *dia tēn enestōsan anagkēn* is, is, on account of the present calamity.

Scholars differ concerning the meaning of the term ἀνάγκην (*anagkēn*) in this verse. Some suggest that Paul urges the believers to stay single in light of the soon coming of Christ, as most translations interpret ἐνεστῶσαν (*enestōsan*) as *impending,* meaning, *which is about to become present*. However, the word in the original text is in the perfect participle active form which undoubtedly means, *what is already present*. Therefore it is sure that Paul is not referring to something that is going to happen, but to some situation that is presently faced by the Corinthians.

The literal meaning of the term ἀνάγκην (*anagkēn*) is *calamity*. Carson affirms that there is firm archaeological and literary evidence indicating the terrible food shortage in Corinth during this period. As a result, panic buying and riots occurred. It caused social unrest and uncertainty of the future. Excavators found eleven inscriptions about this calamity recorded by the person who was three times in charge of grain supply in Corinth. Tacitus, the historian of the Roman Empire also records about continuous earthquakes and famines during this time.[42] So it is a valid reason for connecting the ἀνάγκην (*anagkēn* - calamity) with the danger of famine.

Supporting the aforementioned view, Kistemaker posits another view that the term ἀνάγκην can also refer to the persecutions that Christians have to endure as the end of time approaches.[43] According to MacArthur, the term ἀνάγκην refer to the great Roman persecution which would begin under Nero in the future. However, persecution was a reality the Christians were facing right from the beginning, and not something that they would have to face as the end of the time. Moreover, the perfect participle active form of the word overthrows these arguments. Thus Paul's earlier reason of, individuals continuing in the same status as they wereduring their conversion, best explains the text in its context.

In verse 27 Paul posits a warning to both, married and virgins. Paul says, if a person is already married, he should not seek to be free, and if a virgin, he should not seek a wife (v.27). However, Paul not being a misogamist is not against marriage, nor is he even discouraging those who wish to get married, for in verse 28 he says, *but if you marry, you do not sin, and if a virgin marries, she does not sin*. In verse 9 Paul had already said that if the unmarried people cannot contain themselves, *let them marry*. For Paul, lawful marriage is not a sin. In this instant, whether the unmarried man or women get married or not, their conduct is in harmony with the institution of marriage.

However, Paul gives an indication about the distress such people will face in the future. Verse 28c mentions, *yet those who marry will experience distress in this life. The distress in this life* Paul means is certainly the result of the *present calamity* mentioned in verse 28. It is hard enough for singles to live during the famine. So when two people come together in marriage, their distress will naturally be multiplied.

2.2.1.1.6.1.2 Paul's Theological and Practical Orientation (vv. 29-35)

After imparting his advice to virgin, men and women, Paul gives his theological and practical orientation to the Corinthian believers as a whole. In this section Paul particularly envisions the hardships that the Corinthians must endure. This section also functions as the explanatory section between his opening advice in verses 25-28 and further advice in verses 36-38. The first part of this unit presents an eschatological (theology) framework, and the second part presents the theme of anxiety (practical orientation).

Paul begins the theological orientation with an eschatological connotation that, ὁ καιρὸς συνεσταλμένος ἐστίν (*ho kairos sunestalmenos estin*), literally mean, *the appointed time has been shortened*, which denotes a theology of eschatological immense. There are two words in Greek to denote time such as: καιρος (*kairos*- a fixed/appointed/definite time/a fitting season or opportunity), and χρονος (*chronos* – time). Paul posits that the appointed time has been shortened, therefore the end is nearer.

The imminent *parousia* was a serious concern among first century Christians. Though the Christology of the first century Christians went through different crisis, mainly in terms of doubting the coming of Christ, they were strengthened by Paul and reaffirmed about the imminent return of Christ (I Thess. 4:16-18). In this instant, Paul affirms to the Corinthian Christians that the indestructibility and the unchanging nature of the world is not a firm reality, but it is radically moving towards its imminent end. This becomes clear when verses 29a and 31b are read in unison.

In verse 31b Paul says, παράγει γὰρ τὸ σχῆμα τοῦ κόσμου τούτου (*paragei gar to sch ēma tou kosmou*) literally, *for the form of this world is passing away*. The word *schēma* also mean the outward appearance, fashion, manner of life, way of doing things, or mode of existence. Therefore it is assumed that Paul is talking about the impermanence of the present world.

He also places few poetic lines as he confirms the approaching end of the present world, between the above-mentioned verses. In view of the imminent eschatology, with the phrase ὡς μὴ (*hōs mē* - as though not/as not/as if not) Paul delivers five illustrations in verses 29-31.

1. Those who have wives, be as though they have none (v.29b)
2. Those who mourn, as though they were not mourning (v.30a)
3. Those who rejoice, as though they were not rejoicing (v.30b)
4. Those who buy, as though they had no possessions (v.30c)
5. Those who deal with the world, as though they had no dealing with it (v.31a)

The juxtaposed illustrations afore-mentioned vividly portray the ideal modes of behavior or worldly involvement of human beings. By this, Paul gives a clear eschatological cast with the purpose of reminding the believers that they should not give priority to the things that will pass away.

The first thing Paul talks about is marriage. However, he is not advocating celibacy, separation, or divorce; but the impermanency of it. In the age to come no one will be married, for everyone will be like the angels in heaven. Therefore, marriage is not the most important thing to be considered in Christian life as the other aspects mentioned in verses 29-31, because the present form of the world is not permanent, but will pass away (v.31b). Hence Paul instructs the Corinthian believers to view everything in life such as marriage, sorrow, joy, possession, or business in light of the new era that is to come.

In the second part of verses 29-35, Paul demonstrates his pastoral concern for the entire church as he discusses the theme of anxiety in relation to marriage and service to the Lord (vv.32-35). With the plural personal pronoun ὑμᾶς (*humas* –you) he addresses the entire Corinthian congregation saying, *I want you to be free from anxieties* (v.32a). Paul's advice to both married and virgins in this section is to live in the freedom which the Lord provides.

As per Paul, the unmarried person concerns himself with the affairs of the Lord. He makes this statement as an exhortation, favoring virginity. With freedom in Christ, the unmarried person takes a positive interest in the things of the world and pleases the Lord wherever God has placed him. *But the married man is anxious about the affairs of the world, how to please his wife* (v.33). Paul says that the attention of a married man is divided, as he has to concentrate both on his wife and the Lord. However, Paul is not implying that the concerns of a married man in pleasing his wife is inherently wrong, but points out the demands and responsibilities that cannot be neglected in married life. Therefore the problem Paul sees is not, marriage *per se*, but the danger of becoming too distracted in trying to please the spouse. Taking care of one's family is an important and valid concern, but it should not limit the time a person can spend for the Lord.

Paul is not even considering the married as inferior or the unmarried superior. Both, singles and married men enjoy the same freedom that Christ provides. Both are devoted to the Lord. However, the unmarried man more time since he does not need to worry about the things of this world, but the married man to be concerned for his family, as his marital status demands a particular way of living that involves providing and taking care of them.

In verse 34 Paul applies the same concern to unmarried women and virgin. But here instead of *how to please the Lord* (v.32c), Paul adds, *so that they may be holy in body and spirit* (v.34b). Paul uses this statement parallel to *how to please the Lord* in verse 32c. Paul's use of *being holy in the body* in this instant does not mean that celibate women are pure because they avoid sexual relations that marriage imposes. As marriage is instituted by God himself, sex within marriage is holy. Moreover, keeping away from marriage does not make a person holy by default, since a man or a woman is a combination of body, soul, and spirit. Therefore, whether married or not, all Christians need to be holy before the Lord.

Paul concludes this section with an exhortation-*I say this for your own benefit...to promote good order and unhindered devotion to the Lord* (v.35). Though Paul discusses regarding the distresses in married life, he is not advocating celibacy, separation, or divorce. Paul exhorts the Corinthians about the positive side of being single, about which it was inquired by them. Yet, Paul's argument portrays that, irrespective of one's marital status, one can still live a holy life, without anxiety, and in the freedom which Christ has given us.

2.2.1.1.6.1.6 Further Advice to the Betrothed (vv. 36-38)

After giving theological and practical orientations to the issue regarding marriage and sex, Paul concludes the section with his specific advice to those betrothed. The main question in this section is, does Paul give this advice to the parents, or to the engaged couples? Here too exist different arguments and interpretations.

The first argument is, it is the father or the male guardian who decides whether to give his daughter in marriage. According to this view, the phrase τηρεῖν τὴν ἑαυτοῦ παρθένον (*tērein eautou Parthenon* – to keep his virgin) in verse 37 strengthens the argument, as this suggests to *keep his virgin daughter in his household rather than give her in marriage*. This supports the view that it is the father who decides his daughters' marriage which most likely reflected the cultural situation in ancient Corinth. Further, the verb γαμίζω (*gamizo*) is used twice in verse 38, which means, *to give in marriage* than *to get married*. The latter is expressed by the word γαμέω (*gameo*) in verse 36. Thus it is the father who decides what is best regarding his daughter's marriage. If so, then the verses 36 to 38 will read as:

> [36] If anyone thinks that he is not behaving properly towards *his unmarried daughter*, if his passions are strong, and so it has to be, let him marry as he wishes; it is no sin. Let them marry.[37] but if someone stands firm in his resolve, being under no necessity but having his own desire under control, and has determined in his own mind to keep *his daughter* unmarried, he will do well.[38] so then, *he who gives his daughter* in marriage does well, and he who does not give her daughter in marriage will do better.

The second argument is, it is the man who decides whether to marry the women to whom he is engaged. This view is well taken by NRSV, NIV, NJB, REB etc. Because it seems anomalous to employ the word παρθένος (*parthenos* – virgin) as it is seen in 7:36,37 and 38 if it intends a daughter who is under the care and control of a guardian appointed by their parents or by parents themselves. At the same time, if it means to denote a father, it requires a shift of subject in verse 36. But this argument manages a more consistent subject for the matters discussed in this section and also in the entire chapter because the phrases in these verses are used consistently in verse 9, 28 and 39 to describe considerations appropriate to the engaged couples.

Few other supporting reasons for this argument are as follows. Firstly, it starts with a new section concerning unmarried [virgins], and the issue is whether they should marry or not. In this regard, both men and women are instructed and the decision must be taken by themselves concerning their own marriage (vv.26-28). Secondly, there is no theological, philosophical, or linguistic clue of a new topic introduced in verses 36-38. Thirdly, term παρθένος (*parthenos* – virgin) remains the same from verse 36 as it is used before in the same chapter (7:25, 28, 34). As mentioned above, to use *virgin* to mean *daughter* is totally unusual.

Fourthly, the matter addressed in this section is about the bad conscience of a man who is engaged to a woman. Moreover, verse 36 follows directly from verse 35. Paul says that he does not want to give any instructions to those who want to marry (v.35) and they free to do as they wish (v.36). So it is sure that the addressee is the single man, rather than the father. Fifthly, so far, Paul has not mentioned about the role of a father in marriage. The decision of the father in marriage is contradicting to what Paul had already said in verse 25-35.

In the sixth place, conferring to the first argument, the phrase *he who does not give her daughter in marriage will do better* (v. 38) is totally irrelevant to the context of Paul's argument. From the beginning of chapter 7, Paul corrects the attitude of people changing their marital status for the sake of undistracted devotion to the Lord. For various reasons, Paul had already clarified that those who are single have more time to serve the Lord as they will not be distracted by complications entailed in marriage. However, nowhere does Paul explain that keeping a daughter unmarried has practical benefits for a father in serving God. Therefore, the usage of the word *father* or *guardian* does not fit the context in chapter 7. Thus it will be read as

> [36] If anyone thinks that he is not behaving properly toward his fiancée, if his passions are strong, and so it has to be, let him marry as he wishes; it is no sin. Let them marry.[37] But if someone stands firm in his resolve, being under no necessity but having his own desire under control, and has determined in his own mind to keep her as his fiancée, he will do well.[38] So then, he who marries his fiancée does well; and he who refrains from marriage will do better.

Verse 36 starts with a conditional clause εἰ *(ei* –if) which denotes a reality, and continuous with an indefinite pronoun τις (*tis*-anyone). Its masculine form refers to a man who possesses a virgin [fiancée] not daughter. The verb ἀσχημονεῖν (*aschēmonein* – not behaving properly) literally means behave disgracefully, indecently, or dishonorably. It is an act against Paul's advice to the Corinthians. In Greek culture, the word ἀσχημονεῖν is a euphemism for, sexually indecent acts.[44] Therefore Paul suggests that if their passions are uncontrollable let them marry, which is not sin.

In verse 37, Paul discusses concerning the man who has decided not to marry because of social and financial pressures which probably could be a result of the impending crisis mentioned in verse 26. Be that as it may, while Corinthians preferred celibacy for spiritual reasons, Paul, in contrast, affirms marriage. He says such a man indeed does well. However, he also says that he who refrains from marriage will do better.

Going one step beyond, Paul talks about the binding character of Christian marriage in verses 39-40. Once married, a woman is bound to her husband till his death. But if the husband dies, she is free to marry, but only to a man who is, 'in the Lord' [a fellow believer]. According to Roman law, if a widow who is below 60 years of age, wished to remarry, she must marry within 18 months of her husband's death. However, Paul claiming to have the Spirit of God advices that it is better for a widow to refrain from re-marriage, for she will be more blessed. Thus, Paul once again reiterates that a person can pursue persistent piety to the Lord without making any change in their status.

Summary

In chapter 7, Paul gives his advice to husbands, wives, widows, circumcised, uncircumcised, slaves, free, unmarried, and virgins. Citing the illustration of circumcision and uncircumcision, slavery and freedom, Paul encouraged everyone to remain content with their place in life in which God has called them. Paul laid this down as a rule for all the churches (7:17).

He starts his discussion directing husbands and wives to respect each other's conjugal rights, as they do not have authority over their own bodies. He also advises them not to abstain from sex, except by mutual agreement, and only for an agreed period of time, that too for fasting and prayer. In the next segment, Paul discusses concerning virgins. He relates singleness and marriage to the present crisis and states that entering into a marital relationship is not sinful. He counseled those who marry to expect many troubles because the time in which they live is shortened, and the present world is passing away.

Paul notes that the unmarried people have more time to devote to the Lord's service, than those who are married, who have to provide for the legitimate needs of their families. He urges everyone to live for the Lord without distraction. If a man is unable to control himself with regard to his virginity, Paul advises him to get married and declares that it is not a sin. However, if a man is able to control his sexual desires, and decides not to marry, it is perfectly alright for him to remain celibate.

Paul concludes his discourse on marriage by referring to marriage vows that are for life and are negated only by the death of the spouse. He affirms that widows are free to remarry a fellow believer, but advises her to stay unmarried and enjoy happiness. Those who are virgins should remain in their present state if they have the gift of continence. If not, they should marry.

As a command from the Lord, Paul speaks against divorce. Even in families where one of the spouses is a believer and the other an unbeliever, the couples should stay together and not contemplate separation. If the unbeliever leaves on his or her own accord, the remaining spouse is no longer bound to her marriage vows but is advised to live in peace.

The main argument of Paul against Corinthian's desire to change their present social status is, to remain in whatever status they were at the time of their conversion, since God's call transcends all statuses, and makes it irrelevant. Conversion to Christ creates such a change in one's essential relationship with God, that one need not seek change in one's relationships with people.

2.2.2 Eating Food Offered to Idols (8:1-11:1)

In chapters, 8-10 Paul continues to answer the questions asked by the Corinthians as mentioned in 7:1. These three chapters deal with the problem of, eating food offered to idols. It was a serious concern asked to Paul by the new converts in the Corinthian church. Commentators like Robertson and Plummer,[45] Conzelmann,[46] and Barrett[47] brings this issue in three different situations such as: a) eating food sacrificed to an idol at the temple of an idol (8:7-13; 10:1-22); b) eating food of unknown history that is bought in the market (10:23-27); c) eating food in the private homes of unbelievers (10:28-31). So, Paul in these three chapters corrects the improper way of Corinthians in exercising the freedom with regards to eating of food offered to idols.

One main question that can be raisedis, why does Paul give such an elaborated answer to the issue of eating food offered to idols? To answer this question it is imperative to know the background and the prominence of the meal and idol worship in the socio-political and the religious domains of the first century Roman Corinth.

In Corinth occasions for eating in connection with idol worship or in temple premises was very common. Their celebrations and cultic activities were closely connected with social and civic activities since religion and politics were inseparable from Greek culture. Therefore, though Christians could avoid cultic activities, their civic life invariably entangled them to participate in some festival's sacrificial meals. Moreover, the social practice of eating together was a strong requirement of maintaining one's status quo in the Greco-Roman world and participation in sacrifice was a requirement of holding public office. There was a saying in Corinth that, meals and food were makers of social statuses. It was commonly said among Corinthians that, *you are what you eat, and – more importantly-you are whom you ate with.*[48]

Social meals in the Greco-Roman world was categorized in two: a) Meals on the occasion of social transition such as wedding or funerals, and, b) Meals on celebratory occasions such as birthday of an individual, birthday of a god or goddess, childbirth, reunion of friends, success of adventures, simple meals for the pleasure of entertaining guests, thanksgiving, coming-of-age, election victory, etc.[49] Participation in such gatherings were so important for the social life of Corinthians since the refusal of the invitation was considered as an offense to social ethics. The refusal of common food would consequently lead one to the disapproval of one's present social status.[50]

Corinthian Christians encountered this reality frequently in their socio-religious life. Though it was possible for them to avoid religious festivals, it was mandatory for them to attend other social events because social meals were major means of maintaining social relationships in Corinthian culture. However, most Corinthian believers (especially, *the weak* as Paul introduce *the new converts* in 8:7) did not participate in such social gatherings as there was a strong possibility that food offered to gods would be served in functions like social transition or celebratory occasions. However, another group among the congregation (*the strong,* those who possessed the knowledge, probably the Jewish Christians) sought to demonstrate their spiritual security and liberty by deliberately eating food offered to idols. In this context, Paul's advice to the Corinthian church is to exercise their freedom in Christ, without hurting the weaker brother in the congregation.

2.2.2.1 Paul's Response: "Christians Must Exercise their Freedom within Proper Limits"

In chapter 8:1 to 11:1 Paul gives a strong defense of his apostolic authority with special emphasis on the freedom he possesses. However, Paul's main concern here is not to prove his apostleship, but he mentions about it to prove how he exercises his freedom and authority without hurting others, so that the Corinthians may have proper understanding and acceptance between the *strong* and w*eak* believers in the congregation.

In the name of knowledge and freedom they possessed, the so-called strong believers were advocating consumption of food offered to idols. Some were even attending the cultic meals at the temple deliberately urging that it will build up the weak on the basis of knowledge and freedom they gained through Christ. On the other hand, the weak believers were arguing against it on the basis of conscience. So in chapter 8 Paul specifically talks to the Corinthians about the importance of exercising their freedom in Christ within the proper limit by giving priority for love, rather than the rights they possess.

2.2.2.1.1 In Terms of Eating the Food Offered to Idols, Christians should not Exercise their Rights out of the Knowledge they Possess, but out of Love toward others and Christ

Paul's main argument in chapter 8 is that Christians should not exercise their rights out of the knowledge they possess, but out of love toward others and Christ. Paul establishes this to the Corinthians with two key principle points such as-a) the knowledge Christians possess that feeds arrogance must be overruled by love, and b) the knowledge Christians possess must not be exercised beyond certain limits, because all do not possess equal knowledge, and consequently may commit sin against others and Christ.

2.2.2.1.1.1 Knowledge Puffs Up but Love Builds Up (vv.1-6)

With the first two words in 8:1 (Περὶ δὲ – *peri de*, now concerning) Paul starts dealing with the next question somebody in Corinthians had asked him. The first argument Paul raises is that Christians should not exercise their knowledge and rights over love, because knowledge *puffs up,* but love *builds up*. The issue is mentioned next to *peri de*, which is, τῶν εἰδωλοθύτων (*tōn eidōlothutōn* – the food offered to idols).

The issue of eating food offered to idols was already discussed and directions were given in the first Jerusalem council (Acts 15:29; 21:25). Offering food to the idol was a common practice in the Greco-Roman world.

It was practiced not only in temples but in homes as well. In the temples, it was practiced specifically as part of the religious cult, but in homes, out of fear, because it was believed that evil spirits were constantly trying to invade human beings through food. Therefore, to remove spirits from the food they used to offer it to the gods before it was eaten.[51]

Even a portion of the food/meat offered in the temples were brought home by the devotees. The sacrificial food in the temples was divided into three parts. One part of the food was burned as a sacrifice on the altar. The second part was given to the priest as payment, and the remaining part was taken home by the offerer. This third part was brought home to be eaten by members of the household, or to share it with friends, neighbors, and relatives in the celebration that was followed by the sacrifice.[52]

This was a major issue faced by the early Christians at Corinth that they were unable to participate in any of the common functions or celebrations hosted by their non-Christian friends and relatives. However, on the basis of *knowledge* and right to exercise their *Christian freedom,* some of the Jewish Christian members in the congregation were participating in the common gathering where food was served which was offered to idols. Thus, the Gentile Christians were confused whether the decisions passed on to them must be followed uncompromisingly or is it flexible.

In answering this concern, Paul deals with the issue of exercising Christian freedom on the basis of knowledge. He says, οἴδαμεν ὅτι πάντες γνῶσιν ἔχομεν (*oidamen hoti pantes gnōsin echomen*–we know that all possess knowledge). The Corinthian Christians were very proud of the knowledge they possessed. Fitzmyer posits that the phrase Paul uses in 8:1, *we know that all possess the knowledge,* is a Corinthian catchphrase like many others they had, for example, *for me, all things are permissible* mentioned in 6:12.[53] Paul starts his discussion by using the catchphrase, *we know that all possess the knowledge,* as a strategy to connect with his readers.

This kind of approach is commonly found in the Pauline corpus, especially in 1 Corinthians. This approach enabled Paul to disrupt unnecessary confrontations convincingly and to present his thoughts meaningfully. The expression, *we possess knowledge* was a strong claim raised by the Jewish Christians in the church at Corinthian. Though Paul does not explain about the *knowledge* mentioned in verse1, it could be possible that the claim probably originated out of their monotheistic belief summarized in the Hebrew creed (*Shema*-the proclamation of the oneness of God), Hear, O Israel: the Lord our God, the Lord is one-Deuteronomy 6:4. For in verse 4b Paul says, *there is no God, but one.* Though they possessed this legitimate knowledge, because of the improper way it was exercised, Paul says, ἡ γνῶσις φυσιοῖ ἡ δὲ ἀγάπη οἰκοδομεῖ (*hē gnōsis phusioi, hē de agapē oikodomei* – knowledge puffs up, but love builds up).

Apart from the knowledge about the one living God, they were also exposed to Greek philosophy wherein knowledge was highly esteemed. Though in 1:5 Paul talks about knowledge very positively, in this context, because of its improper usage, Paul suggests that it leads to arrogance. Hence, Paul proposes them to practice love which will enable them to edify and build up each other.

In verse 2 Paul continues to talk about knowledge as a reaction to the behavior of those who think that knowledge is everything. It says *anyone who claims to know something does not yet have the necessary knowledge*. The verb *to know* in the first phrase is in a perfect tense. This indicates that the person who imagines he possesses knowledge has already gained true knowledge. But against the conceited attitude of such people Paul says, they *do not yet have the necessary knowledge*. Here it is important to know what Paul meant by the expressions *something* and *not yet have the necessary knowledge*.

The following verses suggest that the *something* refer to God. No one can have the full revelation of God. Unless God takes the initiative in revealing himself, no one can understand who God is. Eventually, one understands *something* only to a particular degree, but not fully. Hence, true knowledge is not just the acquisition of information about things or even about God, but God's knowledge of human beings (v.3).

Verse 4 was the basis for the Jewish church members to eat food offered to idols, as they knew that there is no life in the idols. Idols were only the figment of somebody's imagination. They are just a piece of stone, clay, wood, or metal. For them, there was no God, but one, and idols were meaningless. This was firmly rooted in their monotheistic belief. The Jewish Christians believed that there is only one God, and only one Lord, Jesus Christ, through whom are all things, and through whom they exist (vv. 5-6). Thus they believed that food offered to idols cannot be contaminated. For this reason, these 'strong' believers who *possessed this knowledge* were exercising their right and freedom with confidence, even sharing in temple banquets.

However, Paul does not consider this as a legitimate exercise of their freedom in Christ. For Paul, their attitude reeked of arrogance, because, though they were doing it knowing that there is only one living God, they were not really concerned about the 'weaker' Gentile Christians among them for whom idols was a part of their life prior to coming to Christ. Therefore it was the responsibility of the mature believers to build them up in Christ with love. However, the unrestrained exercise of their freedom became a stumbling block to those who recently embraced Christianity. Thus Paul validates his first point, Christians should not exercise their knowledge and rights over love, because knowledge *puffs up,* but love *builds up.*

2.2.2.1.1.2 All do not Possess Knowledge, and Unloving Exercise of Rights Leads to Sinning against Christ (vv.7-13)

Paul's second argument is, Christians should not exercise their knowledge and rights over love because all do not possess knowledge, and unloving exercise of rights leads to sinning against Christ. The Phrase 'Ἀλλ' οὐκ ἐν πᾶσιν ἡ γνῶ σις (*alla ouk en pasin hē gnōsis* – but not all/everyone has this knowledge) is a matter of debate among scholars. For it seems that there were gentile believers who did not yet embrace the monotheistic position that the Jewish believers embraced.

However, it is to be noted that many of these Gentile converts at Corinth had been Christians less than two years. Therefore it is not that they did not accept the monotheistic belief, but they were still conscious about their former life as pagans. For, following the phrase *alla ouk en pasin hē gnōsis*, Paul says, *since some have become so accustomed to idols until now, they still think of the food they eat as food offered to an idol; and their conscience being weak, is defiled* (8:7).

By this, Paul emphasizes the habitual life of the newly converted Gentiles who have not yet fully adjusted their outlook to their new situation, as in their former pagan life they strongly believed that idols are literally gods, and not just a statue or image. Carson says that the first-century worshippers never considered the object of their worship as idols or image, but as goddess Athena, believing that she actually existed behind it, and for them, Christians were atheists because they had no object in their places of worship.[54] For this reason, the conscience of the new converts was weak, and for them eating food offered to the idol was akin to desecrating their Christian life.

In verse 8 Paul goes on with the argument of the confident Corinthians who only hold on to the monotheistic and more spiritual view concerning food offered to idols. It is considered as the view of those who possess knowledge because of the shift of 3rd person plural in verse 7 to 1st person plural in verse 8. Thus this verse is well considered as a protest and another catchword of the 'strong' in the Corinthian congregation.[55]

As he continues, Paul first of all says, βρῶμα δὲ ἡμᾶς οὐ παραστήσει τῷ θεῷ (*brōma de hēmas ou parastēsei tō theō* - food will not bring us to God [v.8a]). The verb παραστήσειin this phrase is in its future indicative tense, thus it means, *will not bring close,* which is also used as a legal term. But few versions like KJV, NKJV, NIV, NAB gives emphasis on the present tense, thus reading it as, *does not bring*. However, the manuscript evidence favors the future tense. Therefore scholars explain it in relation to the final judgment day. If so, the argument of the men of knowledge in the congregation is that even if they eat the food offered to idols it will not bring them before God's judgment seat.

Moreover, they believed that, like the idols which are lifeless things, food is a neutral aspect which does not have any spiritual significance. This view is established in the following statement. It says, we are no worse off if we do not eat, and no better off if we do (v.8b). Since food by itself has no moral or spiritual significance, the strong believers in the congregation were saying that they neither lose nor gain anything. In other words, food neither makes a person holy nor a sinner. Jesus also said, it is not what goes into the mouth that defiles a person, but what comes out of the mouth that defiles." (Matt. 15:11).

Therefore, whenever the 'strong' believers were invited to be a part of the celebration held in the temple dining, they would go and eat without their conscience disturbing them. For them idol was nothing more than a piece of chopped stone and the meat was ordinary food. Their faith in God still remained strong. Even Paul is not against it. Because a person whose faith is firm in Christian faith would not see any harm for being part of a festival meal in a temple dining room or in the residence of an unbeliever.

However, Paul strongly rejects the context in which they exercise their liberty as Christians. In verse 9-11 Paul posits the reason for his position with sufficient explanation. Paul's first main argument against such behavior of the men of knowledge is, it will become *a hindrance to the weak* brothers in the congregation. To denote this idea Paul uses the term πρόσκομμα (*proskomma* – stumbling block), literally means, the opportunity to take offence, obstacle, or hindrance.

Further, Paul asks an ironic question to the strong brothers, οὐχὶ ἡ συνείδησις αὐτοῦ ἀσθενοῦς ὄντος οἰκοδομηθήσεται εἰς τὸ τὰ εἰδωλόθυτα ἐσθίειν; (*ouchi hē suneidēsis autou asthenous ontos oikodomēthēsetai eis to ta eidōlothuta esthiein?*- will not his conscience, weak as it is, be encouraged to eat the meat sacrificed to the idol?). The word οἰκοδομηθήσεται literally mean, to build up/edify, i.e., persons with the weak conscience would be encouraged to the extent that they too might eat food offered to a pagan god.

However, Paul asks this question with a touch of irony, because he himself says in verse 9 that such kind of conduct is a stumbling block to the weak. Thus the word οἰκοδομηθήσεται does not denote a positive meaning, and the example of the strong who possesses knowledge is not edification at all. Rather, the edified who take part in such meals consequently, commit the act of idolatry. So Paul says to the men of knowledge that, because of *your knowledge those weak believers for whom Christ died are destroyed* (v.11).

Paul's second main argument against such behavior of the men of knowledge is, they not only destroy the life of their fellow brethren, for whom Christ died but also commits sin against Christ, the Lord of their life. Verse 12 says, *but when you thus sin against members of your family, and wound their conscience when it is weak, you sin against Christ*. The phrase *to wound their conscience* literally means that such kind of activity will mislead the weak brother to believe that they too can eat food offered to idols, which for them was an act of idolatry.

Paul says, such activities are equivalent to sinning against Christ, because Christ not only died for the strong, but also for the weak. Even the weak among them are purchased with the blood of Christ. So it is not only a sin against a fellow believer, but also against Christ. Thus, Paul exposes their arrogance as they freely exercise their rights without considering others.

Finally, Paul concludes the issue of eating food offered to idols by expressing his own conduct in such situation. Paul says, if the food which I eat causes my brother to stumble, *I will never eat meat* [food offered to idols], so that *I may not cause one of them to fall.*

2.2.2.1.2 Paul's Application to Corinthians from his own Life (9:1-27)

The shift of discussion from consumption of food offered to idols in chapter 8 to the defense of his apostolic authority in chapter 9 seems to present the notion that Paul is moving to an entirely new topic. However, at this juncture, Paul does not really require to deal with his apostolic authority since he had already dealt with the authenticity of his apostleship at the beginning of this letter. However, he does so, to explain how he exercises his authority without using it to exploit others. The confusion mentioned above is because of the chapter division at this point.

It needs to be remembered that the New Testament was not written chapter wise, dealing with one theme in each chapter. For example, in this very book (which was not written as a book, but as a letter), the first four chapters deal with the single issue of divisions in the church at Corinthian. Likewise, Paul discusses concerning the spiritual gifts in chapters 12-14. All the books of the Bible were divided into different chapters and verses for the sake of convenience in referencing the location and points in the scripture. Thus, starting a new chapter does not always mean that it is the beginning of a new topic. Moreover, in this instant (chapter 9), the section directly relates to what Paul discussed in the previous chapter.

In the first section (9:1-23), Paul explains why though he had the authority to exercise his apostolic rights he kept it under check, so as not to be a hindrance for the spread of the gospel (vv1-14). He also presents himself as a model for them, that though he was free to exercise his freedom in Christ, but for the sake of Christ, he has humbled himself as a slave, becoming all things to all, in the hope of saving some (vv.14-23). In the second section (9:24-27), Paul exhorts the Corinthian Christians to follow his method of exercising Christian freedom in self-control.

In the previous chapter, Paul deals with the importance of exercising love over one's right for the good of others. To validate his argument in chapter 8, now Paul gives an example from his personal life where he subordinates his rights for the good of the whole (9:1-27).

2.2.2.1.1.2 Christian Freedom must be Exercised in View of Winning People to Christ, than being an Obstacle in the Way of the Gospel of Christ (vv.1-23)

The first thing Paul conveys to the Corinthians in chapter 9 is the exercise of Christian rights, or, that the freedom we enjoy in Christ must not be an obstacle for the spread of the gospel, but must be exercised with the view of winning others to Christ. As he validates his point in this section, he assembles his arguments with diatribe and ample use of rhetorical questions. Paul employs almost 19 rhetorical questions in his endeavor to give an example to the Corinthian believers from his own lifestyle. Among 19 questions, 18 of them covers Paul's first position, i.e., Christian freedom must be exercised with the view of winning people to Christ, than being an obstacle in the way of the gospel (vv.1-23).

Paul employs his rhetorical questions from verse 1 which consist of 4 questions. Each question posited here expects an affirmative answer, thus it characterized with the forms such as Οὐκ (*Ouk* - not) Οὐχὶ (*Ouchi* - not) and Ου' (*Ou* - not).[56] Paul asks, *Am I not free? Am I not an apostle? Have I not seen Jesus our Lord? Are you not my work in the Lord?* The first question indicates his personal liberty. By introducing himself as *the apostle of Christ Jesus* at the beginning of the letter, Paul posits his personal liberty and his apostolic authority which is disregarded by the Corinthians. Thus Paul reaffirms to them that, he is free as other apostles.

The second and third questions indicate the reasons for the authenticity of his apostleship. Paul says, he is called by Jesus and has been a witness of the risen Christ. Paul talks about this because the other apostles and believers were doubtful about his apostleship since he was not one among the original twelve. Hence, Paul often recalls his direct call and witness of the risen Christ in his letters (15:8; Gal.1:16; 2 Cor.11:5; 12:11-12; Rom.11:13 etc). Paul's fourth question indicates his hard work in Corinth in bringing them to salvation. Paul was in Corinth for 18 months and brought them to the salvific knowledge of Christ. Thus, Paul reminds them that they are his spiritual sons and daughters, the fruit of his labor in Christ Jesus.

Since the Corinthian believers were not ready to accept him as an apostle he further says, *if I am not an apostle to others, at least I am to you* (v.2a). By this statement, Paul emphasizes that the Corinthian believers are bound to accept his apostleship. Paul's certainty of this statement is seen in the following sentence that, *for you are the seal of my apostleship in the Lord* (v.2b). With the word σφραγίς (*sphragis*–seal/signet [figuratively, it mean – that which conforms/attest/certifies or authenticates]), Paul reminds the Corinthian believers that their new life in Christ itself is an affirmation, a certificate, or proof of his apostolic status and authority.

After validating his apostleship in verses 1-2, from verse 3-12a Paul posits about the rights of his apostleship through a new series of rhetorical questions. This section consists of 12 questions (vv. 4-12a). Unlike verses 1 and 2, Paul uses the first person plural ομεν (*omen* – we) in verses 4-6. Paul starts this section with a comment that, *this is my defense to those who would examine me* (v.3). There are different opinions among scholars about the right position of this statement in the chapter. The question they raise is, does it connect with the previous verses or the proceeding verses?

Leon Morris suggests that it goes with the previous verse where Paul confirms his apostleship that which is sealed by the Corinthian believers.[57] However, Hurt supports the latter view. According to him, it goes with the proceeding verses whereby it confirms his apostolic rights.[58] The latter view seems to be more applicable to the context because in the following verses Paul posits about the rights he has as an apostle of Christ Jesus.

The first question Paul asks is*, do we not have the right to our food and drink?* This question relates to the basic rights of a human being, which is also connected to Paul's discussion about consumption of food offered to idols. In chapter 8, Paul had already said that if the food which I eat will cause my brother to fall, I will refrain from eating it. However, Paul takes the same concern and proves that he has all the right to his drink and food. One other thing to be noted here is the use of the plural form. In verses 4 and 5 Paul asks, μὴ οὐκ ἔχομεν ἐξουσίαν (*mē ouk ech**omen** exousian* – do **we** not have the right). By the use of the plural, Paul talks about himself and Barnabas as mentioned in verse 6.

Paul's second question in this section is seen in verse 5, *do we not have the right to be accompanied by a believing wife?* The words used for believing wife in the Greek bible is ἀδελφὴν γυναῖκα (*adelphēn gunaika*) literally means, a sister/women. The word ἀδελφὴν can never mean a female life partner but a sister, in this context, a female fellow Christian worker. Further the infinitive περιάγειν (*periagein*), literally mean, to lead around, to have someone with oneself/accompanying oneself). Thus it refers to having women as a companion in the missionary journeys.[59] Even if it is understood as a believing wife, the Corinthians have to agree that Paul has the right to travel with his wife in his missionary journeys, for at the end of the verse Paul mentions the name of Cephas/Peter, one of the accepted leaders among them, who has a wife (Mk. 1:30).

In verse 6 Paul again asks, *is it only Barnabas and I who have no right to refrain from working for a living?* Paul uses the word ἐργάζεσθαι (*ergazesthai*) to denote working which literally means, to toil, to work with one's hand.

Paul was doing ministry without enjoying any support from the community he evangelized. In the first century context, it was a strange thing that a teacher does any form of labor other than teaching. Through this question, Paul reminds the Corinthians that he has the right to get financial support from them but he refrains from enjoying it.

In verse 7 Paul asks another three rhetorical questions that call for a negative answer. Using the example of a soldier, Paul asks, who at any time pays his own expenses for doing military service? In the first century context, a soldier receives his provision from his superior officers who are responsible to meet the necessary needs of his troops. Though Paul does not intend for the Corinthians to take care of his needs, by asking the above question, he defends his right to get help from the people whom he serves.

Secondly, Paul uses the example of a farmer. He asks *who plants a vineyard and does not eat any of its fruit?* Paul says, even a worker who toils in the vineyard has a right to the fruit of the vine. Finally taking the example of a shepherd, he asks, *who tends a flock and does not get any of its milk?* A shepherd manages his family with the daily milk supply from his animal. Comparing himself to a shepherd, Paul argues that being an apostle to the Corinthians he has the right to get material support from them.

From verses 8-12a, Paul elevates the legitimacy of his defense with the backing of Old Testament scripture and a strong theological and spiritual framework. With the question, *do I say this on human authority?* (8a) Paul legitimizes his defense by not resting his case on his own observation. Further, he asks, *does not the law also say the same? For it is written in the Law of Moses, "you shall not muzzle an ox while it is treading out the grain."* (Deut. 25:4). Paul citing this verse from the Old Testament reminds them about a practice that existed among the Israelites in threshing the grain.

Farmers in Israel used to spread the grain on an outdoor threshing floor. It was a flat board weighed down with stones, or people were drawn over the grain by a team of oxen or horses. As the oxen or horses tread out the grain with their feet in a circle, they were permitted to eat as much grain as it desired since they were doing the heavy pulling. Muzzling the oxen while threshing was a serious offense in the Jewish community. If anyone practices it, he was cursed and terrorized in the local synagogue.[60]

Thus, Paul inquires how much more he is worthy to exercise his rights among them as an apostle, and in order to substantiate his argument, he brings theological and spiritual framework in verses 9c and 10. Paul asks, *is it for oxen that God is concerned? If we have sown spiritual food among you, is it too much if we reap your material benefits?* Though these questions expect the answer *no,* Paul never meant that God is not concerned for animals. The simple message Paul want to convey here is that, if God cares for animals, how much *more* does he care for human beings. Finally, Paul concludes this part by saying if we sowed spiritual things in you, is it a great thing if we reap fleshy things of you? The answer is, not at all.

After stating his rights (vv.4-12a), in the next section (vv. 12b-23), Paul discusses about renouncing his rights and gives reasons for the same. Verse 12b clearly portrays that Paul had never made use of any of his rights, for it says, nevertheless, *we have not made use of this right.* Neither in the initial stage of his ministry in Corinth nor as the work progressed, was Paul a burden to them. When he arrived in Corinth during his first missionary journey, he stayed with Aquila and Priscilla and worked as a tent maker for his sustenance (Acts 18:3).

Even when Paul become a full-time preacher of the gospel, he did not make use of his rights but survived with the financial gift brought by Silas and Timothy from the churches at Macedonia (Acts 18:5). About this Paul writes, *and when I was with you and needed something, I was not a burden to anyone, for the brothers who came from Macedonia supplied what I needed. I have kept myself from being a burden to you in any way, and will continue to do so* (II Cor.11:9).

Further, Paul says, *but we endure anything rather than put an obstacle in the way of the gospel of Christ* (I Cor. 9.12c). Using the pronoun *we,* Paul once again refer to himself and Barnabas (v.6), and say that they endure all things/ anything. The root word used for enduring is στέγω (*stego*), which literally means, pass over in silence/keep confidential, or keeping silent out of love for others. And the word ἐγκοπὴν (*egkopēn* - hindrance/obstacle) is used in the New Testament in the military sense which connotes, breaking up a road to impede the advance of a pursuing enemy. This implies an interruption in a course of action, which in this context, refer to any action that disrupts the proclamation of the Gospel of Christ. Thus Paul means to say that, out of their love for them, he and Barnabas did the ministry without causing any kind of hindrance to the gospel of Christ.

After stating another reason to exercise his rights based on the Levitical system (vv. 13-14), Paul once again asserts, *I have made no use of any of these rights* (v.15). Referring to all the rights he had aforementioned Paul says, I have not used those in my ministerial life. Paul supported himself through his own trade during the three missionary journeys (9:6; I Thess.2:9; Acts 18:3; 20:34; II Cor. 12:14). Further, Paul is on the verge of uttering a critical remark but left incomplete. However, in the context of the text, it is probably read as I would rather die than exercising my rights which will cause an obstacle for the spread of the gospel.

This view is well supported by his next comment in verse 16 which says, *if I proclaim the gospel, this gives me no ground for boasting, for an obligation is laid on me, and woe to me if I do not proclaim the gospel.* Paul considers his commission to preach the gospel as an obligation, rather than a matter of boasting. For Paul, the reward of his service is not any kind of material or financial blessings, but being a slave of Christ he proclaims the gospel free of charge. Hence, Paul urges the Christians in Corinth to renounce their rights that makes them to be an obstacle in the way of the gospel of Christ.

Paul's next argument in this section is seen in verses 19-23. In this segment, Paul posits that Christians must exercise their rights only in view of winning people to Christ. Though Paul traveled around and spread the gospel to many people groups, he was totally free with respect to all those peoples. As a free person, he was bringing the light of the gospel to them. Thus Paul starts verse 19 with the statement, Ἐλεύθερος γὰρ ὢν ἐκ πάντων πᾶσιν (*Eleutheros gar ōn ek pantōn pasin* – for [though] I am free from all). By this statement, Paul is referring back to his freedom as already stated in 9:1.

Nevertheless, as he renounced all his rights (12b-18), now he makes it very clear that, πᾶσιν ἐμαυτὸν ἐδούλωσα (*pasin emauton edoulō sa* – I have made myself a slave to all), literally, I have enslaved myself to all. Though it may seem so, yet Paul enslaving himself is not against his own command as stated in 7:23. Being a Roman citizen he had the right to enjoy a wide range of privileges and protections. Few common rights of Roman citizens were as follows. Right to vote in assembly, and stand for civil or public office, right to make legal contracts and hold properties, right of immunity from some taxes and legal obligations, right to appeal in courts and have a legal trial to defend themselves. Most importantly, they could not be tortured or given the death penalty, unless they were guilty of betraying Roman County.

Though in some instant Paul made use of the freedom of his Roman citizenship (Acts 22:23-29; 25:1ff.), he never boasted about that freedom and rights. Irrespective of all these, Paul says his citizenship is in heaven (Phil.3:20-21). On the contrary to his freedom as a Roman citizen, Paul often mentions the real freedom he enjoys as an apostle of Christ Jesus. Yet he says, I made myself a slave to all. The reason for Paul's decision to be a slave to all is described in the next phrase. Paul says, ἵνα τοὺς πλείονας κερδήσω (*hina tous pleionas kerdēsō* - so that I might win more of them). As Paul uses the term τοὺς πλείονας *tous pleionas,* he had the Jews and Gentile in mind.

First of all, Paul says, to the Jews I become as a Jew, in order to win the Jews (v.20a). Paul further addresses them as those who are under the Law. Here Paul speaks of his conduct as an apostle, as he deals with the people of his former religion. It is difficult to understand what Paul really meant by it, as the statement says that Paul undoubtedly lived and dealt with them socially in spite of renouncing all the privileges he had as a Jew (Phil. 3:4-8). However, in our given context, it becomes clear that he practiced certain requirements that were dictated by the Mosaic Law.

Being a Jew he was already circumcised, which was considered one of the important laws in the badges/boundary marks of the Jewish religion. Few examples that support this view is found in the book of Acts where Luke depicts Paul observing Jewish practices such as, cutting his hair at Cenchrea because of a Nazarite vow (18;18); taking Timothy for Circumcision (16:1-3); and purifying himself in the Jerusalem temple (21:23-26). In justifying all these Paul says, to win those under the law, I became like one under the law [though I myself am not under the law] (v.20b). Thus, Paul establishes what he had said earlier, that he became all for the Jews in order to bring them to salvation.

Secondly, Paul says, *to those outside the law, I become as one outside the law* (v.21). The term *outside the law,* was used among the Jews to refer to the Gentiles. Paul is not an antinomian, but he believed that the validity of Mosaic Law has been over-ridden by the death of Christ. As per the New Testament, it is not the Law, but believe in Christ, and obeying his words, is what keeps us in the salvation which is freely given to us during conversion.

Thus, mingling and dining with Gentiles was not a big deal for Paul, moreover, his main intention was to win them for Christ. So he says in verse 22, I have become all things to all, that I might, by all means, save some. Furthermore, he says, I do it all for the sake of the Gospel. Thus Paul validates his first argument in this chapter that, Christian freedom/rights must be exercised with the view of winning people to Christ, rather than being an obstacle in the spread of the Gospel (vv.1-23).

2.2.2.1.2.2 Christian Freedom Must be Exercised with Self-Control (vv.24-27)

As an apt illustration clarifies the entire sermon, Paul here gives the example of an athlete to explain whatever he has said in this chapter thus far. However, with this example, Paul introduces a new idea of self-control which is important in the life of every Christian. Thus, this author considers this as another section where Paul argues that Christian freedom must be exercised with self-control.

Keeping in mind the Greek sports arena, Paul talks about the importance of self-control in the first century Corinthian Christian community. In the ancient Greek world, the Olympic Games were considered an important event. One among the games was Isthmian games that were held around ten miles away from the city of Corinth. This game was held in spring of the first and the third year of every Olympiad. Though the main game in this was horse racing, there were many athletic contests included in it. One of those contests was the running race.

Paul must have witnessed it during his stay in Corinth since he was there for 18 months. And the Corinthians themselves were involved in such games. They were well informed about the long distance runners in the stadium. Though they were well aware of the facts of the games, Paul reminds them that, though all the runners complete the race, only one receives the prize. Nevertheless, all participants exercise self-control in all things.

Paul employs the term ἀγωνιζόμενος (*agōnozomenos*) to denote exercise. The literal meaning of this term is, to strain every nerve, to fight, or to struggle. Preparation for the athletic context is a hard process. But they do that in order to get the prize. Thus Paul asks them indirectly, how much more the Christians should practice self-control as they await an imperishable crown (v.25c). Further, Paul gives yet another example to the Corinthians from his own life starting with a purpose clause, *so,* which mean, for this purpose i.e., to receive an imperishable crown, *I do not run aimlessly, nor do I box as though beating the air, but I punish my body and enslaves it.*

Paul did his ministry with tremendous self-control and help from God. Paul was serious about his conduct as he was engaged in the proclamation of the gospel of Christ. Not only his conduct, Paul says, as an athlete strains every nerve in his body, *I punish my body and enslave it.* Paul did so with another purpose which is revealed at the end of the chapter. He says, as a preacher of the gospel of Christ, *I myself should not be disqualified* (9:27).Thus, to fulfill one's destiny in Christian life, it is pertinent to exercise self-control in our lives.

2.2.2.1.3 Paul's Warning to Corinthians from Israel's History (10:1-22)

After giving an example from his own life, Paul continues his discussion with yet another example taken this time from the desert experience of the people of Israel. Through this example, Paul gets back to the issue of the consumption of food offered to idols and its dangers, as it destroys one's life as a whole, and also causes one to become partners with demons.

2.2.2.1.3.1 Improper Exercise of Christian Freedom Leads to Destruction (vv.1-13)

Paul's first argument in this chapter is that the improper exercise of Christian freedom leads to destruction. Paul posits three main points in this section– indications (vv.1-5), examples (vv.6-10), and exhortation (vv.11-13).

To begin with, in verses 1-5, Paul mentions five signs which proved God's presence with them as they passed through the wilderness after being delivered from the bondage of Egypt. These five signs are, 1) God accompanied them in the cloud (v.1b); 2) God rescued them from the pursuing Egyptians at the Red Sea (v.1c); 3) God guided them through Moses (v.2); 4) God supplied them with food to eat (v.3a); and 5) God provided them water to drink (v.3b).

Paul starts this section (v.1) with a strong indication Οὐ θέλω γὰρ ἀγνοεῖν (*Ou thelō gar agnoein* – for I do not want you to be unaware), literally, for I wish/desire/want you not to be ignorant. The conjunction γὰρ, *for,* in verse 1 indicates that it is connected to the context of the preceding chapter. Further, with the addressing word, ἀδελφοί (*adelphoi* – brothers), he reminds the Corinthians concerning the events that had happen in the life of the Israelites and uses those incidents to warn them of the dire consequences of displeasing God.

With the description, *our ancestors were all under the cloud and all passed through the sea*, Paul mentions regarding the exodus and crossing the Red Sea. Other versions of this event describe that *God led his people by means of cloud by day and a pillar of fire by night* (Ex. 13:21). The cloud protected the Israelites as a covering. The phrase *through the sea*, recalls the miraculous deliverance when God divided the Red Sea to form walls on both sides and made dry land through which they reached the other side.

Further, Paul claims that the wilderness generation also received baptism. It says *all were baptized into Moses in the cloud and in the sea* (v. 2). Paul here compares the Corinthian Christians who placed their faith in Jesus to the Israelites who trusted God as represented by his servant Moses. The phrase *baptized into Moses* does not mean that they were baptized in the name of Moses, but it refers to the loyalty of the Israelites towards Moses and acceptance of his leadership. The phrase εἰς τὸν Μωϋσῆν ἐβαπτίσθησαν (*eis ton Mōusēn ebaptisthēsan* - baptized into Moses) is a Jewish parallel that appears to have been coined by Paul from the Christian idiom, βαπτίσθημεν εἰς Χριστὸν Ἰησοῦν (*baptisthēmen eis Christon yēsoun* – baptized into Christ Jesus), with the intention to strengthen his arguments.

In verses 3 and 4, Paul mentions the fourth and fifth blessings the Israelites experienced in the wilderness. He says, *and all ate the same spiritual food, and all drank the same spiritual drink. For they drank from the spiritual rock that followed them, and the rock was Christ.* It could be possible that what Paul had in mind was that, as the Corinthian believers partook in the Lord's Supper, similarly the Israelites *ate from the same spiritual food* and *drank from the same spiritual drink.* In addition, Paul figuratively says, *that rock was Christ.* Paul here seems to make a connection between the terminology recorded in the Old Testament hymnody (Deut.32:15, 18; Ps. 62:2; 95:1; 89:26; 78:35) and Christ; thus identifying Christ with the rock.[61]

However, irrespective of the care, providence, and protection that the Israelites received from God, yet they distrusted and displeased God. Thus, Paul ends his indications in this section with the dire consequence they faced, *nevertheless, God was not pleased with most of them, and they were struck down in the wilderness* (v.5); which was a relevant lesson and reminder for the Corinthians who were displeasing God by their improper exercise of rights/freedom.

Secondly, as Paul gives few examples to the Corinthians from the life experience of the people of Israel, he particularly considers five historical incidents that happened in their life, which are– their covetous craving for food (Num.11:4); their adoration and idolatrous feasting in front of the golden calf (Exo. 32:4, 6, 19); their involvement in sexual immorality with the Moabite women (Num. 25:1-9); testing the Lord (Ex. 17:7; Num. 14:22; Deut. 6:16); and murmuring against God and his servant Moses (Num. 14:2, 36; 16:1-35).[62]

Paul starts this section by stating, Ταῦτα δὲ τύποι ἡμῶν ἐγενήθησαν (*Tauta de tupoi hēmōn egenēthēsan* – now these things occurred as examples for us). In other words, it means, in view of the indications placed above the life of Israel is an archetype for us. One unique thing seen in this section, especially in verses 6-11, is Paul's use of the plural form. In five places Paul uses the plural form, which communicates that these were examples not only for the Corinthian Christians but for him too.

ἡμῶν (*hēmōn*) - [for] **Us** (v.6a)	Ταῦτα δὲ τύποι ἐγενήθησαν (*Tauta de tupoi egenēthēsan*) – these things happened as examples
ἡμᾶς(*hēmas*) - [so that] **We** (v.6b)	εἰς τὸ μὴ εἶναι ἐπιθυμητὰς κακῶν, καθὼς κἀκεῖ νοι ἐπεθύμησαν (*eis to mēeinai epithumētas kakōn, kathōs kakeinoi epethumēsan*) – might not desire evil as they did.
Πορνεύωμεν (*porne**uōmen***) –**We**(v.8a)	μηδὲ πορνεύωμεν (**mēde *porneu*ōmen**) – must not indulge in sexual immorality
ἐκπειράζωμεν (*ekpeiraz**ōmen***) –**We** **(vv.9-10)**	μηδὲ ἐκπειράζωμεν τὸν Χριστόν, Μηδὲ γογγύζετε, καθὼς καί τινες αὐτῶν ἐγόγγυσαν (*mēdeekpeirazōmen ton christen, mēde gogguzete, kathōs kai tines autōn egoggusan*) – must not put Christ to the test and do not complaint as some of them did.
πρὸς ἡμῶν (*pros hēmōn*) – to **us** (v.11)	ταῦτα δὲ τυπικῶς ..., ἐγράφη πρὸς νουθεσίαν(*tauta de tupikōs ..., egraphē pros nouthesian*)-they were written down as examples

Being the spiritual father of the Corinthian believers, Paul reminds the historical events that happened in the life of Israel. Paul says these things happened as examples for us. The pronoun Ταῦτα (*Tauta* - these things), refers to the first five verses of chapter 10, that the Israelites had all the blessings, but God was not pleased with most of them, and they were struck down in the wilderness. Now from verses 7-11 Paul explicates the reasons behind their fall in the wilderness.

First of all, Paul says, *do not become idolaters as some of them were*. By this Paul reminds the Corinthians about how the Israelites rebelled against God who delivered them out of the Egyptian bondage. Without giving much explanation of their act of idolatry, suddenly Paul moves to another concern, that, these people *sat down to eat and drink and they rose up to play.* The seriousness of the sin (idolatry) is seen in Exodus 32.

When people saw that Moses was delayed in returning from Mount Sinai, they gathered around Aaron and said, make us gods who shall go before us, for we do not know what happened to this Moses who led us out of Egypt (Ex. 32:1). Aaron listened to them and made a calf with the gold they brought, and they said, these are your gods, O Israel, who brought you up out of the land of Egypt (Ex. 32:4). Aaron built an altar before the golden calf and proclaimed, tomorrow shall be a festival to the Lord (Ex. 32:5). The Israelites totally forgetting Yahweh who had rescued them, and considering the golden calf as their redeemer, rose up early the next day, offered sacrifices, brought peace offerings, and sat down to eat, drink, and, 'to play'.

In I Cor. 10:8 Paul alludes to this incident of the Israelites wherein they had indulged in sexual immorality. Their acts of sexual immorality were closely connected to idolatry which was mentioned in the previous verses. Paul talks to them about these things in the context of eating food offered to idols and immorality that existed among them. As mentioned the above phrases such as, κάθισεν ὁ λαὸς φαγεῖν καὶ πεῖν καὶ ἀνέστησαν παίζειν (*kathisen ho laos phagein kai pein kai anestēsan paizein* – the people sat down to eat and drink [v.7]), and πορνεύω (*porneuō* - fornication [v.8]) are closely related because the word παίζειν, *paizein* (to play), itself is a negative word which denotes sexual act as Fitzmyer says, the word παίζειν, *paizein* (to play), has an erotic or sexual overtone.[63]

In the Corinthian context, the incorporation of eating, drinking, and playing was closely related to sexual immorality which was practiced as part of idol worship. Hence, it is related to the issue of consumption of food offered to idols. As mentioned earlier, eating in the temple was a daily routine in the life of Corinthians. Even Christians were invited to such occasions by their friends or relatives to join in the social transition or celebratory occasions. In some cases, the food was served in homes, but mostly the celebration ended by having food in the temple dining itself.

Christians, though not participating in the process of offering sacrifice to idols, shared the joy of their friends and relatives by eating food that was sent to the temple dining by the priest. The food was served with wine by the temple prostitutes. This was followed by dancing, singing, and finally culminated in sex with these temple prostitutes who were considered sacred. Furthermore, reminding the Corinthians about sexual immorality committed by the Israelites, Paul warns that we should refrain from such acts as a result of which twenty-three thousand Israelites died in the wilderness.

Paul mentions two more examples from the life of Israelites in this section. Verses 9 and 10 say they *tested* and *grumbled* against God. By this

Paul is referring to Israel's frequent testing of the Lord's patience during their wilderness journey. After defeating the king of Arad, the Israelites become overconfident and were unwilling to make a circuitous journey around Edom. They expressed their impatience towards God by blaspheming against God and criticizing Moses. In response, God sent poisonous snakes and many were destroyed. In verse 10 Paul talks about their murmuring against God and his servant Moses, which is considered as another form of testing Him because it originated from their lack of trust in Moses and God Himself.

Through these examples, Paul tells the Corinthians that, like the Israelites tested God, we should not test Christ by refusing to accept his divine guidance in our life. Paul also says, do not grumble against Christ, as it reflects our dissatisfaction with Christ. People of Israel through their improper behaviors such as idolatry, sexual immorality, testing, and grumbling displeased God, as a result of which they were destroyed in the wilderness. Using these as examples, Paul exhorts the Corinthians that improper exercise of Christian freedom will lead to their own destruction.

2.2.2.1.3.2 Improper Exercise of Christian Freedom will Lead us to become Partners with Demons (vv.14-22)

Paul had closed the previous section with an exhortation to the Corinthians saying, if you think that you are standing, watch out that you do not fall into the same danger that Israelites fell and destroyed themselves (vv.12-13). Now in verses 14-22, Paul starts yet another section raising his next argument that calls for the proper exercise of Christian freedom. He addresses those who considered themselves as *strong.* Paul draws their attention once again to his argument as he resumes his discussion on idolatry.

It starts with the conjunction Διόπερ (*Dioper* – therefore). In this instant, the word is considered as a very strong *inferential conjunction* because of the combination of words δι and ὅπερ. The position of inferential conjunction at the beginning of this section suggests that Paul brings a logical conclusion to what he had said in the preceding section where he showed by way of example that Israel's idolatry had caused their overthrow in the desert, despite their sacraments.[64] However, in this section, Paul brings a sub-supporting point for his argument to the proper use of Christian freedom.

Paul starts it with a straightforward prohibition, φεύγετε ἀπὸ τῆς εἰδωλολατρίας (*pheugete apo tēs eidōlolatrias* – flee from the worship of idols). This is Paul's basic exhortation about eating food offered to idols, repeating what he had said in 6:18 - *shun fornication.* At first glance, it might seem contradictory to what Paul had said in his earlier statement (8:9). But it is not a contradiction because Paul allows the mature believers to eat in pagan temples, but with limited freedom. Firstly, he permits freedom as long as it does not become a hindrance to the new convert (the weak brothers). Secondly, since idols are nothing, and the strong have the knowledge that idols do not really exist, they were free to eat whatever food was placed before them.

However, in 10:14, Paul addresses the issue of idolatry itself. Thus Paul explicitly says, flee from the worship of idols, because it is God's commandment to not worship idols (Exod. 20:4-6; Deut. 5:8-10). Paul specifically addressing then mature believers says in verse 15, *I speak as to sensible people…* Fitzmayer considers this as a generic introduction to his main argument in this section that he belongs to Christ as he partakes in the Holy Communion.[65] Paul continues his discussion in verse 16 with a rhetoric question, the bread that we break, is it not a sharing in the body of Christ? The answer is certainly 'yes,' because they all are partakers of the same bread. With this Paul clarifies that, since the bread we partake is one, we who are many are one body. The church in Corinth consisted of Jewish and Gentile Christians who formed one body, the body of Christ. Thus Paul says, *we who are many are one body* (v.17). By this Paul also conveys another message that there should not be any division between them on the basis that we, the knowledgeable are *strong,* thus are permitted to eat the food offered to idols, and they being ignorant are *the week*, therefore are not permitted. For, partaking in the Lord's Supper rules out the possibility of any member attending pagan festivals in the temple where idols are kept.

Intending to argue his case one step further, Paul once again alludes to the people of Israel and says, consider the people of Israel, are not those who eat the sacrifices partners in the altar? In the Old Testament, when the Israelites offered sacrifices on the altar, in effect they were identifying themselves with what was offered on the altar and with the Lord, on whose altar the sacrifice was offered (Deu.12:6-7; 14:26; Lev. 3:1-17; 7:11-36; I Sam. 9:12-13). Thus Paul says, eating the food offered to idols in a pagan temple leads a person to become a partner with demon himself because they are not offering it to God but to an idol.

It is true that idols are nothing, but only wood, metal, stone, or clay. However, the Gentiles offered sacrifices thinking that they are offering it to their gods, which is a sacrifice to demons. Therefore Paul says, those who are strong in their conscience, which allows them to freely associate with idol worshippers and eat the food offered to idols are forgetting the connection of such food with the subjective convictions of the idolaters, who offer sacrifice to the demons.

In verse 22 Paul says, *you cannot drink the cup of the Lord and the cup of demons. You cannot partake of the table of the Lord and the table of demons*. However, the so-called mature believers in the church at Corinth were becoming partners with demons, as they used their freedom to eat the food offered to idols, on the basis of knowledge. Thus, Paul validates his argument that improper exercise of Christian freedom will lead one to become partners with demons.

2.2.2.1.4 Paul's Final Word on the Issue of Eating Food Offered to Idols (10: 23-11:1)

Paul's discussion in this section (10:23-11:1) is his conclusion to the argument which he began in chapter 8. On the basis of Paul's arguments, some Corinthian Christians thought that he was giving contradicting advice; as in some instance he agrees with the strong, and in other, he disagrees with them. Nonetheless, Paul had given his advice in order to avoid causing the weaker brother to fall into sin. However, some among them still could not understand what Paul was trying to convey to them. Thus, in this section, with a series of imperatives and explanatory comments, Paul makes a distinction between the essential and the nonessential aspects in Christian life.

2.2.2.1.4.1 Though it is lawful, Christians should Restrain from Exercising their Liberty, because neither it is Beneficial, nor does it Builds up (vv.23-30)

The slogan at the beginning of the section, Πάντα μοι ἔξεστιν (*panta moi echestin* – all things are lawful for me), is seen elsewhere with a restrictive comment (6:12), but *for me* not all things are beneficial [though *for me* – which is omitted in some text, however, the copyists uses it in MSS such as ℵ[2] C[3], H, Ψ, and in Koine text-tradition].[66] Paul used this slogan in 6:12 in relation to the liberty the Corinthians exercised in their social life. However, in this instance, he uses it in relation to eating food that was sold in the marketplace. On the basis of questions asked by the Jews who were challenging Paul on Christian liberty, he responds to them with an addition to the slogan, *but not all things are beneficial and not all things build up*. Furthermore, Paul gives reasons, why it is neither beneficial nor building up either those who eat this food or others.

Paul posits his main reason in verse 24, it is neither beneficial nor builds up because the *strong* in the Corinthian congregation were doing it for their own advantage or benefit. They were doing it out of their pride and rivalry to others, as they freely exercised their freedom on the basis of knowledge they possessed. But Paul advises them with a command, *do not seek your own advantage, but that of the other* (v.24). Paul's intention was that the Corinthians who are strong in their conscience should not practice it for the benefit of others. Hence, he should curtail his usage of freedom/liberty in Christ.

On the contrary, he gives another command, *eat whatever is sold in the meat market without raising any question on the ground of conscience, for the earth and its fullness are the Lord's* (vv.25-26). In the Corinthian meat market, the main source of meat was the temple. Because of the excess of meat left in the temple by the devotees, it was sent to the markets to be sold, which was another source for the temple economy. Thus, it was well known that the meat available in the market has been offered to idols. However, there was no reason to think that no other meat or food was sold in the markets other than that comes from the temple.

However, the Jews in Corinth were hesitant to buy non-kosher meat from the market because it was forbidden for them. For food to be kosher, the animal has to be killed individually by a trained Jew known as a *shochet*. Before buying, it was customary for the Jews to inquire from the shopkeeper whether the meat was kosher or not. However, in opposition to their religious teachings, Paul commands them to eat whatever is sold in the meat market without raising any questions on grounds of conscience. Since the Jewish Christians in Corinth nullified the spiritual significance of food offered to idols, Paul commands them to eat this meat, as it also does not have any spiritual or religious significance.

In verse 26, quoting from Old Testament (LXX of Psalms 24:1), Paul gives a theological reason for what he has just said in verse 25, *for the earth and its fullness are the Lord's*, which was a part of standard Jewish blessing of food.[67] By this Paul meant that, even though the meat is offered to idols [who does not exist], it does not belong to them, because everything on earth ultimately belongs to God who created it. Thus it is permissible for a Christian even to eat at the home of an unbeliever, without raising any questions *on the ground of conscience*.

However, Paul gives this command with an exception expressed in verse 28 – *But, if someone says to you, this has been offered in sacrifice, then do not eat it, out of consideration for the one who informed you, and for the sake of conscience*. Here Paul presents a situation in which a Christian might face in the dining room of a gentile host. The information about the idol meat can be given by the Gentile host, or an unbeliever, or by a diligent Christian. Verse 29a suggests that it is possibly a weak Christian. In any case, Paul commands them that, once having known the source of the food presented before them they must refrain from eating it, else their negligence will lead them to sin not only against the one who has informed them, but also against God himself (8:12).

So Paul says, though the conscience of the one who is invited is strong, considering the conscience of the informer, *do not eat it*. In the next verse (v. 30), Paul says, even in the case of one partaking the food which is offered to idols *with thankfulness* it is wrong because it can cause insult to others. Both, Jews and Christians offered prayers to God before eating, in reverence to God as the giver of the provision. Nevertheless, if the strong is criticized for the meal hosted by a Gentile, his prayer becomes ineffective because the conscience of the one criticizing is weak. By this Paul reminds the Corinthian Christians to exercise their freedom sensitively, because the improper exercise of freedom will lead those whose conscience is weakto judgment. Consequently, he himself becomes a sinner. For these reasons Paul says, though it is lawful, Christians should restrain from exercising their liberty to eat the food offered to idols because neither is it beneficial, not does it builds up.

2.2.2.1.4.2 Because it neither Glorifies God nor Pleases others or Leads others to Salvation (vv.31-11:1)

Finally, in this section, Paul concludes his discussion about the issue of the consumption of food offered to idols. With a sentimental expression followed by three imperatives, Paul exhorts the Corinthians to live their life for the glory of God.

In the phrase, *whether you eat or drink, or whatever you do*, Paul includes all areas of life of a Christian. Whether it is social or religious, they must live in such a manner that it elevates Christian values. Paul's first command is, πάντα εἰς δόξαν θεοῦ ποιεῖτε (*panta eis doxan theou poieite* – do everything for the glory of God [v.31b]). Every behavior of a Christian must be to bring glory to God. In Christian life, not only our words and deeds, but our behavior also is equally important. If our intention is not right, whatever we do, will not glorify God. Thus Paul says, Christian life should not be motivated by food laws or any kind of happiness that quenches his physical appetite. Rather Christian life should be lived for God's glory, by exercising one's rights and privileges appropriately.

The second command Paul gives is, *give no offense to Jews or to Greeks or to the church of God* (v.32a). Though the kind of offense is not specified here, it is understood that Paul is talking about the improper use of Christian freedom. With the improper use of one's freedom/rights, Paul says no one should fault against a Greek or Gentile, or even the church of God. The church at Corinth consisted of Jews and Gentiles. Then what could be the reason for Paul to use three different nouns – *Jews*, *Gentiles*, and *the church of God*. Paul uses the first two nouns, *Jews* and *Gentiles* to refer to the unbelievers outside the church, and the phrase, *to the church of God*, denotes the mixture of Jews and Gentiles converts within the church.

By this, Paul commands the Corinthian Christians to conduct themselves well, not only for the benefit of those inside the church but also for the benefit of those outside. This they needed to do without prioritizing their own advantage, but with the intention of winning others to Christ. With the phrase *so that they may be saved*, Paul means to say that the main objective of a Christian life must be the salvation of others. Paul as an apostle and a faithful ambassador of Christ tirelessly proclaimed the gospel and explained the way of salvation to others. So, Paul encourages the Corinthian believers also to do everything in such a manner that will cause others to come to Christ.

Finally, Paul commands the Corinthians, *be imitators of me, as I am of Christ* (11:1). As he gives this concluding remark on the discussed issue, Paul ends it with another imperative *beimitators of me*. By this Paul sets an example and beseeches his readers to follow him as he follows Christ. In chapters 8:13-9:21 Paul had implicitly proposed himself as a model for the Corinthians to follow. In 11:1b Paul gives the ultimate reason for his call to the Corinthians to follow him. He says I imitate Christ.

The life in Christ eliminates any suggestion of pride and arrogance because the life of Christ was an ultimate example of humility, obedience, love, care, and concern for others (Phil. 2:5-11). Thus Paul validates his final argument on the issue of consumption of food offered to idols, by stating that, though it is lawful, Christians should restrain from exercising their liberty to eat the food offered to an idol, because it neither glorifies God, nor pleases others, nor leads others to salvation.

Summary

Paul's discussion on the issue of consumption of food offered to idols consisted of three chapters. In each chapter, Paul validates his points with skilled arguments to prove the dire consequences of the improper exercise of Christian freedom/rights, as the freedom which some *strong* Christians exercised, became a stumbling block for their *weaker* brothers and sisters in faith. So in chapter 8, Paul warns them not to lead a weaker brother astray by eating food in the temple, for if it disturbs the conscience of a weaker brother, they are not only sinning against their fellow believer, but also against Christ himself. In chapter 9, after a careful argument on this same issue, Paul concluded with a strong expression of his decision to abstain from eating such food, in order to keep a weaker brother from falling into sin.

In close connection with chapter 8, Paul explains about the matter of his apostolic rights and the way how he exercises it, in chapter 9. As he tracks the flow of thoughts from chapter 8 to 9 he carefully drafts it with a series of rhetorical questions which ultimately expect a positive answer from his recipients. He asks questions like, do we not have the right to our food and drink? Do we not have the right to be accompanied by a believing wife? Is it only Barnabas and I who have no right to refrain from working for a living? Does a soldier serve at his own expense? Does a farmer not eat his own grapes? Does a shepherd refrain from consuming the milk products of his flock? After the careful delivery of all these questions with the fine touch of strong rhetoric, he proves his argument by quoting the Law of Moses, which forbids muzzling the ox when it is threshing. People who work in the fields share in the harvest; so also Paul and his associates who sow spiritual seeds have the right to reap the material harvest from the Corinthians. Workers in the temple receive their sustenance from the temple. Likewise, as the Lord commands the preachers of the gospel should derive their living from it.

However, Paul refuses to avail himself of the right of material support from his people. He wants to preach the gospel without being dependent on anyone's material support. Thus he is not obligated to anyone, is able to boast, and can freely preach the gospel. He belongs to no one and is free to win various people to Christ: the Jews, those under the law, those without the law, and the weak. Paul is all things to all people. Apart from giving example from his own life experiences, he uses imagery borrowed from the field of sports, he exhorts his readers to run the race to obtain the prize. He applies the illustrations to himself and says that he does not run without looking intently at the goal. He disciplines himself so as not to be disqualified. Thus validates, though he has all the freedom to exercise the aforementioned rights he renounces it for the sake of the gospel of Christ and bringing others to Christ.

After raising the need of exercising one's right in a proper way from his own life - experience, in chapter 10, Paul once again reaffirmed his argument through the historical event that happened in the life of the people of Israel during Moses' time. Paul asserts that all the Israelites who left Egypt under the cloud passed through the sea and were baptized into Moses. All these people ate the same spiritual food and drank the same spiritual drink from the spiritual rock that accompanied them, namely, Christ. Yet, because he was displeased with them, God scattered their bodies across the desert floor. Through the historical events, Paul relates in chapter 10 serve to alert the Corinthians about the dangers of idolatry. He recalls the incident of the Israelites eating and drinking when they worshiped the golden calf, a festivity that degenerated into pagan revelry. During their journey through the wilderness, they tested God's patience. As punishment, many were bitten by poisonous snakes and others were killed by an angel. The Corinthians are instructed to take note of it so that they do not submit themselves to idolatry.

After delivering a direct command to flee from idolatry, Paul instructs the readers to observe the significance of the Lord's Supper. They must know that partaking of the cup and of the bread demonstrates unity. Eating food offered to idols make the believer a participant or partner with demons. Paul shows the utter inconsistency of drinking from the cup of demons and from the cup of the Lord. The Corinthian believers (the strong) interpreted and applied *All things are permissible* to eat the meat bought at the meat market which is neither beneficial nor builds up. Because they were practicing it for their own advantage to quench their physical appetite without considering the conscience of the weak among them.

Finally, Paul concluded his discussion on food offered to idols with a closing note – do everything for the glory of God, without being an offense to the Jews, Gentiles, or to the Church of God.

2.2.3 Appropriate Behavior for Men and Women in the Christian Worship (11:2-16)

After prohibiting the Corinthians from eating food offered to idols, Paul now moves on to address three kinds of abuses in their own assembly, such as - issue of head covering or hairstyle of women while praying or prophesying (11:2-16); abuse of Lord's Supper and the poor in the common gathering (11:17-34); and unhealthy exercise of spiritual gifts, especially, speaking in tongues in the assembly (chap. 12-14).

As he begins his instruction in the matter of worship, Paul, first of all in chapter 11:2-16, deals with the worshippers, both men and women, who pray and prophecies against the custom of the church of God. However, as Paul was asked specifically concerning submission of women within the church context, he focuses his attention on the matter of women and their conduct while praying and prophesying in the church.

2.2.3.1 Paul's Response: "Men and Women, Veiling and Unveiling, respectively, their Head while Praying or Prophesying Disgraces their Head"

In view of the aforementioned concern, Paul recommends few advices to be followed by members of the Corinthian Church on the ground of theological, physiological, and sociological realities, in order to reason out the relation of men and women to Christ and God.

2.2.3.1.1 Men Should not Veil his Head because they are the Image and Reflection of God (v. 4,7)

Paul starts this section with a word of admiration about the Corinthian Christians. Paul starts verse 2 with the phrase, *I commend you.* The root word used for commend is 'Επαινῶ (*Epainō* [1st person. singular, present, indicative, active]), which literally means, *I praise you.* So far in this letter, Paul corrected many of the mistakes which they were practicing in their sociological and ecclesiastical life. However, as he begins this section for yet another correction, he begins it with a word of appreciation, because though he cannot approve of their practices, he admits that Corinthian believers, in general, have been practicing what he has already taught them (v. 2b).

Two words are very important in this verse – *everything* and *traditions.* There exists considerable discussion on what did Paul mean by these expressions. However, the possible answers are, the word πάντα (*panta* – all things/everything) and παραδόσεις (*paradoseis* – traditions)[68] refers to the apostolic teachings that Paul had taught the Corinthians while he was with them. In this context, it can even refer to the proper conduct during worship. However, they were praised by Paul since they maintained the tradition just as he handed it over to them.

In verse 3, Paul then begins his argument with a theological paradigm of *head* that he has not mentioned elsewhere. With the metaphorical representation of *the head*, Paul introduces three kinds of relations, such as - Christ to man; husband (man) to wife (woman); and God to Christ. The metaphorical usage of κεφαλὴ (*kephalē* - head) is always understood as a symbol of authority or hierarchy. However, Fee comments that the word κεφαλὴ (*kephalē* - head), is not understood as authority, but as source or source of life.[69]

The idea of the head as the source is well displayed in verses 8-9. It proves that Paul's main intention in this section is not to prove the hierarchical order of authority, but relational aspects, i.e., the relation of one's being as the source of other's existence. Thus Paul states the relation of a woman, man, and Christ. Kistemaker view it as the authority because Christ has authority over the man, man has authority over women, and God over Christ. For him, authority is not about the superiority of one party and the inferiority of the other, but equality and inter-dependency, as Christ in his essence is equal to God the Father, so also women in her being and worth is equal to man.[70]

Therefore, though the head signifies authority, it also includes a reference to origin and equality that affects a continued relationship. As Paul brings the metaphor of head to discuss about the problem concerning conduct of women, he brings men into the scene for the theological reason to prove the source/headship/authority of God over Christ, Christ over man, and man over woman; and to exemplify the way for men and women to owe their respect towards each other and to Christ as they come together for worship.

As Paul continues, first of all, he says, *any man who prays or prophesies with something on his head, disgraces his head* (v.4). The background of the passages in this section is closely connected to the culture, dress code, and practices of Corinth. The city of Corinth consisted of a mixed population of Greeks, Romans, Jews, and people from other nations. The church at Corinth must have adopted the customs and practice of the pagans in their church gatherings.

Since Paul talks about prophecy, it is clear that Paul is not discussing about the private meetings, because the gift of prophecy was given for the edification (common good of the people) of the church as a whole. And by prayer, Paul mean here is not the private prayer, but the prayer in public which is loud and audible to all.

Then, addressing the men Paul says, you should not veil your head while praying and prophesying. The phrase κατὰ κεφαλῆςἔχων (*kata kephalēs echōn*– with something on his head), literally, having something down from his head/ having hanging down from the head. So Paul is not referring to just keeping something on his head, but something hanging down from his head, and which covers his head fully. In either case, it is not good, because he disgraces his head by doing so.

Men covering their head was practiced as part of their status, civil or legal position they held. Many first-century statues have been discovered depicting men covering their head, such as the statue of a man praying to gods, Augustus in the Julian Basilica of Corinth, and Nero, etc. Even the Roman magistrates used to cover their head as part of their religious, civil, and legal roles. The elite group in Corinth also practiced the same in their socio-political and religious life. Even homosexuals of those days used to cover their head with long hair.[71]

Paul possibly corrects their misconduct because, men who were not part of the elite group, were forcefully following their old custom in their new religious life, as they prayed and exercised the gift of prophecy. They might have done this to demonstrate their dignity and power within the church. However, Paul calls such conduct as καταισχύνω (*kataischunō* - disgrace), literally, put to shame, disfigure, or dishonor.

In verse 7 Paul says, *a man ought not to have his head veiled, since he is the image and reflection of God.* As per Paul, the action of men covering their head was equivalent to concealing his status as the image and glory of God. Though it was practiced by the pagan converts to present their status as being from the elite community, they were, in fact, disgracing themselves by concealing the image of their creator, and the status of being a child of God, which they have received in and through Christ. Therefore Paul instructs the men in the church not to cover their head.

2.2.3.1.2 Women Should Veil her Head because they are the Reflection of Men (vv. 5-6, 7b-10)

Paul's second argument in this section is given in relation to women and their conduct during Christian worship. Verse 5 says *any woman who prays or prophesies with her head unveiled disgraces her head.*

The phrase *any woman who prays or prophecies*, spell out the equality of women with men in Christ. Unlike Old Testament times where men were the recipients of the covenant of God and the representative for women; in the New Testament, women and men were considered equal before the Lord. This is evident as Paul describes regarding the role of men and women in the religious functions such as *praying* and *prophesying*.

However, Paul gives some instructions to the women as they exercise these religious activities in a common gathering. Though Paul had said that the husband (man) is the head of his wife (woman), in light of verse 5, it means her own physical head. Further, he says, *with her head unveiled, disgraces her head.* In the first century, women covering their head was a part of the culture. Especially, in public, if a woman failed to do this, it was a dishonor to herself and a disrespect to her husband. Thus, the Corinthian women followed the custom of covering their head to express respect toward themselves and to their husbands.

A possible question that arises in this context is, does Paul give this instruction to married women only? B. W. Winter supports that it is meant for the married women since it was a custom practiced by the married woman outside the homes in the Roman culture.[72] On the contrary, Fitzmyer comments that the phrase πᾶσα δὲ γυνὴ (*pasa de gunē* - but every woman) expresses a wider range of category of woman, both married and the unmarried.[73] Referring to the Corinthian custom of head covering, Paul exhorts the Christian women to conduct themselves by veiling their head even as they pray and prophecy in the common gathering.

Further, Paul says, *it is one and the same thing as having her head shaved* (v.5b). Cutting or shaving the hair was practiced to humiliate an adulterous woman. It is mentioned in the writing of Dio Chrysostom, a first-century Roman author, that a woman caught in adultery was shorn by the authorities of the island of Cyprus in order to identify her as a prostitute.[74] Thus, what Paul is saying is that, as a woman with an uncovered head in public is a shame to her husband, so too a shorn and shaven head is to herself.

Later in verse 6, Paul gives a chance for women to make a choice: *for if a woman will not veil herself, then she should cut off her hair; but if it is disgraceful for a woman to have her hair cut off or to be shaved, she should wear a veil.* Paul places two choices before the women such as: κειράσθω (*keirasthō* - to shear/to cut off) κατακαλυπτέσθω (*katakaluptesthō* - to cover up/to veil). Thus Paul makes his argument clear that women in Corinth who are not willing to cover their head while praying and prophesying during a church worship service, should have their hair cut off. On the contrary, if they wish to avoid being a disgrace to herself and to her husband, they must cover their head in the church.

In verses 8 and 9, giving the example of the creation order, Paul mentions two other supporting reasons for women to cover their head. He says,

Man is not made from woman *but* *Woman* is made *from man* (v.8)	Man is not created for the sake of woman *but* *Woman* is created *for the sake of man* (v.9)

The phrase γυνὴ ἐξ ἀνδρός (*gunē ex andros* – woman from man) is in the case of the genitive of source. The words ἐξ ἀνδρός is the source from which the head noun γυνὴ originates. Thus alluding to the creation history in the book of Genesis, Paul validates man as the *source* of woman, *woman is made from man*. Likewise, the phrase γυνὴ διὰ τὸν ἄνδρα (*gunēdia ton andra* – for the sake of man) in the accusative case in Greek language, refer to the direct object. So the noun γυνὴ, in this phrase referring to the direct object διὰ τὸν ἄνδρα to which it stands related. The direct object always answer to the question of whom? or what? Thus, it becomes clear the *action* (creation of woman) is for the sake of man.

In verse10, Paul gives one more reason for a woman to cover their head, *for this reason, a woman ought to have a symbol of authority on her head, because of the angels*. The expression διὰ τοῦτο ὀφείλει (*dia touto opheilei* – for this reason), is a strong evidence that Paul is connecting his discourse in verse 10 with the theological and biblical argument expressed in the preceding verses (vv.7-9).

However, the construction of the phrase*, a woman ought to have a symbol of authority on her head, because of the angels,* is a matter of debate among scholars, and there exists various proposed interpretation of this text. With regards to the phrase, *a symbol of authority*, Hooker says, with head covering a women displays the new freedom she receives in Christ as she engages in public worship.[75] However, as Paul's main concern in this section is not about the freedom one has in Christ, this view is ruled out.

Hurley suggests that the expression of authority has been linked to the creation account in Genesis 1:26-28 wherein both, male and female, had received the command to rule the created things in heavens and on earth.[76] However, the text does not provide any further explanations. Moreover, in I Corinthians 11, head covering is viewed as a symbol of honoring oneself, and as a means of submission to one's husband; rather than as an expression of authority. Thus, it could be interpreted that, by covering her head, a woman exercises control over it, and not expose it to indignity. On the contrary, if she unveils, everyone has control over it and can embarrass her by gazing at her. Hence, Robertson and Plummer translate it as, a woman ought to have authority over her head,[77] which seems more suitable to the context.

With regards to the phrase, διὰ τοὺς ἀγγέλους (*dia tous angelous* – because of the angels), Rose comments that it refers to the bishops (presbyters) interpreting ἀγγέλος as, angels of the church, as mentioned in the book of Revelation.[78] However, as per Fitzmyer, this argument scarcely suits the context of chapter 11.[79] Fitzmyer, quoting from Meyer and Roesch posits that woman ought to cover her head in imitation of the angels, because in the book of Isaiah it is mentioned that the Seraphims, as subordinate beings, cover their feet and loins in the presence of the Lord; which this author thinks is not an apt argument, given the context of the text.[80]

Tertullian and many modern commentators view this in terms of the fallen angels. They understand ἐξουσία (*exousia* – authority), as a sign of modesty to conceal a woman's seductiveness from the angels.[81] However, this interpretation is irrelevant to the context of Christian prayer, because nowhere in the New Testament the word ἀγγέλος have such a negative connotation.

Most scholars[82] suggest that it refers to the angels who are considered assisting the gatherings of public worship, wherein an angel function as the mediator of the prayers of holy people. These angels are explained further at times as cosmic guardians of the order of the world, or even as those addressed, as in Genesis 1:26, Let us make human being; though God never refers to anyone here as, angels.

Nevertheless, the above explanation seems preferable, as Fitzmyer says it could be because of Paul's rabbinical training that he asks women to cover their head. Evidence from Qumran also says that an unveiled women in a sacred assembly is like a bodily defect which should be excluded because the holy angels who are present at worship services are offended by defects. In their presence, a woman must not expose the glory of man. If she was to pray or prophecy with uncovered head, she would be exposing herself, *the glory and reflection of man* and so would not be glorifying God.[83] Thus, Paul authenticates his second point, women should veil her head because they are the reflection of men.

2.2.3.1.3 Paul's Conclusion from the Natural Physiology of Man and Woman (vv.11-16)

Paul concludes his discussion on the issue of, women covering their head while praying and prophesying in church worship, with a note of physiological and natural dimensions. While the physiological dimension qualifies the inter-dependent nature of man and woman, the natural dimension calls the woman to still hold on to societal conventions, which is normal and theological (as mentioned in vv.3,8-9), that is, to present herself as honorable and respectful in her social and ecclesiastical life.

Verse 11 expresses that, *in the Lord woman is not independent of man, or man is independent of women.* Having discussed the reasons for woman to cover her head while praying and prophesying, in verse 11, Paul introduces the right relation of woman to man and man to woman. Although, Paul agrees with the Jewish tradition and the biblical argument from Genesis that calls woman to be submissive, Paul says, *in Christ*, neither man nor woman is independent of each other.

Paul posits his above statement with a Christian consideration i.e., ἐν κυρίῳ (*en kuriō* - in the Lord). All believers, male and female, are in the Lord and are alike under the Lord. Though the role of men and women are different in function and relationship, in spirituality and importance they are the same before the Lord. Thus the verse teaches that men and women are complementary in every area of their life; even in ministry, they work together as a divinely ordained team.

After stating the inter-dependence nature of men and women *in the Lord*, in verse 12 Paul describes yet another aspect of inter-dependence which they have physiologically, i.e., through the biological origin of man and woman. It says, *for just as woman came from man, so man comes through woman.* The phrase ἐκ τοῦ ἀνδρός (*ek tou andros* - from man [the means of origin]), refer to the creation account of woman mentioned in verse 8b and Genesis 2:21-23. As also the second phrase ἀνὴρ διὰ τῆς γυναικός (*anēr dia tēs gunaikos* – through woman [the means of origin]).

In both the cases, the subject (man and woman [genitive substantival]) indicate the means through/by which the verbal action is accomplished. Thus, the inter-dependency of man and woman is even evident in grammatical analysis, that both, man and woman are *the means* or *the instruments* of the biological existence of each other, and their ultimate origin/source is from God. Thus in the first part (vv. 11-12) of this section (vv. 11-16), Paul proves the physiological inter-dependent nature of man and woman in the Lord.

However, in the second part (vv.13-16), Paul gives his final word about the importance of women covering their head in the church. Though the previous section described about their reciprocity in terms of the biological nature of man and woman, Paul here commands the woman to cover her head as she prays to God.

The section starts with a strong imperative Εν ὑμῖν αὐτοῖς κρίνατε (*en humin autois krinate – judge* for yourselves). Paul employs the imperative at this point with the intention to encourage the Corinthians to look at the facts that he has given on the basis of the theological and physiological reasons mentioned in verses 2 to12. With two rhetorical questions, Paul further challenges the Corinthian Christians to conduct themselves properly in their ecclesiastical activities.

The first question Paul asks is, *is it proper for a woman to pray to God with her head unveiled?* On the basis of decorum that needs to be followed in God's presence, Paul asks them, whether it is proper for a woman to pray to God with her head uncovered. As mentioned earlier, the phrase *head unveiled,* remarks the way a woman needs to uphold her feminine honor and dignity in public by wearing a head covering, and most importantly in the church as she prays and prophecy.

The second rhetorical question is in verse 14, *does not nature itself teach you...?* This question presents the natural order of God's creation. By nature, man and woman are different from each other. Barrett comments that the difference in the nature of man and woman is evident in the quantity of hair God has assigned to each.[84] Even pagan writers and philosophers also speak of the difference in the hair of men and women given by God and the need of keeping it as it was a part of their religious and social life.[85]

Though Paul talks about the man in this verse, his main intention was to highlight the importance of women covering her head, by humiliating men for their misconduct of growing hair and covering their head in their social life and church activities. Further, Paul says, the long hair given to a woman is for her glory. In verse 15b, Paul gives a supporting reason for women to cover her head, ὅτι ἡ κόμη ἀντὶ περιβολαίου δέδοται [αὐτῇ]. (*hoti hē komē anti peribolaiou dedotai [autē]* – for [her] hair is given for a covering). The Greek word ἀντὶ which means *instead*, suggests another reading, i.e., her hair is given instead of a veil. Thus, hair is equivalent to a veil or a covering.

However, in the previous section (vv.5-6), Paul emphatically tells women to cover their head in public as they pray and prophecy. If they fail to cover their head with a veil, they renounce the authority of their husband and dishonor the divine principle of headship described in verse 3. So Paul encourages the Corinthian women to veil their head, in addition to the long hair, which portrays their respect and submission to their husbands.

Paul ends his discussion with a strong statement *if anyone is disposed to be contentious - we have no such custom, nor do the church of God* (v.16). Paul knew that everyone in the congregation may not be ready to follow what he had shared with them so far. Thus, knowing the argumentative nature of the Corinthian Christians, Paul says, if anyone wants to talk further about the issue of head covering and disturb the ecclesiastical sanctity and order, we have no such custom, nor do the church of God.

Summary

The matters discussed in 1 Corinthians 11:2-16 is a much-debated topic, and it is very hard to come to a definite interpretation or conclusion. Though Paul began with a note of appreciation for rightly following the tradition which he had handed over to them, it has now become clear that there were arguments and struggles in terms of women covering their head during the time of worship.

Like other issues, this issue of *head covering by women* came about after Paul had left Corinth. Though Paul mentions about the immodest conduct of man, his main objective was to correct the wrong practice of women in the church. Thus, the example of men is employed here only as a rhetorical tool to substantiate his argument as he strove to correct the error in the church. Paul had mentioned the theological aspect (the hierarchical order of God to Christ, Christ to man, and man to woman), also with the same intent.

As he came to a close of his discussion, Paul gave a strong warning to the women in the church (v.13). He finally ended his arguments on this topic with a very unusual statement, if anyone is disposed to argue, we have no such custom, nor do the church of God.

2.2.4 Abuse of the Lord's Supper (11:17-34)

During his last Passover meal with his disciples in the upper room, Jesus instituted the Lord's Supper and handed over the tradition to them with a command to observe it as a remembrance until his coming. Christ's institution of the Lord's Supper on the day of Passover was not an accidental event. The Israelites observed the feast of Passover to remember and celebrate their miraculous deliverance from the land of Egypt after 400 years of slavery. God had protected them when on God's command they had applied lamb's blood on the doorposts and lintels of their homes. Hence they celebrated the passing over of the angel of death with roasted lambs, unleavened bread, and bitter herbs.

However, Jesus during the last hours of his earthly ministry handed over to his disciples a new tradition in memorial of his impending death, which would deliver from eternal death. He transformed the Passover feast into a new celebration that proclaimed a greater deliverance. As Jesus commanded, the disciples in turn, handed over this tradition of, the Lord's Supper, to the early Christian community who practiced it in their gatherings, followed by the fellowship meal, also known as the love feast.

The love feast was a congregational meal meant to emphasize the need of having fellowship, affection, and mutual caring among the believers. However, for several reasons, gradually they lost the spirit of fellowship and caring in their gatherings. Since communion was observed by the early Christians after the love feast, it is pertinent to look into the broader and immediate context which paved the way for the Corinthians to turn the Lord's Supper into a gluttonous and drunken revelry.

The broader background of the issue lay in the Christological crisis which the early Christians faced. The reluctance of the disciple to move out of Jerusalem into Judea and to the uttermost parts of the earth reveals that they were looking forward to the sudden *parousia* of Jesus Christ. They misunderstood the message conveyed by the angels at the time of Jesus' ascension (Acts 1:11). Thus, even after the infilling of the Holy Spirit (Acts 2:1-4), without giving much importance to the great commission of Lord Jesus (Matt. 28:19-20), they stayed in Jerusalem waiting for an imminent return of Jesus, and the establishment of his physical kingdom.

With one mind and spirit, the messianic community was also patiently waiting for the coming of the Lord before their death. Hence, believers started to sell their property and offer the money at the feet of the disciples (Acts 5). There was no division between poor and rich, Jew and Gentile, slave and master etc. They constantly devoted themselves to the Lord in prayer, fasting, and fellowship. However, Jesus did not return as they expected. Gradually, the original disciples and the initial lot of believers who patiently waited for the coming of the Lord died and passed away to glory.

Thus, the remaining ones started to doubt about the coming of the Lord. As a result, their hearts were filled with distrust and several questions arose concerning the hope they had in Christ Jesus. Certain questions that emerged in their mind were, will Jesus ever come back? If and when he comes, what will happen to the faithful Christians who waited patiently for his coming, and passed away? What will happen to those who are still alive? Due to these and many more such reasons, the Christology of the first century Christians were in chaos. It is assumed that Paul wrote I Thessalonians (considered to be the first written book in the New Testament) as an answer to the questions of the first-century messianic community to make them stand secure in their faith in Christ Jesus (I Thess. 4:16-18).

However, there existed a lot of confusions and crisis as they were already diverted from the life which Christ expected from them. Hence, they lost the love and concern they had for each other and the true spirit of fellowship (love feast) that they used to have after partaking the Lord's Supper. Believers become more self-centered and started to accumulate land and possession for themselves. As a broader background, this change in attitude played a very important role about which Paul deals within the section below.

2.2.4.1 The Immediate Context of the Problem (vv. 17-22)

Verses 17-22 serve as the immediate context concerning the abuse during the Lord's Supper which was followed by the love feast. The Corinthians were having the love feast and observing the Lord's Supperin a wrong manner because of the effect of the Christological crisis they faced in the first century. It was commanded by the Lord to observe it as a remembrance of his sacrificial death, till his coming. However, the wealthy believers in the congregation brought their own food and drink for themselves and ate them before the arrival of the poor believers, thus consequently turning the sacred fellowship into a voracious and drunken revelry. Thus, Paul deals with this serious issue in the church at Corinth and tries to correct their wrongdoings practiced during their common meal and the celebration of the Lord's Supper.

The immediate context of the abuse is sandwiched between the negative comments, *I do not commend you* in verses 17 and 22. The verb οὐκ ἐπαινῶ (*ouk epainō* - I do not praise), is in contrast to the positive praise 'ἐπαινῶ δὲ ὑμᾶς (*epainō de humas* – but I praise you) at the beginning of the chapter. Though Paul praised the Corinthians at the beginning for following the tradition, now he deprecates them for the reason mentioned at the second half of verse 17. Though the actual problem is not mentioned here, Paul compresses the unseemly behavior of the Corinthians with an understatement, ὅτι οὐκ εἰς τὸ κρεῖσσον ἀλλὰ εἰς τὸ ἧσσον συνέρχεσθε (*hoti ouk eis to kreisson alla eis to ēsson sunerchesthe* – that you come together not for the good, but for the worse).

However, in spite of the difficulty in determining the actual problem, the verb συνέρχεσθε clarifies that it has to do with their *coming together*. The verb συνέρχεσθε is used five times between verses 17-34 [vv.17,18, 20, 33, 34]; which is used as a technical term to denote the people of God coming together for worship. Thus, it is clear that the concern Paul discusses in this instance is regarding something that happens when they come to worship God as a church.

The problem of the Corinthian congregation was not that they were not coming together for worship, but the attitude that governed them in such gatherings. The literal meaning of the word [adjective] ἧσσον (*ēsson*) is, inferior or lesser. Since the word describes the action of the noun, it can either mean that their gatherings were not for their betterment, but for humiliating or making others look inferior/lesser. The tradition of the Lord's Supper was given to the church not only to remember the salvific work of Christ but also to remember and live as members of the same body. But the church members, based on class and social status, were divided among themselves.

In verse 18, Paul presents a vivid picture of their fractions. It starts with the phrase, πρῶτον μὲν γὰρ (*prōton men gar* - first of all). The phrase, *first of all,* is a technical term used to denote the logical movement of a particular topic from one level to the other with succeeding points. Paul as a trained rhetorician used lots of rhetorical tools in his writings. In this instance, starting with the phrase πρῶτον μὲν Paul presents the major issue that existed among the Corinthians.

Paul says, when you come *together as a church*, I hear that *there are divisions among you*. The phrases in verse 18 such as συνερχομένων ἐκκλησίᾳ (*sunerchomenōn humōn en ekklēsia* – together as church) and σχίσματα ἐν ὑμῖν (*schismata en humin* – divisions among you) itself shows the seriousness of the problem among them. The church is the body of Christ, bought by Christ with a prize, to function together as a single entity without any anomalies. However, the church at Corinth was divided among themselves. Though Paul does not want the Corinthian congregation to track any kind of discriminatory strife, in verse 19 Paul posits that indeed it is inevitable among them, so that the genuine Christians among them can be differentiated.

Stating this Paul moves to the root problem in the congregation. He starts it with the phrase Συνερχομένων οὖν ὑμῶν (*eunerchomenōn oun humōn* – when you come together) which is often repeated in this section. The implied purpose of their *coming together* was to have fellowship (love feast) and to celebrate the Lord's Supper. But Paul says you come together not really to eat the Lord's Supper. The meal before the Lord's Supper was supposed to be a sign of their unity, love, and care for others. However, due to class division among them, the love feast lost its true nature and turned into gluttonous and drunken revelry.

As mentioned earlier, they lost the true characteristics of their Christian life because of the delay in *parousia* and other related issues. Thus, believers become more self-centered and started to accumulate wealth and possession for themselves. The number of poor members among them gradually increased. These poor Christians were constantly opposed and humiliated by the rich Christians both, in society, and in the church. Even as they partook in the Lord's Supper, this class division was evident, as the rich believers proceeded to have their meal without waiting for the poor brethren.

Verse 21b says *each of you goes ahead with your own supper*. The pronoun ἕκαστος (*hekastos* – each one, [nominative, masculine, singular]), at the beginning of the verse emphasizes the self-centeredness of the believer during the fellowship meal. Another phrase that shows their individuality is ἴδιον δεῖ πνον (*idion deipnon* – one's own supper). Thus they made it not the Lord's Supper, but their own supper, because there was no unity and concern towards their poor brethren as they come for the fellowship meal and celebration of the Lord's Supper. As a result, one group (the poor) goes hungry, and the other group (the rich) becomes drunk. They turned the sanctity of the fellowship meal and the Lord's Supper into a mockery by humiliating the poorer members of the body of Christ.

As mentioned earlier, the fellowship meal was an unavoidable factor in their gatherings. In the book of Acts, it is mentioned that the early Messianic community came together in their homes and shared their food as they enjoyed common meals (Acts 2:46). Sharing food with one another was considered as the hallmark of the Christian gatherings. One way it helped the community by nurturing and maintaining the unity among them as they partook in the Lord's Supper. However, when Paul wrote this letter, the Corinthians were not practicing it as it needed to be. Thus, Paul concludes this section (the immediate context of the issue) by condemning their improper behavior by raising few questions as mentioned in verse 22.

First of all, Paul asks, *do you not have homes to eat and drink* (v. 22a). This is a rhetorical question asked with the intention to get a positive answer from the Corinthians. Through this rhetoric question, Paul annoyingly interrogates the wealthy believers in the congregation and tells them that if they want to eat and drink in order to satisfy their appetites, they need to do it in their homes. He indirectly conveys the message that such wealthy believers who do not have any love or concern for the poorer members in the church, should not even attend the love feast, because they were neither honoring God nor the poor, who are also members of the body of Christ.

The second question Paul asks is, *do you show contempt for the church of God and humiliate those who have nothing* (v. 22b). The church in Corinth consisted of members from both classes, the rich and poor. However, the poor were more in numbers than the rich. Paul asks the rich, are you looking down on those who are poor in the church of God? The phrase ἢ τῆς ἐκκλησίας τοῦ θεοῦ (*hē tēs ekklēsias tou theou* – the church of God) shows the seriousness of the issue because of the irregular practice of the rich believers.

All believers in the church are like different parts of the same physical body. Like each part in the human body is important and have its own function, similarly, all members, whether rich or poor, master or slave, Jew or Gentile, are equally important in the body of Christ. Thus, through this question, Paul conveys a serious offense which the rich believers committed. Humiliating a poorer member of the church is like humiliating Christ because all are equal before Christ. As believers come together to celebrate the Eucharist, they should not be driven by racial, social, or sexual predispositions.

Since the Corinthians were not having the right attitude while celebrating the love feast or while partaking the Lord's Supper, Paul ends this section with two successive questions - *what should I say to you? Should I commend you?* Through these questions Paul indicates that in this instance he is not able to make a positive statement about them, but underscores his disapproval of their misconduct by repeating his earlier remark made in verse 17, ἐν τούτῳ οὐκ ἐπαινῶ (*en toutō ouk epainō* - in this I do not praise you) (v. 22c) .

2.2.4.2 Paul's Response: "Believers Must Examine themselves when they Participate in the Lord's Supper"

After rebuking the Corinthians for their irregularity in the common gatherings, in verses 23-32 Paul proceeds to the crux of the early Christian tradition concerning the institution of the Lord's Supper. Paul uses this as the basis for his comments regarding their misconduct in the common gatherings. He uses it as the core aspect of his argument because their misconduct has in effect nullified the true meaning of Lord's Supper and concern for others. Thus, in this section through two main arguments, Paul exhorts the Corinthians that they must examine themselves before participating in the Lord's Supper.

2.2.4.2.1 Believers Eat and Drink the Bread and the Vine in Remembrance of the New Covenant Christ made with them (vv. 23-26)

To substantiate the main argument of verses 23-34, in verses 23-26 Paul gives his first supporting argument that the Corinth believers must examine themselves when they participate in the Lord's Supper because *they partake in it (eat the bread and drink the vine) in remembrance of the new covenant Christ has made with them.*

The verses given in this section are the precept used for the observance of the Lord's Supper. It starts with the words of Paul saying, *for I received from the Lord what I also handed on to you* (v.23a). Though Paul's perplexity is seen in verse 22, as their spiritual progenitor, Paul from verse 23 onwards teaches them the significance and the proper manner of celebrating the Lord's Supper in their common gatherings. It is true that the tradition of Lord's Supper had already taken shape among the messianic community even before Paul received his call from Christ on the road to Damascus. To the Corinthians Paul had already passed this tradition while he came and evangelized among them. However, now Paul quotes an earlier tradition which he had received and passes it with the authority of Christ since they were not practicing it in its true sense.

To stress the importance of practicing it in the right way, Paul claims that the tradition that he had passed on to them was received from the Lord himself. The phrase παρέλαβον ἀπὸ τοῦ κυρίου (*parelabon apo tou kuriou* – received from the Lord) shows the source (*apo tou kuriou* – from the Lord [genitive of source]) from which he received the tradition. It was a major question concerning his apostleship that he was not a direct disciple of Jesus Christ. Though Paul preached the gospel, the other disciples were not ready to admit him as one among them because he was not a direct recipient of the words and deeds of Jesus.

However, in all his writings with much emphasis, Paul addresses himself as the apostle of Christ Jesus. In the letter to the Galatians, he says that the gospel he proclaims is not of any human origin. Neither it is taught or sourced by any human, but received it through the revelation of Jesus Christ (Gal.1:11-12). Employing the same argument, Paul in I Corinthians says that the tradition that he has passed on to them was received from the Lord. However, since the Corinthians did not give it much importance, once again specifically acknowledging the Jesus tradition Paul says in verse 23a, *for I received from the Lord what I also handed on to you.*

Verse 24ff clearly explains the tradition that Jesus passed on to his disciples. On the day Jesus was betrayed he took a loaf of bread and after giving thanks he broke it and said, this is my body that is for you, *do this in remembrance of me*. He also took the cup and said, this is the new covenant in my blood, *do this* as often as you drink it, *in remembrance of me*. The phrase τοῦτο ποιεῖ τε εἰς τὴν ἐμὴν ἀνάμνησιν (*touto poieite eis tēn emēn anamnēsin* – do this in remembrance of me) is used twice in this section.

The Corinthian Christians were not observing the Lord's Supper in the proper manner, for as believers they were expected to remember the death of Christ and reflect on its implications to their socio-religious life. Hence, Paul repeats the Jesus tradition as a reminder to the Corinthians that the celebration of Lord's Supper is an act of remembrance of the death of Christ that needs to be observed in its true manner until his coming. Through the phrase *touto poieite eis tēn emēn anamnēsin* – do this in remembrance of me, Paul exhorts the believers to refrain from turning the Lord's Supper into an occasion for gluttony and drunkenness.

He exhorts them to examine themselves thoroughly so that they may be able to partake in it the right manner, keeping the sanctity and serenity with love and concern for others, since all members, whether Jew or Gentile, rich or poor, master or slave, are one in the covenant community through the broken body and shed blood of Christ. Thus Paul validates his first point, believers must examine themselves before they participate in the Lord's Supper because they eat the bread and drink wine in remembrance of the new covenant Christ made with them.

2.2.4.2.2 Believers Participating in the Lord's Supper in an Unworthy Manner brings Judgment Upon themselves (vv.27-32)

After his exhortation to the Corinthians about the proper manner of celebrating the Lord's Supper (vv.23-26), Paul now gives further teachings on the same to convey the necessity of introspection as they partake in it. The supporting argument of Paul in this section is that believers must examine themselves before they participate in the Lord's Supper because participating in the Lord's Supper in an unworthy manner brings judgment upon themselves.

The present unit is dominated by the theme of judgment. As Paul begins to discuss about it, he starts the unit with the strong conjunction Ωστε (*ōste hōs* – so that). The word Ωστε is a consequence clause that expresses the result of the action of the main verb. The main verbs in verse 27 are ἐσθίῃ (*esthiē* - to eat) and πίνῃ (*pinē*- to drink). The adverb ἀναξίως (*anaxiōs* – unworthy) depicts the manner in with the action is done. Therefore, the result is, *they eat and drink judgment against themselves* (v.29b). Thus through the conjunction, Ωστε Paul vibrantly substantiate that the main theme of this section is *judgment* that follows everyone who partakes in the Lord's Table in an unworthy manner.

Since the Lord's Supper is celebrated in remembrance of the death of Christ, the believers are expected to participate in it the appropriate way. Thus Paul says, examine yourselves before partaking in the Lord's Supper (v.28). The word Δοκιμαζέτω (*dokimazetō* - examine) literally means, to prove yourself. Though not pure, the word is a forensic term. Ordinarily, it means to put to the test. Commonly, such kinds of tests are done not by self, but by another person.[86] However, in this instance, as a command, Paul says to the Corinthian believers to prove themselves right in terms of both their works and faith before God as they come together to celebrate the Lord's Supper.

The command, to prove yourself, is not only applicable to the believers at Corinth but to the members of the church universal. The verb (to prove/ to examine) in its present active tense indicate the way one must approach the Lord's Supper with a constant proper examination that holds true for all Christians everywhere. Hence, he continues with the phrase γὰρ ἐσθίων καὶ πίνων (*gar esthiōn kai pinōn* – for whoever eat and drink [v.29]).The conjunction *for* in this verse connect this sentence with the previous sentence and speaks of the need of proving oneself before partaking the communion elements. Failure of διακρίνων τὸ σῶμα (*diakrinōn to sōma* – discerning the body) consequently leads a person to eat and drink judgment against themselves. Judgment happens only if a person discerns not the body.

The phrase *without discerning the body*, in verse 29 is often interpreted differently. Mainly four ways the word σῶμα can be understood. Firstly, the literal body of Christ (the physical body that Christ had from the time he was conceived at the womb of Mary until his ascension). Secondly, the symbolic body (the bread which he broke and said, this is my body), thirdly, the mystical body (church), and finally, the individual bodies of believers. The word in its context well explains that *the church* is in view as Paul mentions about the need of discernment before participating in the Lord's Supper.

Scholars like Bornkamm, Käsemann, Kümmel also takes the same position that it refers to the congregation of believers as *the body* of Christ.[87] Supporting to this Fee also says that the phrase ἐκ τοῦ ἄρτου (*ek tou artou* - one loaf of bread) is identified as the participating solidarity of the Church/community of believers.[88] The church as the body of Christ, hence, must discern themselves to be away from the judgment of which Paul speaks in verses 30-32. Paul reminds the Corinthian Church about the dire consequences of not judging the present irregularities that prevail in the unity and brotherhood among them.

The result of their neglect to examine themselves is evident in the following verses. As Paul comes closer to the end of his discussion, he points out the sad effects of the abuse of the Lord's Supper in the physical and spiritual life of the Corinthian believers. Paul might have received this information along with the problems and questions reported to him. Thus he makes the comment, *for this reason, many of you are weak and ill, and some have died.* Given Paul's Jewish background, we can deduce that sickness here relates to divine punishment for sinful conduct and transgressions (Exo. 4:11; Deu. 32:39; Sir.27:27-29; 2Macc. 4:38; Mk. 2:1-12; Jn. 9:2 etc).[89] However, it is not to be understood that Paul is promoting Lord's Supper as medicine for a life without sickness or as an antidote for immortality.

Hence, judging oneself as a member of the body of Christ, before participating in the Lord's Table, is very important. Identifying himself with the addressees Paul says, if we subject ourselves to judgment (self-examination) we would not be judged (v. 31). In the next verse, Paul interprets the meaning of the verb *judged*. It says, when we are judged by the Lord, we are disciplined. The Lord judges us with the purpose to discipline and educate us, so that we may not be objects of the eschatological judgment. The phrase kept aside *from the world* has a negative connotation, for it refers to those who oppose God. Thus, Paul concludes this section by emphasizing his main argument that believers must examine themselves while participating in the Lord's Supper because participating in it in an unworthy manner brings self-condemnation.

2.2.4.3 Paul's Concluding Remarks (vv. 33-34)

As he concludes his discussion of the Lord's Supper, Paul once again returns to the divisive situation in the Corinthian community as described in verses 18-22. With the phrase *when you come together* that echoes from verse 17, Paul explains how their meeting should be conducted, and how the believers must behave with each other in their common gatherings. If the meeting is meant to share their meals and celebrate the Lord's Supper, Paul encourages them to do it in an appropriate manner.

In verse 33b Paul says *when you come together to eat, wait for each other*. Awaiting the arrival of all members and sharing the meal with them is mandatory for the Church, as they observe it in remembrance of the broken body and the shed blood of Christ. Employing the word ἀλλήλουςἐκδέχεσθε (*allēlousekdechesthe* – wait for one another), Paul reintroduces the proper mode of partaking in the Lord's Supper that must characterize their common gatherings.

With the word τις (*tis*- anyone) Paul addresses both, the rich and the poor, to eat and drink at homes if they do not want to share their meal with others in the communal gathering. Paul also conveys the message that partaking in the Lord's Supper is not meant to satisfy one's physical appetite, but it exemplifies a spiritual desire for fellowship with fellow brethren and Christ. Thus Paul in this section by urging them, if you do so, when you come together, it will not be for your condemnation.

Summary

In chapter 11, Paul discussed two main concerns regarding proper behavior. The first concern was in relation to worship (especially in terms of women covering their head while praying or prophesying), and the second concern was in relation to the proper manner of celebrating the Lord's Supper.

While dealing with their improper conduct during worship (vv. 1-16), Paul mentions the impropriety of a man praying and prophesying with his covered head and a woman doing the same with an uncovered head. With sufficient theological reasons Paul teaches that a woman should have her head covered, else she should have her hair completely cut off, which obviously would be a disgrace to her. Paul also taught that man is the glory of God, and woman is the glory of man. The woman is taken from man, and man is born from woman, but all things are from God. Long hair is a disgrace to man but is a woman's glory.

In the second part of the chapter (vv. 17-34), Paul dealt with the irregularity of Corinthians as they came together for the love feast/fellowship meal and the celebration of the Lord's Supper. He remarked that when they came together for the Lord's Supper, the poor remained hungry, while the rich got drunk. Thus, as per Paul, they undermined the concept of consideration and love for others, which was the core of Christian life.

Based on what he had received from the Lord, Paul instructed them to observe it in its true nature - with the love of God and concern for fellow brethren. Paul urged them to examine themselves before they participated in the Lord's Table, as lack of self-examination caused them to sin and resulting in divine judgment as evident in some becoming weak, some falling sick, and some dying. Paul reiterated that self-examination which led to repentance would consequently prevent God's judgment. Paul concluded his discourse with an admonition to satisfy their appetites at home so that the Lord's Supper can be observed properly (vv.33-34).

2.2.5 Spiritual Gifts (12:1-14:40)

Chapters 12-14 of 1 Corinthians deals with another problem that was disturbing the proper functioning of the body of Christ in Corinth. The spiritual function of the church was in disarray because of the misunderstanding of the functions of various spiritual gifts. This prompted some church members to ask Apostle Paul for clarifications. As in the previous chapter, here too Paul deals with their conduct in Christian worship. Though the main motif of Paul in this segment is to correct their wrong understanding about spiritual gifts and its usage, it also has a broader theological framework that starts from chapter 8. In fact, it is even closely connected to chapter 1, as from the beginning of this book, we observe a specific group of people who boasted about themselves as being spiritually *strong/the spirituals,* and who did not respect the spiritually weak members in the community.

2.2.5.1 Paul's Response: "The Gift of Speaking in Tongues must be Exercised Properly in the Common Gatherings"

As mentioned above, the so-called group of *spirituals* in the church at Corinth, who positioned themselves in the esteemed statuses, were thinking that speaking in tongues was the most important spiritual gifts among all other gifts. As a result of such wrong understanding and its propagation, some believers were misusing this gift without understanding its proper purpose and the way it needs to be exercised among various other gifts.

Given the exclusive status conferred on speaking in tongues, believers in the congregation were eager to receive and exercise this gift, over all other spiritual gifts. Thus, Paul in these two chapters (chapters 12-14) responds against such misguided believers and gives his advice on the proper function and exercise of the gift of speaking in tongues. He also reminds them about all the different facets that constitute the church, the body of Christ.

2.2.5.1.1 Introductory Remarks (vv.1-3)

The church at Corinth was like many of the churches today, seriously affected by misunderstanding and misuse of spiritual gifts, especially the gift of speaking in tongues. One chief evidence of spiritual immaturity of the Corinthian Christians was reflected in their lack of discernment while the gifts were exercised among them. They were actually ill-informed about the varieties of spiritual gifts and its different functions. It seems that even they misunderstood the pagan practices which have supernatural effects, as the work of God. Given this scenario, and on being specifically asked, Paul felt the need to educate them about spiritual gifts and its various functions.

Verses 1-3 serves as the introduction to the entire section. Verse 1 starts with the phrase Περὶ δὲ (*Peri de* – now concerning). This phrase indicates that Paul is now addressing a new issue brought forward by the Corinthians in their letter to him. Though in the Greek text it is only mentioned as τῶν πνευματικῶν (adj. *tn pneumatikōn* – the spiritual/pertaining to the spirit), it is clear that Paul wants to inform them about spiritual gifts, than spiritual matters or spiritual individuals; since throughout the following chapters (12:2-14:40) Paul mainly discusses regarding various spiritual gifts and its purpose and proper usage.

As he gives his advice, Paul softens himself and his audience by addressing them as ἀδελφοί (*adelphoi* – brothers [brothers and sisters/fellow Christians]). Throughout the section, Paul constantly corrects the Corinthians concerning their failure in recognizing their mistakes. He also criticizes them for their lack of knowledge and defective understanding about the gifts of the Spirit, its purposes, and functions. Thus with the intention of making them aware of the seriousness of the issue, Paul says, οὐ θέλω ὑμᾶς ἀγνοεῖν (*ou thelō humas agnoein* – I do not want you to be uninformed). Through this phrase, Paul gives a strong indication to the Corinthian believers, just as he had done in 10:1.

From verse 2 onwards, Paul begins the process of correction in relation to their query regarding the issue of spiritual gifts. However, before dealing with the issue at hand, Paul reminds them about their ignorance due to their past way of life. By using the term ἔθνη (*ethnē* - pagans) literally- nations (a Jewish term used to denote the human race that does not worship YHWH, the God of Israel), Paul reacts to the pagan background of the Corinthian Christians. Paul reminds them that once they were ignorant (v.1), were enticed, and led astray to idols that could not speak. With the phrase τὰ εἴδωλα τὰ ἄφωνα (*ta eidōla ta aphōna* – the mute, speechless, or silent idols) Paul possibly mean that they were led astray by demons who caused them to experience ecstatic passions as an implied agent. That is to say, before coming to Christ, they were stumbling in darkness, being led by evil powers until they were delivered by the Spirit of God through their confession, Jesus is Lord.

Thus Paul says in verse 3, *I want you to understand thatno one speaking by the Spirit of God ever says "let Jesus be cursed!" and no one can say "Jesus is Lord", except by the Holy Spirit.* Paul talking about the spiritual life of the Corinthian believers say that, once they were pagans, but now they are led by the Spirit of God. Thus, by employing an inferential conjunction διὸ (*dio*– therefore), Paul corrects their ignorance in terms of discerning the works of the Holy Spirit, and brings his opening argument to a conclusion.

Paul brings to their attention two balanced clauses that indicate what cannot be said about Jesus by someone who is speaking with the Spirit and what can be said about Jesus by someone who is speaking without the Spirit. The Corinthian church members were now no longer pagans, but those who were possessed by the Spirit of God. Thus Paul validates in the introductory section that, the presence of the Spirit of God, in power and gifts, makes it easy for the Corinthians to understand about the ultimate purpose and proper usage of all the spiritual gifts.

2.2.5.1.2 It must be Considered and Exercised Equal with Verity of other Spiritual Gifts which are Activated by the Same Spirit (vv.4-11)

Paul's first argument regarding the exercise of speaking in tongues is mentioned in 12:4-11. In these verses, Paul encourages the Corinthians to consider and exercise the gift of speaking in tongues equally with verities of other spiritual gifts which are activated by the same Spirit. By listing out the number and kinds of spiritual gifts, Paul tries to bring about an awareness to stop giving importance to any particular spiritual gift or considering one gift over the other. With his first statement itself (v.4a), Paul disqualifies such thinking of the Corinthian believers.

Verse 4c says, *now there are varieties of gifts, but the same Spirit*. The term Διαιρέσεις (*diaireseis* – varieties/divisions) is in the plural form, which itself shows the manifold ways of God's blessings to his people in the form of varieties of gifts. The use of the adversative particle δὲ (*de* - but), right after the term Διαιρέσεις (*diaireseis* – varieties/divisions) clearly denotes the variety of gifts in contrast to one Spirit which is the source of all spiritual gifts. It is the Spirit who enables the body of Christ to exercise it properly in unison.

Further, Paul says, *and there are varieties of services, but the same Lord* (v.5). Greek word διακονία (*diakonia*) is employed to denote Christian *service*. The term literally means services that are performed within the context of the church. All kinds of services rendered to the body of Christ are equally important for its proper functioning. No church member can boast of having received a greater gift or a higher position than other members, because all gifts and positions are from the same source, the Lord.

Then Paul moves to the next category saying, *and there are varieties of activities, but it is the same God who activates all of them in everyone* (v.6). The Greek phrase used to denote activities is ἐνέργημα (*energēma*), which literally means, work/task. It is God who energizes/activates his people for all those different difficult tasks.

Paul brings out the diverse spiritual gifts listed in verses 4-6 under the manifestation of the Spirit in verse 7, wherein it says, *to each is given the manifestation of the Spirit for the common good*. Though the gifts are different and given as the manifestation of the Spirit, it is given for the common good of the community.

After giving a brief explanation of the variety of gifts, sources, and its purpose, in verses 8-11, Paul lists out different kinds of spiritual gifts that are manifested in the Christian assembly. This is the first occurrence of such listing in the Pauline corpus. Nine spiritual gifts are mentioned in these verses. A structural display of these spiritual gifts will help us to understand it better.

To one is given	**Through the Spirit**	*The utterance of wisdom* (v.8)
To another	**By the same Spirit**	*Utterance of Knowledge* (v.8)
To another	**By the same Spirit**	*Faith* (v.9)
To another	**By the one Spirit**	*Gifts of healing* (v.9)
To another		*Working of miracles* (v.10)

To another		*Prophecy* (v.10)
To another		*The discernment of Spirits* (v.10)
To another		*Various kinds of tongues* (v.10)
To another		*The interpretation of tongues* (v.10)

Though verse 10 gives the list of five spiritual gifts, it does not provide any emphasis on Spirit, as mentioned in verses 8 and 9. However, verse 11 fills the gap of verse 10 by relating all these gifts to the same Spirit. It says, ALL THESE ARE ACTIVATED by the SAME SPIRIT. The phrase πάντα δὲ ταῦ τα (*panta de tauta* – all these/ all these things) stands in emphatic position at the beginning of the verse, and connect all the gifts mentioned in verses 8-10 to the same Spirit by which they are activated. Thus, it becomes clear that the main emphasis of the entire paragraph is to postulate the diversity of spiritual gifts and its manifestation through the same Spirit.

Consequently, Paul nullifies the argument of some of the Corinthian *strong* believers who held the view that, the gift of speaking in tongues is the greatest gift among all the gifts of the Spirit. Therefore Paul encourages them to consider and exercise the gift of speaking in tongues with the verity of other spiritual gifts which are activated by the same Spirit.

2.2.5.1.3 Like Many Members United in the Single Body with Different Functions, Speaking in Tongues must be Exercised in Recognition of the Function of other Gifts in the same Body (vv. 12-31)

After the brief depiction of the Holy Spirit and the spiritual gifts that he distributes to the believers, Paul in this section (vv.12-30) speaks about the church and its unity as a single body. With the metaphorical description of church in terms of the human body with its different members and its various functions, Paul tries to make the Corinthians to understand that, like many members are united in a single body but each organ has a different function, so too, speaking in tongues must be exercised in tandem with other gifts given to different members of the one body, the church.

According to the progression of Paul's thoughts and arguments, the present section can be divided into four subsections (vv. 12-13, 14-26, 27-30, and 31). The first section (vv.12-13) sets forth the metaphoric explanation of the diverse spiritual gifts, its functions, and the Spirit that unites all these together.

Paul gives twofold elaboration of the imagery in these two verses. Verse 12 emphasizes the diversity, and verse 13, the unity. Verse 12 is a clear example of Paul's usage of Greek philosophical ideas in his writings. The use of *distinction* (e.g. the One and the Many) was very common in the Greek philosophy.[90]

Starting with the conjunction γὰρ (*gar* – for), to fill the gap between verses 11 and 13ff. Paul expounds his teachings on spiritual gifts.

In verse 12, Paul, through the metaphor of the human body says, though it has many members, it is a single entity. Further, it says, *so it is with Christ.* In Christ, members refer to the individual believers (*many members* - diversity). However, in its totality, all believers are one in Christ. Thus, like different members in the body has its own distinct function, but contributes to the working of the entire body, similarly, in the body of Christ every believer, though having different spiritual gifts, serves the entire church.

In verse 13, through another imagery, Paul gives further explanation for the unity of all spiritual gifts. It depicts that, neither racial origins (Jews or Greeks) nor social status (slaves or free) makes any believer more privileged than the other since all are baptized into one body and made to drink one Spirit. Though each believer is bestowed with different gifts, services, and activities, all are part of the single organic body.

In the second section (vv.14-26), Paul starts the elaboration of the imagery by personifying some parts of the human body such as foot, hand, ear, eye, and head. As he proceeds to elaborate, Paul repeats the same idea which he had mentioned in verse 12b. However, in verse 12b it was stated as a matter of faculty i.e., the body is one, and the one body has many members. However, in verse 14, Paul blends the two themes (one body and many parts/members) with a negative contrast - *the body does not consist of one member but of many* (the one body is not one member, rather it consists of many essential parts that have different roles). Paul develops the imagery in two directions (vv.15-20 and 21-26) with the primary concern to indicate the many members of the body with different functions.

Verses 15-20 describe how the body with its many members has been created to function effectively as a single unit. With the hypothetical illustration specified in verses 15 and 16, Paul imagines an inferior part of the body grumbling against a more important part of the same. Two such identical sentences are found in this section.

v.15 - If the **foot** would say, "Because I am not a hand, I do not belong to the body" - *That would not make it any less a part of the body*
v.16 - If the **ear** would say, "Because I am not an eye, I do not belong to the body" - *That would not make it any less a part of the body*

The analogy does not provide any hint about the superiority of one member over the other in a human body. It even disqualifies the idea that any part of the body can deny their place in the body. Paul says, though the foot and ear may argue that they do not belong to the body, their argument is invalid because it would not make them any less a part of the body.

To emphasize the differences and importance of various members of the body, Paul now employs few parallel rhetoric questions in verses 17-20. First two questions are mentioned in verse 17. He asks *if the whole body were an eye, where would the hearing be? If the whole body were hearing, where would the sense of smell be?* The first question stated in verse 17 is a question to the ear, since it says, *because I am not an eye, I do not belong to the body* (v.16). Thus Paul asks a counter question *if the whole body were an eye, where would the hearing be?*

No member in the body can detach themselves thinking that they are inferior to the other. If the entire body would be only eyes, it won't be able to function smoothly. Indeed it won't be even called as a body (v.19), as a body is the combination of many members with different functions. Thus, each member of the body is equally important though they play different roles. It is God who arranged the members in the body as he chose (v.18). Paul closes the section (vv.19-21) with the same arguments which he had expressed in verses 16-18.

After the skillful narration about the equal importance of each member of the human body, Paul begins a subsection (vv.22-26) with the phrase *on the contrary*. By this phrase, Paul highlights the indispensable role of the weaker parts of the human body. Though they are less honorable, we clothe them with greater honor. Paul might have had the internal organs in his mind as he says, the weaker/less honorable.[91] Paul says, our less respectable members are treated with greater respect (v.23b). However, the more respectable members εὐσχήμονα (*euschēmona* – lit. elegant in figure of shape) stands in contrast with the other. They neither need any covering nor any adornment. This rules out the stated discord (vv.15, 16, 21) between the human body parts mentioned in verses 15, 16, and 21.

Paul ends this section with a note of mutual reciprocity and positive side of verse 25, i.e., all parts of the body should have equal concern for each other. Kistemaker considers this verse as the most beautiful texts in first Corinthians since it describes the effect genuine care can have on the members of the Christian church.[92] However, through the continued illustration in verses 12-26, Paul tries to convince the members of the Corinthian congregation that their arrogance hampers the unity of the church. They should not consider one greater than the other on the basis of the spiritual gift with which they are blessed with. The core intention of the metaphor and analogy used in this section was to make them aware that, in spite of their wrong understanding that speaking in tongues is the most important gift, all the spiritual gifts are equally important, and given for the edification of the church.

In the third section (vv.27-30), Paul brings to a conclusion the discussion started in verse 12. After exhorting the Corinthians through the metaphoric usage of a human body, its different parts and functions; here in verse 27 Paul says, *now you are the body of Christ and individually members of it*. By this Paul asserts that the physical body with its unity in diversity is like the body of Christ, which is the Church.

The following verses explain that different ministries, activities, and gifts operate together for better functioning of the church. Verse 28 says *God has appointed in the church first apostles, second prophets, third teachers, then deeds of power, then gifts of healing, forms of assistance, forms of leadership, and various kinds of tongues*. In this verse, Paul clearly exposes what he meant by *individual members*(v. 27), by listing out different kinds of services and gifts through which the church as a body is enriched. A further clarification of the same is done through a list of question mentioned in the following verses (vv.29-30).

Paul asks, *Are all apostles? Are all prophets? Are all teachers? Do all work miracles? Do all possess gift of healing? Do all speak in tongues? Do all interpret?* The simple idea Paul conveys to the Corinthians is, the church is a combination of people who are apostles, prophets, teachers, and people with other gifts. All are not blessed with the same gift or similar kind of ministries, but verities of gifts and ministries, all of which are equally important in the body of Christ for the common good of all believers. Thus, Paul concludes this third section validating that, many members with different functions are united in the single body. Therefore, the gift of speaking in tongues must be exercised in recognition with other gifts in the same body.

With this final note Paul consequently enters the fourth and last next section (v.31) that begins with a strong imperative, and also serves as the transitional verse to the next chapter, *but strive for* [be zealous for] *greater gifts. And I will show you a still more excellent way.*

2.2.5.1.4 All Spiritual Gifts must be Exercised with Love, because Love Never Ends but the Gifts will come to an End (13:1-13)

In chapter 13 Paul explains what he meant by *I will show you a still more excellent way,* mentioned in 12:31. Fitzmyer comments that, though chapter 13 is a continuation of chapter 12, it is often viewed as problematic since it interrupts Paul discussion on spiritual gifts started in chapter 12.[93] However, there is not many digression as in the other case (Like chp. 9 between 8 and 10), but is intricately related to the preceding and proceeding chapters. For, through this chapter, Paul awakens the interests of Corinthians towards the greatest virtue of Christian life but was found lacking, as they gave importance to exercising the spiritual gifts without having true love for one another.

Thus, Paul gives a rhetorical speech on love to the Corinthian believers to practice it in their Christian life. It is considered as an important instruction on the basic reality of Christian morality. In its present context, chapter.13, while acting as a comment on the endowments of the Spirit in chap. 12, also discusses the basic element of Christian experience and on a level far higher than that of chapters 12 or 14. Love, as elucidated in chapter 13, is something that surpasses all spiritual gifts. Thus Paul presents love as the highest/greatest of all divine gifts.

Chapter 13 is best understood through the study of its three sub-sections: a) the basic requirement for the exercise of spiritual gifts (vv. 1-3); b) the characteristic of love vv. 4-7; and c) the superiority of love over spiritual gifts (vv. 8-13).

As posited above, the first section talks about the basic requirement for the exercise of spiritual gifts listed in chapter 12. Paul starts this section with a conditional clause 'Ἐὰν (*ean* – if). It further explains the verb λαλῶ (*lalō* - I speak) in terms of the indirect object γλώσσαις (*glōssais* – tongues) with the genitive cases that follows such as: τῶν ἀνθρώπων (*tōnanthropōn* - of the men) and τῶν ἀγγέλων (*tōnangelōn*– of the angels). The tongues of mortals [men] seem to mean, the way men speak eloquently. However, since the context of the text lies on the improper usage of the gift of speaking in tongues (12:28-30 and 14:1-25), the phrase is not a simple expression of the eloquence of speech, but *speaking in tongues* itself. Thus the phrase *the tongues of men* mean human speech that is inspired by the Spirit but unknown to the speaker and the hearer.

There are still lots of doubts regarding the second phrase, *the tongues of angels*. Fitzmayer suspects that Paul may be alluding to what he heard in his vision, *the things that no human can express* (II Cor.12:2).[94] However, we don't have any mention of angels in that verse and there is no way that the tongues Paul discusses here is uttered by such beings. Moreover, Fitzmayer makes another comment that it is Paul's rhetorical hyperbole with irony, as Paul joins the terms which are contradictory to paint the complete picture of those who exercise the gift of speaking in tongues. In the Corinthian context, it means that those who spoke in tongues thought that it is the heavenly speech, speaking in God's own language since the one who speaks in tongues speaks to God, not to man.

Considering these two aspects Paul says, if I speak in the tongues of men (communicate eloquently) or in the tongues of angels (unintelligible language), *but do not have love,* I am a noisy gong or a clanging cymbal. Thus, Paul presents love as the maxim in Christian life, because the Corinthian believers were carried away by their wisdom that led to quarrels and rivalry (1:10; 3:4), and knowledge that led to the destruction of their own brothers for whom Christ died (8:2, 11).

The two following verses also start with the conditional clause followed by contrasting sentences.

v.2 - And if I have prophetic powers, and understand all mysteries and all knowledge, and if I have all faith, so as to remove the mountains,-	**but** *do not have love,*	I am nothing.
v.3 - If I give away all my possessions, and if I hand over my body so that I may boast,-	**but** *do not have love,*	I gain nothing.

Both these verses, like the preceding ones, emphasize the importance of love. From mortals and angels depicted in verse 1, Paul in verse 2 widens the range to three of the gifts that are mentioned in 12:8-10. He mentions the gift of prophecy, which was considered significant to some extent by the Corinthians; the gift of knowledge, the favorite one especially to the strong among them; and the gift of faith, with a qualifying verb - *that can move mountains*.

The emphasis of these gifts are seen in Paul's use of adjectives πάντα or πᾶ σαν (*panta*-all or every/*pasan*- all or every). If the persons who are exercising such gifts in it fullness do not have love, it makes the person as nothing before God. In verse 3, Paul gives the best example of one's self-sacrifice. If a person gives away all his possession, including his body, but do not have love, he gains nothing. Thus, Paul confirms *love* as the basic requirement for rightly exercising the spiritual gifts.

The second sub-section (vv.4-7) depicts the characteristic of true Christian love with fifteen Greek verbs which includes two affirmative descriptions, eight negative characteristics, and five positive ones.

Affirmative	Negative	Positive
Love is – Patient	*Love is not* – Envious	*But* – Rejoice in Truth
Kind	Boastful	Bears all things
	Arrogant	Believes all things
	Rude	Hopes all things
	It does not – Insist on its own way	Endures all things
	Irritable	
	Resentful	
	Rejoice in wrongdoing	

Verse 4a renders two affirmative characteristics of love. The Greek word used for the first characteristic is μακροθυμεῖ (*makrothumei* - patient) which literally means, to be forbearing with respect to actual offenses and injuries one receives from others. Such kind of love enables a Christian to demonstrate a readiness to take someone's disagreeable character traits in advance and to exhibit enduring tolerance.

The next word is, kind. This is the only place the word χρηστεύεται (*chrēsteuetai* – to be kind) is used in the New Testament.[95] This word commonly expresses a generous welcome or active goodness that one person renders to the other person. In Pauline theology, both these terms represent the two sides of the divine attitude toward humankind. On one side it expresses God's loving forbearance, and on the other, his kindness. Thus, it communicates the message that Christians must conduct themselves in the same manner with others.

Verses 4b-6a indicates how love does not behave. Employing the adverbs such as: οὐκ (*ouk* – not) and οὐ (*ou* – not) Paul lists out eight characteristics. It says love is not envious or boastful. It literally means, love is not intolerant of rivalry or unfaithfulness, and it does not engage in self-glorification. Love is not arrogant, which means, it does not puff itself up. Love is not rude, literally, it does not behave discourteously, suffer shame, or incur disgrace. It also does not insist on its own ways, it is not irritable or resentful, it does not rejoice in wrongdoings. True love helps Christians to be away from these dangers, and to have stability and consistency in life

With five positive characteristics of love (vv.6b-7), Paul concludes the present section. Except for the first verb, all other verbs in this section are accompanied by the object πάντα (*panta* - all things). The section starts with an adversative conjunction δε (*de* – but) that unites the preceding and following verses that express opposite meanings. Starting with δέ Paul lists out five positive characteristic such as — [love] rejoices in truth, bears all things, believes all things, hopes all things, and endures all things.

All these five characteristics expose the behavioral problems of the Corinthian believers. The main emphasis is about the lack of love, for love does not behave in the way they were behaving with each other. Thus he ends the section by saying, love is devoted to truth in everything. With regard to *all things* within God's righteous and gracious will, love protects, believes, hopes, and endures what others don't

The last section (vv. 8-13), describes love's superiority over spiritual gifts. As Paul re-emphasizes the permanency of love, he redirects the thinking of the Corinthians on the true nature of spirituality, and also brings their mistaken emphasis of speaking in tongues within the framework of the primacy of love in Christian conduct.

In this sub-section, Paul concludes with another set of contrasts. Paul's main argument here is, unlike the spiritual gifts which function only within the framework of the present eschatological time, love would continue to exist, both now, and forever. Hence, love is superior, not only because it has all the five positive characteristics explicated above, but also because of its never-ending nature.

The present segment starts with the phrase Ἡ ἀγάπη οὐδέποτε πίπτει (*hē agapē oudepote piptei* - love never ends (v.8a), which itself announces the never-ending nature of love. In all of Pauline corpus, the emphatic adverb οὐδέποτε (*oudepote* – never) in the phrase occurs only here. With this Paul stresses the abiding and superior quality of love over all the spiritual gifts listed in 12: 8-10.

Despite the ongoing description of love that Paul mentioned earlier, he sets forth three spiritual gifts in contrast to the ever-abiding quality of love. Except prophecy, the other two gifts were favorite to the Corinthians. Pau says, *but as for prophecies, they will come to an end*; *as for tongues, they will cease, as for knowledge, it will come to an end.*We need to note how the gifts of prophecy and knowledge come to an end.

The Greek verb used in both the case is καταργέω (*katargeō* - lit. to abolish) which indicates that these gifts are going to *be abolished,* that something will put an end to these two gifts. Verses 9 and 10 give further explanations about these gifts. When the perfect comes, these gifts (καταργηθήσεται-*katargēthēsetai,* the partial/powerless) will be rendered inoperative. However, speaking in tongues will *cease* by itself. By this Paul explicates that all the endowment of Spirit will come to an end. Everything that we know and do, even the exercise of the spiritual gifts will have very little importance, or no relevance at all, in the future life.

In verse 11 and 12, picking up the themes of the perfect and the partial, Paul gives a better explanation of the temporality of the gifts through an analogy. Employing first person singular Paul says, when I was a child, I spoke, thought, and reasoned like a child. But when I become an adult, I put an end to childish ways. The adult does not continue to talk, think, or reason like a child. Through this analogy, Paul illustrates that there will come a time when the gifts will pass away.

Finally, in verse 13, Paul gives a formula that puts an end to the discussion of love by highlighting its permanency and superiority over spiritual gifts. It says, *and now faith, hope, and love abide, these three; and the greatest of these is love*. Though spiritual gifts remain in the present time, they will not continue beyond the end of times. Thus, Paul ratifies the permanency and greatness of love over spiritual gifts. However, since spiritual gifts are given to the church for the common good, being Christians, the Corinthian are advised to exercise their spiritual gifts with love, because love never ends, but the gifts will come to an end.

2.2.5.1.5 Exercise the Gift of Prophecy in the Common Gatherings because Prophecy Edifies the Church, but Speaking in Tongues Edifies only One's Self (14:1-5)

Having proved the greatness and everlastingness of love, Paul, in chapter 14, talks about two gifts in particular. The chapter begins with an exhortation to pursue love, which is the basisfor exercising all spiritual gifts. In verses 1-5 and 20-25, Paul specifically urges the Corinthians to seek prophecy in contrast to tongues, because prophecy is understandable, it edifies the church, and even brings others to Christ. Thus, the first five verses of this chapter serve as the basic contrast and the central themes that follow.

This section (vv. 1-5) starts with an imperative that serves as a transitional phrase from the preceding, to what follows. Keeping abuse of the gift of tongues as the issue, Paul begins by saying, *pursue love and strive for spiritual gifts (14:1a)*. Two verbs (Διώκετε [*diōkete* - pursue] ζηλοῦ τε [*zēloute*- strive/desire earnestly for]) in this verse are connected with the adversative particle δὲ (*de* – and) that shows the emphasis on love in this context. Paul emphatically says that any person who strives for spiritual gifts must first pursue love. The literal meaning of the verb διώκετε in this instance is, to chase after, or to press on.

After presenting the importance of love, in verse 1b Paul mentions the gift of prophecy in contrast to tongues, and says, *especially that you may prophesy*. In verses 2 to 4, Paul gives the reason for his advice and provides three explanation for each case.

Speaking in **Tongues (vv.2-4)**	Do not speak to other people - *but to God*
	For nobody understands them – *since they are speaking mysteries in the spirit*
	Who speak in a tongue build up themselves

Prophecy (vv.2-4)	Speaks to other people
	For the up building, encouragement and consolation of others
	Those who prophecy build up the church

The chart above makes clear that Paul's emphasis on the gift of prophecy is for the edification of the church. The gift of tongue edifies the speaker but not the congregation, because it is not understandable, as they are speaking mysteries to God in the Spirit. On the contrary, the gift of prophecy is given to the church with the purpose of edifying the church as it is addressed to the people.

In verse 5b, Paul gives one more reason to choose the gift of prophecy over the gift of tongue, *one who prophesies is greater than one who speaks in tongue*, because it is understandable to the people. However, Paul's statement of the greatness of prophecy is made with one exception, *unless someone interprets* [the tongue]*, so that the church may be built up.* Thus Paul says to the Corinthians to exercise the gift of prophecy in the church, because, prophecy edifies everyone, whereas speaking in tongues edifies only one's own self.

2.2.5.1.6 Those who Exercise it in the Church Pray for the Gift of Interpretation so that the Entire Congregation will be Edified (vv. 6-19)

The argument in this section (vv.6-19) indicates that the real problem is not the gift of tongues or the gift of prophecy, but the edification of the community. In the absence of the gift of interpretation, Paul says that the gift of the tongue is unintelligible, and thus does not edify the church. So in this section, Paul prioritizes the importance of the gift of interpretation in a congregation where speaking in tongues is explicitly exercised.

Starting with a hypothetical assumption, Paul makes the issue very clear to the Corinthians. Paul asks them, *brothers and sisters, if I come to you speaking in tongues, how will I benefit to you (6a).*On one hand, it expresses that so far Paul didn't appear in their midst speaking in tongues, and on the other hand, it presents his rejection of their criterion for being spiritual. The reason for his rejection is expressed in the second clause, *how will I benefit to you.* Paul knew that unless he speaks to them in revelation, or knowledge, or prophecy, or teaching, they will not be benefited.

In verses 7 and 11, Paul furthers his discussion with few analogies. Firstly, he talks about flute and harp, two lifeless musical instruments that produce sound. He mentions these two, as these were commonly used on special occasions in the Hellenistic world, consequently, the Corinthians were familiar with it. Taking these as examples, he asks, *if they do not give distinct notes, how will anyone know what is being played?* Whether it is flute or harp, if the musician does not produce a distinct/pleasing sound, the audience will not understand and appreciate. So, too it is with speaking in tongues.

Secondly, Paul takes an example from the realm of warfare, wherein the trumpeters/bugle blowers on the city wall alerted the citizens about the approaching army. Verse 8 says, *and if the buglegives an indistinct sound, who will get ready for the battle?* Bugles were used in the battle to give a warning call to the soldiers and to make them alert. However, if it is not played rightly, instead of getting ready for the battle, they may go on with their duties. In this manner, Paul conveys to the Corinthians the utter futility of speaking in tongues which do not communicate a clear spiritual message in a common gathering (v.9).

The final analogy is the phenomenon of different languages. This was also very common to the Corinthians because the city was a cosmopolitan center. So with the word φωνῶν (*phōnōn* -sounds/voices), Paul brings in the idea of different sounds the human tongue was meant to make. None of the languages in this world is without meaning to those who speak them. However, if the listener is a foreigner, it won't make any meaning to him unless someone interprets it. Thus, Paul concludes his analogies with a final note, *so with yourselves; since you are eager for spiritual gifts, strive to excel in them for building up the church (v.12).*

Two main emphases are seen in this verse. First, s*ince you are eager for spiritual gifts.* It clearly indicates the enthusiasm of the Corinthians to have spiritual gifts, especially, the gift of speaking in tongues. In the second part, Paul urges them, *strive to excel in them for building up the church.* Paul does not criticize the Corinthians' pursuit of spiritual gifts, especially the gift of tongues; but he recommends them to have the proper motive for such pursuit and striving. The expression, *to excel in them* demands, that whatever gifts they have, it must work together for the betterment of the community as a whole. In nutshell, Paul advises them, if they crave for the gift of speaking in tongues, they also need to pray for the gift of interpretation, so that the church is edified.

Paul talks about this in detail in verses 13-17. Verse 13 starts with the phrase, *therefore.* This phrase connects the present section with the preceding one. In the previous section, Paul's main advice to the Corinthians was to strive to excel in the spiritual gifts with the purpose of building up the church. By employing the conjunction Διὸ (*dio* – therefore), Paul gives further guidelines to the Corinthians to be followed, especially in relation to the exercise of speaking in tongues. The one and only guideline Paul gives to the Corinthians is to *pray for the power to interpret,* for speaking in tongues without interpretation is like *speaking into the air (v.9d).*

So, Paul brings the application from his own life in verses 14-15. The first clause in verse 14 is conditional. He says if he speaks in tongues, only his spirit would be praying, and his mind will be unproductive. By making this observation, Paul actually implies what was happening in the church at Corinth. Contrary to the above, Paul says, both, a person's spirit and his mind must equally be engaged in order to be productive. Hence with a question, Paul begins verse 15, *what should I do then? I will pray with the spirit, but I will pray with the mind also; I will sing praise with the spirit, but I will sing praise with the mind also.*

The next verse gives the result of not practicing what was said in the previous verses. Starting with the phrase *otherwise,* Paul says, you might pray and praise in the utterance of tongues but ἰδιώτου (*idiōtou* – others/outsider), literally, an unskilled or ungifted person won't be able to say 'Amen' to it.

Therefore, for the sake of others in the congregation, it must be interpreted. If not, it benefits only the one who exercises the gift, but it never builds up the church (v. 17).

Paul concludes this section with yet another personal note - I speak in tongues more than all of you; but in the common gatherings, I would rather speak five words with the mind than ten thousand words in a tongue so that others will be encouraged/edified (vv. 18, 19). Thus Paul corroborates his main argument in this section by saying, those who exercise the gift of speaking in tongues in the church should pray for the gift of interpreting also so that the entire church is edified.

2.2.5.1.7 Exercise the Gift of Prophecy in Church if there is no one to Interpreter the Tongue, so that the Unbeliever will be Convinced of their Sins and Worship God (vv.20-25)

Having proved the incapability of tongues-speaking, in edifying the church, Paul in this section discusses about the effects of tongues and prophecy on unbelievers. As in verse 6, Paul begins this section also with the vocative (the case of address), *brothers [and sisters]* followed by three imperatives such as – *do not be children* in your thinking; rather, *be infant* in evil, but in thinking *be adult*. For, though some in the church spoke in tongues, as far as true spirituality was concerned, their life in society and within the church was unacceptable. So, Paul continues his argument to persuade them to seek the gift of prophecy instead of the gift of speaking in tongues. Tongues in the context of church worship, not only was unintelligible but was also alienating the unbelievers and strengthening their unbelief.

Referring to the life of Israelites from the Old Testament, Paul reminds the Corinthians that the result of God speaking to the Israelites in a non-Jewish language ended up in their disbelief (v. 21). Now, in New Testament times, the Corinthians are speaking in tongues while outsiders are present in the church, thus causing them to abandon the Christian fellowship as a gathering of mad people. Thus Paul interprets tongues as a sign in a negative sense with regard to unbelievers expressing their unbelief and hardness of heart.

On the contrary, Paul says, prophecy is not for unbelievers, but for believers; as the conversion of unbelievers through prophecy is a sign of God's presence among them. Hence in verses 23-25, Paul gives reasons for using the gift of prophecy, as against the gift of speaking in tongues, in the context of church fellowship.

Paul's first reason is against the gift of tongues mentioned in verse 23. It says, *if, therefore, the whole church comes together and all speak in tongues, and outsiders or unbelievers enter, will they not say that you are out of your mind?* Since the language of the unknown tongue is unintelligible, when an unbeliever hears it, he will conclude that the believers are out of their mind and subsequently go away from God. However, Paul's second reason is in favor of the gift of prophecy which brings an unbeliever closer to God. For, through the exercise of the gift of prophecy, the unbeliever's heart will be disclosed and they will bow down before God and worship him. Thus, Paul authenticates his main point in this section, in the context of church worship, exercise the gift of speaking in tongues only if there is an interpreter, else, exercise the gift of prophecy; so that unbelievers in the church will be convinced of their sins, and worship God.

2.2.5.1.8 Paul's Concluding Remarks (vv. 26-40)

The irregularity of Corinthians in their common gathering was a serious issue, which is explicitly addressed by Paul from the beginning of this letter. They were not maintaining the sanctity of church activities. In this section (vv. 26-40), Paul gives them further instructions concerning how proper decorum must be maintained in the church. This passage talks about the proper order of exercising the spiritual gifts in common worship. Paul especially gives special directives to those who exercise the gifts of tongues and prophecy, which in its essence are the same.

This section starts with a question that is very similar to the question previously asked in verse 15, *what should be done then, my friends?* (v.26a). Paul asks this question in the background of disharmony and disorder in the Corinthian congregation as a result of individualism and singularization of the spiritual gifts. Thus, with a number of directives, Paul encourages the Corinthians to follow order and sanctity of worship in church gatherings.

Before giving his instructions, Paul presents the imaginary scenario of a prayer meeting, wherein everyone exercises their gifts, such as hymn, lesson, revelation, tongue, and interpretation. A hymn may be referring to prayer or praise as mentioned in verse 15. Lesson refers to instructions in Christian faith/truth. The person exercising the gift of revelation passes on some further understanding of God's self-communication to the congregation. Tongues are the mysteries, and its interpretation is by someone else. Paul's argument here is that, if everyone exercises their gifts together, it results only in confusion, and no one is edified. Thus with the intention to create order and harmony, Paul exhorts them to exercise their gifts in an orderly fashion, and for the edification of everyone present.

In verses 27-33, Paul specifically gives directions regarding the maintenance of order and harmony in Christian worship. The first direction is given in regards to the exercise of speaking in tongues (vv.27-28). Paul says, *if anyone speaks in tongues, let there be only two or at most three, and each in turn (v.27a)*. Beginning with the conditional clause *if*, Paul says let there be only two or three, and each in turn. With these numbers, two or three, Paul denotes that everyone should not speak in tongues together. If there are more individuals with the gift of tongues, only two or three must speak, and too, turn by turn.

At the same time, says verse 27b, *and let one interpret.* It signifies that Paul allowed the Corinthians to exercise the gift of tongues provided there is an interpreter. When someone speaks in tongues, the other must interpret it into a language that is understood by all, so that everyone present may comprehend what is being communicated in the common gathering. If there are no interpreters, Paul says, *let them be silent in the church and speak to themselves and to God* (verse 28). By this last phrase, Paul advises them to keep silence in the church and not create confusion; however, they are free to speak with themselves and to God in their mind/spirit.

Paul's second direction is given with regards to the gift of prophecy (vv.29-31). The direction to those who prophecy is similar to those who exercise the gift of tongues. Even in this case, Paul allows two or three to prophecy, and someone interprets it. It denotes that even the prophets are also subject to the scrutiny of others. Those with the same gift of prophesying are advised to discern carefully the prophetic preaching made publically, and when the prophesying stops, if someone has received a revelation, he must interpret it before the congregation.

The order and benefit of the exercise of prophecy are given in verse 31. It says, let it be done *one by one* so that all may *learn* and *be encouraged.* The result is twofold: a) orderly exercise of prophecy helps other to learn by conversing, listening, and inquiring; b) all may receive encouragement from the prophetic utterance. In verse 32, Paul gives justification for his guidelines given in the aforementioned verses.

Paul also makes a clear distinction between prophecy and ecstasy. He says *the spirits of prophets are subject to the prophets* (v.32). The phrase πνεύματα προφητῶν (*pneumata prophētōn* – spirits of prophets), means, the spirit that is possessed by the prophets, or, the prophetic Spirit by which the prophets speaks through their own spirit. Paul's point in this verse is that, though the content of prophecy is the product of the Divine Spirit, the prophetical utterances are totally subjected to the speaker in terms of timing. Paul validates his line of reasoning with a theological reason in verse 33, wherein he says, *for God is not a God of disorder but of peace.*

Thus Paul concludes the discussion of disorder in Christian worship, especially with regards to speaking in tongues and prophesying, saying, *be eager to prophesy, and do not forbid speaking in tongues; but all things should be done decently and in order (v.39b-40).* Giving prominence to the gift of prophesy, Paul exhorts the Corinthians to be eager to prophesy. However, he warns them not to forbid speaking in tongues, provided there is an interpreter. No one can stop the exercising of any spiritual gifts in the church, but maintaining sanctity and harmony is extremely crucial. Therefore Paul ends by saying, *but all things should be done decently and in order* (v.40).

Summary

Just as the Corinthians had deprived almost everything else, they also had deprived the nature, purpose, and use of spiritual gifts. Thus in chapters 12-14, Paul reminded the Corinthians of the spiritual gifts they had received, and how it must be exercised in the church, and for the benefit of all present. As he began his discussion, Paul reminded them of their pagan backgrounds in which they have often led astray to the mute idols. But as believers they should know that only through the power of the Holy Spirit they are able to say, "Jesus is Lord" i.e., it is through the Spirit's work they came to the salvific knowledge of Jesus Christ. And it is the same Spirit, the same Lord, and the same God who has provided them spiritual gifts for the common good of the church. Therefore, Paul reminds them to exercise it reverently keeping the order and harmony for the benefit of all of them especially the gift of tongues considering equal with the verity of other spiritual gifts which are activated by the same Spirit.

In chapter 13, Paul talks about love and its importance as Christians exercise the spiritual gifts. In conditional sentences, Paul lists the gifts of tongues, prophecy, knowledge, faith, giving money to the poor and a physical body to the flames. But without love these gifts are nothing. Paul describes love positively as patient and kind but then resorts to saying what it is not. It cannot be jealous and does not brag. It is not proud, rude, selfish, or easily provoked; it bears no ill and takes no delight in wrongdoing. It protects, trusts, hopes, and endures. It never fails. Although love is eternal, the gifts of prophecy, tongues, and knowledge are temporal and are set aside. Thus, Paul validates the permanency of Love and urges all the Corinthians to exercise the gifts with love.

After proving the permanency and superiority of love over all the Spiritual gifts, Paul teaches his readers to follow the way of love, to strive for spiritual gifts, among which the gift of prophecy is outstanding. Anyone who speaks in a tongue addresses God, but the person who prophesies addresses the people and edifies them. By using analogies taken from the areas of music, battlefield and language, Paul illustrates the purpose of tongue-speaking. He mentions the flute, harp, and trumpet and explains their function; and he states that languages are not without meaning. But if spoken words make no sense to the listener, both he and the speaker remain foreigners to each other. Paul then urges the readers to seek those spiritual gifts that edify the church.

The tongue should be interpreted so that it may become intelligible and they will be edified. Those who exercise the gift of the tongue also pray to get the power of interpretation. Because without interpretation, tongue is of no use in the common gatherings. But the Corinthian believers were not concerned about it, hence the worship was without order and harmony. Therefore, Paul instructs the Corinthians to follow guidelines for orderly worship so that the members of the church are strengthened, edified and built up together in the Lord. Giving specific number Paul asks them only two or at the most three tongue-speakers may speak, provided that someone interprets. Most importantly, if there is no interpreter Paul says, let the one who exercises the tongue be silent in the church. Likewise, he also warns the prophets, let two or three prophets should speak in turn for instruction and encouragement. Even in this case, when one speaks the mysteries let the other discern what is said is from God or not. He concludes his teaching by exhorting the Corinthians to be eager to prophesy and not to forbid tongue-speaking, but to do everything in a decent and orderly manner for God is a God of order and peace.

2.2.6 Resurrection of the Dead (15:1-58)

Chapter 15 is the longest chapter in all of Paul's epistles, and the entire chapter deals with the subject of resurrection. This passage is read in the context of church's celebration of the Feast of the Resurrection of Our Lord, both in antiquity and in the mainline churches today. In this chapter, though Paul mentions both, the resurrection of Jesus and the resurrection of believers, he is not trying to prove the resurrection of Jesus, but uses it as an example for his argument to prove that all Christians will be resurrected, just as Jesus was resurrected from the dead. So, those, who are in Jesus Christ and pattern their lives after him, can hope for a glorious resurrection in the future.[96]

In answering the questions concerning the resurrection of believers, Paul uses the Greco-Roman style of rhetoric to establish his thesis. According to Anthony C. Thiselton, in the rhetorical form, Paul's statement in 15:1-11 is considered as *narratio* where Paul narrates the death and resurrection of Jesus Christ that provides a base and foundation for his further argument. Verse 12-19 is the first *refutatio* which explains the "unacceptable and disastrous consequences of denying the currency of the very concept of resurrection."[97] Verse 20 is the first *proposition* (listing of the prepositions) which is followed by first *confirmatio* (vv.21-34): the confirmation of Christ's resurrection as the first fruits of the resurrection of those who share his life and death.

The third main block within this chapter concerns the logical possibility or conceivability of the resurrection of the dead (vv.35-58). In rhetorical terms, he further designates its two subsections as the second *refutatio* (vv.35-49), and verse 50 is the second *propositio* and the second *confirmatio* (vv.51-57), after which a very brief *peroratio* (v.58) sums up and concludes the argument.[98] Thus, this whole chapter is structured in the Greco-Roman rhetorical style.

2.2.6.1 Paul's Response: "Believers should not Doubt about the Resurrection of the Dead"

Though at the beginning of chapter 15 Paul does not explain the contextual reason for his lengthy reflection on the resurrection, the issue is made clear from verse 12 onwards. Therefore, verses 1-11 can only be understood in the light of verse 12ff. Verse 12 begins with the expression, "how can some of you say that there is no resurrection of the dead?" Fee rightly describes this in other words as, "you believed in the resurrection of Christ (vv. 1-2, 11), how is it that some of you are [now] denying the future bodily resurrection of believers?"[99]

Paul's question i.e., πῶς λέγουσιν ἐν ὑμῖν τινες (*pōs legousin en humin tines*), "how can some of you say… ?" expresses his astonishment as in Galatians 4:9.[100] The reason for Paul's astonishment is that the Corinthians earlier believed Paul's proclamation of Christ's resurrection - ὅτι Χριστὸς ἐγήγερται[101] ἐκ νεκρῶν (*hoti Christos egēgertai ek nekrōn*) "Christ has been raised from the dead" (1 Cor. 15:1, 11), but now doubts had crept in. He contends that, if they did not believe in the resurrection of the dead, it is absolutely contrary to his proclamation "that Christ has been raised from the dead." Therefore, with specific arguments, Paul encourages the Corinthian believers not to doubt the resurrection of the dead.

2.2.6.1.1 The Core Message of the Gospel is the Death and Resurrection of Jesus Christ (vv.1-11)

The first reason Paul set forth is, Christians should not doubt the resurrection of the dead, because, the central message of the gospel is the death and resurrection of Jesus Christ. Paul was the one who proclaimed the gospel in Corinth and brought them to Christ. Now, based on the gospel preached to them, and what they had believed, Paul proves to the Corinthians about the assurance of the resurrection of the dead.

The initial expression in verse 1 (Γνωρίζω δὲ ὑμῖν, *gnōrizō de humin* – now I remind you), demonstrate that the Corinthians have forgotten what was proclaimed/preached to them beforehand. The latter part of the verse narrates the theme, its content, and their response to Paul's proclamation.

Theme	Content	Response
Gospel	Proclamation of the death and resurrection of Christ	They - Received - Standing on it - Being Saved

Paul reminds them about τὸεὐαγγέλιον (*to euaggelion* - the good news) that was preached to them. As mentioned above, it is through the preaching and teaching of Paul that the Corinthians came to faith. In 4:15 Paul rightly says that he became the father (spiritual progenitor) of the Corinthian community through the gospel. The content of the good news, though not mentioned directly, indirectly is included in the term τὸ εὐαγγέλιον. The message of salvation is further explicated in vv. 3–4. Paul endorses the shared pre-Pauline tradition which both, proclaims the death and resurrection of Christ, and also interprets it in terms of the transforming power of God as the message is explained intelligibility within the framework of their scriptures.[102]

In verse 1b, the response of the Corinthians is presented by Paul in three relational clauses. This is followed by another response that shows the result of their believing in Paul's preaching (v.2a). The first relational clause is ὃ καὶ παρελάβετε (*ho kai parelabete* – and which you received). This reflects the past by which Paul expressed the effect of the gospel in the essence of Christian tradition, especially among the Corinthians. The second relational clause is ἐν ᾧ καὶ ἑστήκατε (*en ō kai hestēkate* – in which also you stand). This clause reflects the present condition of Corinthian Christians. The term ἑστήκατε χομμυνιχατεσ the effect of a past action that continues into the present. Thus, it expresses that the Corinthians have been living according to the gospel that was preached to them.

Finally, Paul reminds them about how the proclamation of good news resulted in their life. In verse 2a Paul says, δι' οὗ καὶ σῴζεσθε (*di ou kai sōdzesthe* - and through which you are saved). This again shows that the gospel is not something that was just preached to them in the past, but it also has present soteriological importance. This clause thus depicts the future effect of their faith in the content of the gospel preached in the past.

After employing three conditional clauses, Paul uses two omre conditional clauses in verse 2b such as– εἰ andεἰ μὴ (*ei* – if and *ei mē* - if not/unless), that reflects, unless they hold firmly to what was preached to them (in which they are presently standing and being saved), their faith is in vain. Paul brings this argument because some believers were confused and not believing the gospel as it was proclaimed to them. Therefore in verses 3-11, Paul gives them a detailed explanation of the good news that was preached to them in the past.

In verse 3a, Paul once again emphasizes the technical Greek terms for tradition, παρέδωκα (*paredōka* – handed over) and παρέλαβον (*parelabon* – received) to express that the gospel/good news was already preached to them. From verses 3b-9, Paul mentions the content of the gospel, and the proofs of Christ' resurrection in a chronological order. In verse 3b-4, Paul gives the threefold content of the gospel which he had preached to the Corinthian community, i.e., *Christ died, he was buried and he was raised.*

Verses 5-8 details about Christ' appearance to different people in a chronological order. Christ appeared to Cephas, then to the twelve, and then to more than five hundred brothers and sisters. This was a fact that everyone agreed upon. Paul says, most of them to whom Jesus appeared are still alive.

Though few doubted Jesus' resurrection, Paul invites them to enquire for themselves. In the following two verses (vv.7-8) Paul adds Jesus' appearance to James, to all the apostles, and finally narrates his own experience. Though Jesus did not appear to Paul as he appeared to other apostles and disciples, referring to his Damascus experience he includes himself to a kind of actual resurrection appearance, with others in this series.

After combining the enumerated resurrection appearances with his own experience, Paul concludes by saying that, whether it was he who brought them to Christ, or the other apostles, probably Cephas and Apollos (1:12; 3:4-5). Though, Paul argues that he worked harder than any other disciple (v.10b), in order to emphasize the tradition they received that proves the resurrection of Jesus Paul says, whether it is I or they, we proclaimed and you believed (v.11). Therefore Paul says that they should not doubt the resurrection of the dead, for the very core of the gospel message is the death and resurrection of Jesus Christ.

2.2.6.1.2 If there is no Resurrection, Christ is not Resurrected, Our Faith is Futile, and We are False Preachers and you Still Live in your Sins (vv.12-19)

Paul's second argument to the Corinthians on the issue of doubting the post-mortal existence is if there is no resurrection, then even Jesus is not resurrected, consequently, our faith is futile, and we still live in our sins. Though the Corinthians believed Paul's proclamation that ὅτι Χριστὸςἐγερταιἐκ νεκρῶν (*hoti Christos egērtai ek nekron* - "Christ has been raised from the dead" [1 Cor. 15:1, 11]), to his astonishment, they still doubt the resurrection of the dead. He argues that, if they did not believe in the resurrection of the dead, it is absolutely contrary to his proclamation "that Christ has been raised from the dead." Therefore Paul counter-questions them with a conditional clause, *if Christ is proclaimed as raised from the dead, how can some of you say there is no resurrection of the dead?* (v.12).

Scholars suggest several proposals on the expression ἐν ὑμῖν τινες (*en humin tines* - "some of you" in verse 12.[103] Fee comments that "most likely the τινες (*tines* – someone)[104] are the same as those in 4:18 and elsewhere (e.g., 9:3), who have had a significant influence within the community and are responsible for its prevailing anti-Pauline sentiments."[105] According to M. Mitchell, they were only a faction.[106] David E. Garland avows that "Paul addresses a conviction held by some of the community's members."[107] Thus, it could be concluded that the ἐν ὑμῖν τινες (*en humin tines*) are some of the community members who have had a significant influence within the community, and are responsible for its prevailing anti-Pauline sentiments.

The position of this anti-Pauline group was ἀνάστασις νεκρῶν οὐκ ἔστιν (*anastasis nekrōn ouk estin* - "there is no resurrection of the dead"), meaning, that the dead do not rise, thus implying that both, those who are already dead, and those who shall yet die, will not have a post-mortal existence that involves their present bodily form.[108] However, what they denied about the resurrection and the reasons behind their denial is ambiguous, but could be understood only by making inferences from Paul's reply. It is palpable that Paul is reacting to a local heresy of denying the possibility of the resurrection of the dead.

There are several theories that have been postulated as to the possible origin of this deviation. The first theory says that the opponents were Jews who had a Sadducean theology that rejects the resurrection altogether.[109] The second theory states that the Corinthians were influenced by Greek philosophy, which talks about the immortality of the soul but rejects the resurrection of the body.[110] The third theory argues for the Gnostic attack among the Corinthian believers. It is believed that some of them had adopted incipient Gnostic views[111] and had actually denied the resurrection of Christ.[112]

The fourth theory is based on the teachings of Hymenaeus and Philetus who lived in Ephesus and are mentioned in 2 Tim. 2:17-18. They were the forerunners of the "over-realized" eschatology.[113] According to this belief, the resurrection had already taken place long time ago in a spiritual sense, in the case of "spiritual" believers. Thus, they denied the doctrine of a bodily resurrection and thus destroyed the faith of some believers.[114]

The fifth view is given by Fee and Kistemaker. They say that the possible reason for denying the resurrection of the dead is because of their misunderstanding of the fact regarding their sacramental union with Christ. They might have believed that as a result of their sacramental union with Christ they had already received present immortality.[115] For them Christ's resurrection was spiritual, and with Christ they also were raised from the dead at the time of their baptism. Thus, for them, the resurrection had already taken place and had only passing significance. They did not accept it as a tenet of the Christian faith.[116]

Thiselton and Garland give the sixth possible reason. According to these two authors, a group of Corinthians found themselves unable to believe in any kind of post-mortal existence, perhaps similar to certain Epicurean maxim which Paul mentions in 15:32b, "let us eat and drink, for tomorrow we die."[117] The Epicureans believed that the soul can no longer exist after the dissolution of the body (Acts 17:18-21, 32).[118]

As per the seventh theory, the Corinthians failed to comprehend how an earthly (terrestrial) body that is physical and perishable, can be made suitable for a heavenly (celestial) realm that is spiritual and imperishable. Earthly bodies and heavenly existence are altogether incompatible, as different as chalk from cheese. The Corinthians fail to understand, then, how the resurrection of the dead makes sense, given this inherent polarity between the earthly and the heavenly spheres.[119]

There is no sufficient evidence to specify one definite solution in exclusion to others. Most commentators believe that the Corinthians' error is not rooted in some deliberate doctrinal rebellion, but in honest confusion, given their Greek worldview. J. Wilson comments that Paul is making "explicit, probably for the first time, a new line of thought on the basis of his Jewish presuppositions but contrary to their Hellenistic presuppositions."[120] Thus, it could be inferred that Paul's argument is against a group of people who resort to the Greek worldview.

However, in verses 13-19, Paul gives a series of logical arguments against Corinthians' doubt regarding post-mortal existence. Throughout this segment, the connective δὲ (*de* - but) continues the unfolding logic with another contrast ἄρα (*ara* - then/therefore).[121] Ἄρα is an inferential particle which indicates a clear logical consequence such as: then, therefore, so, consequently etc.

As stated earlier, Paul's argument appears to adopt the Hellenistic-Roman rhetorical form of elaboration. He places the *confirmation* of the rationale (15:1-11) prior to the statement of the *theme* and *the rationale* itself (v. 12); and then provides *elaboration through several arguments*, for example, *from the contrary* (15:13-19).[122] Thus, in 15:13-19, Paul argues the reality of the resurrection of the dead by demonstrating the absurdity, even futility, of working from the premise of those who deny the resurrection of the dead. Therefore, from verses 13-19 Paul elucidates the serious consequences of denying the resurrection of the dead.

Paul begins his argument with an expression that starts with a conditional clause εἰ δὲ ἀνάστασις νεκρῶν οὐκ ἔστιν (*ei de anastasis nekrōn ouk estin* - if there is no resurrection of the dead), and marshals all his reasons against their doubts about the resurrection. Paul's first argument against their disbelief is, if there is no resurrection of the dead then, οὐδὲ Χριστὸς ἐγήγερται (*oude Christos egēgertai* - "not even Christ has been raised" [v.13]). Paul's use of the double negative οὐκ and οὐδὲ in the two parts of this verse with the conditional clause indicates that their understanding of resurrection is contrary to the reality. Thus, the clause "if there is no resurrection of the dead" contrasts the fact that there is a resurrection.[123]

However, preempting the critics deny this fact, then Paul draws for them the inescapable conclusion, in that case, even Christ's physical body did not rise from the grave either.[124] Thus, Paul's logical argument in this verse is, "let's allow that your position is correct, i.e., there is no resurrection of the dead, which consequently mean, "no one has, or ever will rise from the dead, including Jesus." Paul already has in mind the causal connection between Jesus' resurrection and that of the believers. It indicates that to deny the resurrection of the dead, is to deny the resurrection of the one who makes any and all resurrections possible.[125] Paul uses an old syllogism[126] to prove his argument:[127]

> Major premise:[128] All men are mortal
> Minor premise:[129] Christ is a man
> Conclusion:[130] Therefore Christ is mortal.
>
> Major premise: All mortals die
> Minor premise: Christ is mortal
> Conclusion: Therefore Christ died
>
> Major premise: Christ rose from the dead
> Minor premise: Christ is a man
> Conclusion: Therefore a man rose from the dead (hence, the resurrection of the dead is possible!).

Using these syllogisms, Paul asserts that Christ in his human nature, by being raised from the dead, overcame the destructive power of death; therefore other human beings receive the same victory over death through resurrection.

Paul's argument in this verse shows how the Corinthians' premise (there is no resurrection of the dead) affects the Christian doctrine of Jesus' resurrection and the Christian *kerugma* of it (vv. 1-11), as their denial of the possibility of post-mortal existence, logically excludes the resurrection of Jesus too. However, Paul concludes that Jesus has been raised, for when he had proclaimed the gospel, they believed (v.11); hence, there must be a resurrection of the dead.

The second consequence of denying the resurrection of the dead is depicted in verse 14. It says, if you doubt the post-mortal existence, then, κενὸν τὸ κήρυγμα ἡμῶν (*kenon to kērugma hēmōn* - "our preaching is empty" or worthless [v.14]). Here the emphasis lies on the futility or baselessness of his preaching. Jerome Murphy comments that in Paul's lexicon (I Cor. 15:10, 58; II Cor. 6:1; Phili 2:16; I Thess 2:1; 3:5) κενός (*kenos* - empty) means "nonproductive." Thus, Paul is telling that his preaching brought nothing new into being, and the Corinthians are unchanged.[131] Employing the phrase τὸκήρυγμα ἡμῶν "our preaching" Paul directs the Corinthians to what is said in verses 3-7, and declares, it has no foundation if Christ is not raised; or, he is pointing to the futility of their preaching as an activity, since it has no basis in truth.

Thiselton asserts that τὸ κήρυγμα ἡμῶν in this context denotes neither simply, our preaching, nor, our proclamation; but specifically, our proclamation of the gospel. It looks back to the verb κηρύσσομεν (*kērussomen* – we preach) of v.11, and refers to the content of what is proclaimed.[132] Kistemaker rightly says that gospel, without the tenet of the resurrection has no message of redemption.[133] Possibly here it is a case of both (content and activity), and since both are equally important, Paul says, denying the resurrection of the dead indicates the uselessness and baselessness of the Christian Gospel.

The third logical argument of Paul is presented in verses 15-16. It says, if there is no resurrection for the dead, εὑρισκόμεθα δὲ καὶ ψευδομάρτυρες τοῦ θεοῦ [*heuriskometha de kai pseudomartures*- "we are even found to be false witnesses of God" (vv.15-16)]. The phrase κατὰ τοῦθεοῦ [*kata tou theou* – about God/of God (v.15b)], although can mean "about," the ordinary meaning of "witnessing against" makes sense here.[134] The concept, speaking against someone, is a legal terminology. It is used when a witness swears an oath to affirm the truth of his testimony. In this instance, Paul's argument is that, if one denies the resurrection of the dead, or if indeed the dead are not raised, then, he/she witnesses against God by saying that he raised Christ[135] from the dead, whom he did not raise."[136]

However, there is an argument whether the genitive "of God" is objective,[137] subjective[138] or Possessive.[139] By subjective, it can signify that they were sent forth by God himself to preach and practice deceit. However, God does not commission people to represent him deceitfully. Fee comments that although it is possible that the genitive "of God" is objective (we are false witnesses about what God did or did not do), it is also possible that it is possessive (we are bearing false witness in God's name, as those sent from God).[140] However, Orr asserts confidently that the objective genitive[141] for τοῦθεοῦ (*tou theou* – of God/God's), concerning God, seems to fit the context better than a subjective genitive (in God's service).

Thus, the objective connotation implies that if Christ's resurrection is false, then, those who proclaim it as a tenet of faith are liars, consequently, Paul and his co-workers were giving a false report of what God had done in Christ. However, for Paul, Jesus' resurrection was not his (Jesus') own doing, but God's vindication of the work of the Son; which means, the denial of resurrection of the dead ultimately leads to a denial of the gospel altogether, and levels an accusation against God himself that he did what in fact he did not do.

Paul's fourth logical argument is, if there is no resurrection of the dead, then, κενὴ καὶ ἡ πίστις ὑμῶν ματαία ἡ πίστις ὑμῶν [*kenē kai ē pistis humōn, mataia ē pistis humon*- "your faith also is empty, worthless, or futile" (vv.14b&17a)]. The opening clause in verse 17 repeats the hypothetical protasis/conditional clause, "If Christ is not raised." (v.14a). The apodosis/main clause, in this case, picks up the last clause of v. 14 ("empty is your believing") in order to elaborate on it. By the change of adjectives with which the clause now begins, Paul emphasizes the utter futility of their own situation if their basic premise is incorrect. The futility of their "faith" has to do with both, the living and the dead.

Paul's use of two adjectives κενὴ in verse 14 and ματαία in verse 17 with the noun ἡ πίστις are argumentative. O'Connor comments that by using ματαία Paul intensifies the force of κενός. For him ματαία means, ineffective.[142] For Kistemaker, κενός means "useless" and ματαία means "worthless." The difference is that the Greek adjective κενή, translated"useless," expresses emptiness, and the Greek adjective ματαία, translated "worthless," connotes aimlessness.[143]

According to Fee, the force of ματαίαto denote the first, your faith is without effect, which differs in some degree from, your faith is κενή "empty" in v.14b. The ματαία concerns the fruitlessness or pointlessness of Christian faith (the futility of their faith in terms of its effects) if there is no resurrection, and therefore no resurrection of Jesus Christ too; κενή concerns its lack of content or without substance.[144] Thus, both the terms, ματαίαand κενή give diverse meanings and explanations to validate Paul's argument that, your faith is ineffective and without essence.

The fifth logical argument of Paul is in verse 17b. It says, if there is no resurrection of the dead, then ἔτι ἐστὲ ἐν ταῖς ἁμαρτίαις ὑμῶν [*eti este en tais hamartiais humōn* - "you are still in your sins" (v.17b)]. This argument refers to the Corinthians who were alive at that time. Thiselton comments that it is unusual for Paul to use 'sins' in the plural, since he more regularly views sin as an attitude, stance, or state, in contrast to a mere series of actions. However, the preposition ἐν "in" underlies this more structural aspect.[145]

Paul's argument is that the denial of their future, that they are destined for resurrection on the basis of Christ's resurrection, has the net effect of a denial of their past, that they have received forgiveness of sins on the basis of Jesus' death. As in Rom. 4:25 and 5:10, the death of Jesus as "for us," including both justification and sanctification, is inextricably bound together with his resurrection, so also, to deny the one is to deny the other. Without the resurrection of Jesus, his death alone has no atoning, redemptive, or liberating effect in relation to human sin.

Thus Kistemaker posits it in another way that, if Jesus is not raised from the grave, he is dead; a dead Jesus is unable to justify believers and unjustified believers remain in their sins.[146] The justification of believers rests directly on the resurrection of Jesus. Without the risen Jesus, there is no justification, without justification, there is no living faith, and without living faith, there is no forgiveness of sin. Thus, Paul reminds the Corinthians that, if you doubt the resurrection of the dead, you are still in your sins.

The sixth consequence of denying the fact of the resurrection is mentioned in verse 18. It says if you deny the resurrection of the dead, ἄρα καὶ οἱ κοιμηθέντες ἐν Χριστῷ ἀπώλοντο [*ara kai hoi koimēthentes en Christō apōlonto*- "Indeed, also those who have fallen asleep in Christ are lost" (v.18)].

This consequence refers to the Corinthians who died as believers (11:30). The phraseἄρα καὶ underlines Paul's identification of further logical consequences in this *refutatio* of the counter-statement. ἄρα, in this verse means "as a result."[147]

The use of the metaphor 'sleep' for death, on the part of believers who are "in Christ" was important in earliest Christian faith, because the logical "grammar" of sleep (κοιμάω, *koimao* - sleep) carries with it the expectation of awaking to a new dawn and a new day, i.e., the expectation of resurrection and the gift of renewed life (v. 51). It also anticipates the triumphant hope of the removal of the sting (τὸ κέντρον, v. 55) of death when God, through Christ, has dealt with sin (v. 56).

Pannenberg adds: "The familiar experience of being awakened and rising from sleep serves as a parable for the completely unknown destiny expected for the dead."[148] The new day brings its surprises as well as its new life. It is crucial to note that this clause is a continuation of v. 17. The end result of the Corinthian's position is that the dead in Christ, that is, those who died in Christ, have in fact "perished." The second aorist middle indicative ἀπώλοντο (*apōlonto* - perish) indicates, regularly they have perished. Thus, Paul reminds the Corinthians of the consequences of their disbelief that, those who died in the Lord would never "awake" from sleep, and are lost permanently.

In verse 19, Paul places the seventh disastrous consequence of denying the resurrection of the dead. It says, if there is no resurrection then, ἐλεεινότεροι πάντων ἀνθρώπων ἐσμέν (*eleeinotepoi pantōn anthrōpōn semen* - "we are of all men most to be pitied."). This verse adds a final addition to the point of vv. 17-18 and flows especially from the conclusion reached in v. 18. Nevertheless, the precise nuance of the protasis is not easy to determine. Literally, it reads *if in this life in Christ we are those who hoped only*. Whether the "only" modify or qualifies the whole clause, the phrase "in this life" (NIV), or more specifically the verb itself, emphasizing that in this life we have only hoped in Christ but with no real future are debated.

However, Fee comments that "more likely it is the former, since 'hope' is always a positive term in Paul's extant letters and the second option makes it somewhat negative."[149] Thus, the adverb μόνον "only," though placed after the perfect periphrastic construction (i.e., a participle with the verb "to be") ἠλπικότες ἐσμὲν (*ēlpikotes semen* – our hope) is best taken with the entire clause to mean, "If all our hopes in Christ are confined to this life…"

The word ἐλεεινότεροι means, more pitiable, or more to be pitied, followed by the genitive of comparison πάντων ἀνθρώπων (*pantōn anthrōpōn* – every men) than all human beings (not simply, πάντων). Fee rightly points out that Christians are to be pitied if there is no post-mortal existence, and the persecutions and hardships that the Corinthians faced were futile. Thus, the thrust of Paul's argument is that by believing in Jesus' death and resurrection, we have placed our trust in Jesus Christ to forgive us our sins.

However, if Jesus is not raised from the dead, Paul says not only have we forfeited the present forgiveness, but have lost our hope for the future as well. In addition, if we have believed in the future when there is no future, then of all human beings, we are the most to be pitied, not because Christian existence is interested only in the future, but because the loss of the future means the loss of the past and the present as well. Thus, Paul reminds the Corinthians that denying Jesus' resurrection, is equal to denying the Christian life altogether.

The aforementioned logical arguments of Paul show that the denial of the post-mortal existence is a serious defect in the Christian faith. Paul developed his arguments in verses 13-19 largely in negative terms, showing what would be the consequence if Christians did not believe in the resurrection of the dead. Paul's thesis in verses 12-19 is that, since his readers already believe that Jesus has been raised from the dead, they should also be convinced that believers will rise with Him.

Jesus' resurrection entails the resurrection of the dead. Paul declares that to deny our resurrection, is to deny Jesus rising from the dead. He presented seven *arguments* to demonstrate how futile Christian faith would be *if there is no resurrection of the dead.* If there is no resurrection of the dead, then Jesus has not been raised from the dead (vv. 13, 16), our preaching is worthless (v.14), our faith is futile and worthless (vv.14,17), we are false witnesses of God (v. 15), you are still in your sins (v.17), those who died in Christ have perished (v. 18), and, we are to be pitied more than all human beings (v. 19). Thus, Paul elucidates the seven unacceptable and disastrous consequences of denying the resurrection of the dead.

2.2.6.1.3 If there is no Resurrection, it Affects not only the Facts of Christ' Resurrection but also the Order of things that Need to Take Place at Parousia and Afterwards (vv. 20-29)

In the previous section, Paul exposed the dreadful consequences of denying the possibility of resurrection. However, the seven consequences placed by Paul against their arguments were hypothetical. Now Paul begins this section with an affirmative sentence that includes the theme of verses 1-11. It says, Νυνὶ δὲ Χριστὸς ἐγήγερται ἐκ νεκρῶν (*nuni de Christos egēgertai ek nekrōn*– but in fact, Christ has been raised from the dead. The literal meaning of the phrase, Νυνὶ δε is *but now*, which is again understood in a logical sense.

The reasons for Paul's affirmation of Christ' resurrection is given in the following verses. All these reasons not only affirm the certainty of Christ's resurrection, but also Christ's resurrection as the guarantee of future events, especially the certainty of the resurrection of the dead. Though the second part of the verse consists of only three words in Greek (ἀπαρχὴ τῶν κεκοιμημένων, *aparchē tōn kekoimēmenon* – the first fruit of those who have died), it is filled with meaning.

Paul employs this statement assuming that his readers are acquainted with the Old Testament teachings on the first fruit. In the Old Testament background, firstfruits were meant to be offered to God in recognition of his faithfulness in terms of the agricultural activities and providing crops in the due season. It also indicated that the first bunch of the upcoming grain harvest would be followed by the rest of the sheaves. Thus, Paul proves that the resurrection of Christ as the first fruit raised from the dead is the guarantee for all those who die in Christ.

In verses 20-21, Paul gives further explanation of the metaphor mentioned in verse 20. By this, he also provides an inherent implication of the inevitability of the resurrection of the dead. Both the verses are described in perfect double parallelism where verse 21 alludes to the account mentioned in Genesis 3. Kistemaker calls it as a typical semantic parallelism in which Paul connects man and death in the first clause and man and resurrection of the dead in the second. In the parallelism, he compares Adam (through whom death came) with Christ (through whom life comes).[150] A better understanding of this parallelism is presented in the table below:

For since	Also
death	the resurrection of the dead
came through a human being	come through a human being
for as	So
all in Adam	all in Christ
die	will be made alive

After proving the inevitability of Corinthians' understanding of the resurrection of the dead in verse 20, Paul reemphasizes his argument in 21-22 saying, since death came to this world through one man (Adam), the resurrection of the dead come through another man (Christ).

In verse 23 Paul once again makes the resurrection of Christ as an absolute necessity for the resurrection of all the dead in Christ. After the parallel explanation of death and life, respectively through Adam and Christ, Paul says, the bodily resurrection of the dead will take place in its own order. What did Paul mean by the term, *order*? The Greek word used for order is τάγματι (*tagmati* - order), which is a technical military term for detachment of troops. The background of Paul's usage of this term is evident in the following verses.

Verses 23-28 shed light on Paul's main argument regarding the resurrection of the dead and the order of this event as a whole in the eschatological clock.

The order of the events starts with Christ. In Paul's words, Christ is the first fruits, then at his coming those who belong to Christ, then comes the end. In verse 20 Paul had already said, *Christ has been raised from the dead.* The perfect passive phrase ἐγήγερται (*egēgertai* – has been raised) signify that the action has already taken place. Thus the order of event has already started. The next event is the coming of Christ and the resurrection of those who belong to him. Then comes the finale, when Christ hands over the kingdom to God the Father.

Verse 24c-28 explains the order of events that need to take place right before Christ hands over the kingdom to his father. Alluding to the Christological tradition from LXX (Ps. 110:1), Paul says in verse 25, that Christ must reign until he put all his enemies under his feet. Paul emphasizes the necessity of Christ' reign which is currently in effect by employing δεῖ (*dei* – it is necessary), the impersonal verb. Shedding light on the biblical perspective of *Christ's rule* that began with his resurrection, Paul in this instance, by employing δεί underlines the need for *it* until the fulfillment of Psalms 110:1.

Though the verb δει is considered as an impersonal verb that does not have a determinate subject, it is indirectly understood that δει stands in favor of the phrase ἄχριοῦ θῇ (*achri ou the* - until he has put) which is, the rule of Christ. Thus Fitzmyer calls δει as both, the apocalyptic impersonal and a scriptural enforce.[151] The reign of Christ must continue until he destroys every ruler, every authority and power (v.24c). By the destruction of these three entities along with the ultimate enemy of humanity (death, v.26), the opposition to the rule of Christ will be eradicated totally. The final redemption of humanity comes through Christ's act of demolishing all the rulers, authority, power, and death. The last enemy in this order (list) is death, and it takes place by the resurrection of the dead. And then, the kingdom will be handed over to the Father and God will be all in all.

So, the order of events starts with the resurrection of Christ as the first fruits of those who have died, then the resurrection of the dead in Christ, followed by the destruction of all rulers, authority, and power, after which the kingdom will be handed over to the Father. Thus Paul validates that the Corinthian's' doubt concerning the resurrection of the dead, not only affects the fact of Christ' resurrection, but also *the order* of things that need to take place at Parousia and afterward.

2.2.6.1.4 It is the Hope of Resurrection that Enables the Christians to Put themselves in Danger Every Hour (vv. 30-34)

This section details Paul's argument regarding the resurrection of the dead through the presentation of concerns such as physical danger, laxity, and corruption of character. Paul begins this section with a query, *why are we putting ourselves in danger every hour?* Through the use of first person plural,

Paul includes his co-workers along with him in the life struggle they face every day of their life, hoping for a future resurrection. The verse clarifies that it is the hope of a future resurrection that enables them to put themselves in danger every hour as they proclaim the gospel of Christ in the corrupted world. The denial of resurrection, hence, makes the life and ministry of Paul and others, illogical.

Though the life struggles of his co-workers are not mentioned particularly, Paul's own struggles as part of his apostolic ministry are vividly portrayed throughout his epistles. A detailed list of Paul's struggles is given in II Corinthians 4:8-11 and 11:23-27. The reason behind Paul's endurance was the hope he had on the fact of the resurrection of the dead. The emphasis of Paul's hardship is made clear in the phrases such as πᾶσαν ὥραν [*pasan hōran* – every hour [v.30]) and καθ' ἡμέραν (*kath hēmeran*–every day (v.31)].

Paul was happy to put his life in danger for the sake of the gospel because he knew that, though he loses his life in this world, it will be resurrected at the coming of Christ. The hope Paul had was no human hope, but divine. In verse 32, Paul says, *if with merely human hope, I fought with wild animals at Ephesus, what would I have gained by it?* The concluding clause in this verse is noticeable. Paul's question, *what would I have gained by it?* shows that if there is no resurrection, he has wasted his life. Thus, Paul exhorts the Corinthians that, without resurrection their earthly struggles are meaningless.

Paul also employs a crucial philosophical argument of Epicureans in verse 32. The sentence (*if the dead are not raised, Let us eat and drink, for tomorrow we die*), features a condition that is contrary to the reality. The expression, *if the dead are not raised*, itself is a surety of the resurrection of the dead. Paul employs it for the sake of argument to display the reality. Alluding to Isaiah 22:13, Paul further says, let us eat and drink, for tomorrow we die. Taking an incident from the life of Israelites, Paul exhorts the Corinthians not to behave like the Israelites, who when surrounded by a foreign army, instead of seeking strength from God, rebelled against Him, by eating meat and drinking wine saying, let us eat and drink for tomorrow we will die at the hands of our enemies.

So Paul warns the Corinthians, *do not be deceived* by those who reject the facts of resurrection and enjoys their life in the world by eating and drinking. They do so since they do not have any hope for a post-mortal existence. Paul advises the Corinthians not to be carried away by such teachings because *bad company ruins good morals*. The fundamental idea Paul passes to the Corinthians is that the adoption of deviant doctrine which denies the resurrection of the dead will cause them to lose their future inheritance in the Kingdom of God. Consequently, Paul encourages the Corinthians to be filled with the same hope that he has in his life, i.e., the hope of a future resurrection which enables him to face all struggles and dangers for the sake of the gospel every hour, and every day.

2.2.6.1.5 If there is no Resurrection, there is no Possibility for those who Died in Christ to have a Glorified Body (vv. 35-58)

As Paul deals with the issue of Corinthian's doubt concerning the resurrection of the dead, in this section, he responds to them by explaining the nature of resurrection using analogies from Nature [(seeds growing, different kinds of bodies (vv.35-41)]; the application of the analogies (vv.42-49); and the assurance of resurrection through Christ' victory over death (vv.50-58).

With the strong adversative ('Ἀλλὰ, *Alla* - but) at the beginning of verse 35, Paul begins a new argument in this section with two sets of inter-related analogies that are further applied in verses 42-49 to prove the fact of post-mortal existence. The indefinite pronoun τις (*tis* – someone) at the beginning of the section, though not providing proper identification of those who do not believe in the resurrection, gives the notion that they are believers in the same congregation, but influenced by Greek philosophy. Though the Greek philosophers believed in immortality of the soul, they denied the immortality of the human body.

Verse 35 records for us the twin doubts of these church members. Their first doubt was regarding resurrection itself, and the second was regarding the kind of bodies the resurrected ones would have. Therefore Paul, through analogies, explains about different kinds of bodies. As he answers their questions, Paul uses a harsh vocative in verses 36-37 to address those who doubted the resurrection of the dead. The phrase ἄφρων (*aphrōn* – foolish man) is a sarcastic title given to those who professed to be, wise.

However, Paul asks them how foolish can they be, for at this juncture, they don't even understand the basic reality that, unless the seed dies, it cannot come to new life. As Paul explicates this analogy, he puts the Corinthians as the agents of the action saying, what *you sow* does not come to life unless it dies (v.36), and when *you sow you do not sow* the body that is to be, but a bare seed (v.37). Thus Paul says that the natural order of plant itself shows how God designs its life as it sprouts from the soil. A farmer never plants the body of a plant that is to be, but a seed. After a while, this seed sprouts out from the ground to a new form.

In verses 38-39, Paul describes the different kinds of earthly bodies that God in his wisdom has designed, such as, seeds, fishes, birds, animals, human beings, etc. Then in verse 40, Paul distinguishes between the glory of these earthly bodies (plants, fishes, birds, animals, etc.) and the glory of the celestial bodies (sun, moon, stars, etc.). Paul says, each has its own glory, and the glory of the earthly bodies is different from the glory of the heavenly bodies.

In verses 42-44, Paul, applies the above analogies, to the earthly body/form that we now have, and the new kind of body that we will have when resurrected. Below is tabulated a list of differences between our earthly body and our heavenly body.

Earthly	**Heavenly**
Perishable	Imperishable
Dishonor	Honor
Weak	Power
Physical	Spiritual

Thus, Paul validates his argument concerning the security of the resurrection of the dead. The word οὕτως (*outos* – thus) in verse 42a, reflects that, like the glory of sun, moon and stars differs, so too, the glory of the resurrected body will be different from the earthly body. In verse 42b Paul says, what is sown is perishable, what is raised is imperishable. Our physical bodies are perishable, but it will be restored with imperishable nature at the time of resurrection. The dissolution of the human body is a matter of dishonor since humans were crowned with glory and honor to rule God's creation. Nevertheless, at the time of resurrection, it will raise with a much more glorious inherent that will never perish.

In verses 45-49, Paul gives scriptural support (Gen.2:7) for his analogical argument in verses 35-44 regarding the resurrection of the dead. The content of these verses is also connected to verses 21-22, wherein Paul compares Adam and Christ in a different manner.

Adam	**Christ**
The first man, Adam	The last Adam
Become a living being	Become a life giving spirit
From the earth	From heaven

The above comparison shows that it is not the spirit which came first, but the physical body. The first man (Adam) was created from the earth, therefore he is earthly (present body of human beings); while the second man (Christ) is from heaven (the post-mortal body of believers). Christ, the last Adam, who is from heaven, will change the bodies of believers into the likeness of his glorified, imperishable, body. Human beings have borne the image of the first man, Adam, with which they cannot enter into the kingdom of God. Verse 50 states, flesh and blood cannot inherit the kingdom of God, nor does the perishable inherit the imperishable. Thus it is imperative for the dead to rise, to be clothed with the heavenly body, in order to inherit the kingdom of God.

Thus Paul's argument is unequivocally ratified, if there is no resurrection of the dead, then, there is no possibility for the dead in Christ to be clothed with an imperishable, glorified body; through which one can inherit the kingdom of God.

Summary

Paul wrote this longest chapter on post-mortal existence to rectify Corinthians' wrong beliefs and its dire consequences. The first reason for the resurrection of dead Paul gives in verses 1-11. If there is no resurrection the core message of the gospel which is the death and resurrection of Jesus is in vain. Paul reminding Corinthians of the gospel he proclaimed to them. He summarizes its content by mentioning Christ's birth, death, burial, resurrection, and appearances. He notes that he delivered to them this gospel that is in harmony with the Scriptures. He enumerates Jesus' appearances to Peter, the Twelve, the five hundred brothers, James, and Paul himself. Paul does not deem himself worthy to be called an apostle, but he says that by the grace of God, finally Christ is appeared to him and become the preacher of his resurrection. It is Paul who brought the Corinthians to Christ. Thus, if they doubt the resurrection of the dead it is a question to the gospel they received, in which they stand and being saved.

Paul's second argument in this chapter was similar to the first one. In verses 12-19 he says, if there is no resurrection, Christ is not resurrected, consequently, our faith is futile, Paul and his fellow workers are false preachers and the Corinthians are still living in their sins. Paul equates the resurrection of the dead with that of Christ and asserts that if the one is not true, neither is the other. If Christ is not raised, then the preaching of the apostles is useless and so is the faith of the Corinthians. If this is so, then the Corinthians are still in their sin and are objects of shame.

With certainty, Paul continues his proclamation of the resurrection of Christ in verses 20-29 saying, if there is no Resurrection, it affects not only the Facts of Christ' Resurrection but also the Order of things that Need to Take Place at Parousia and Afterwards. All his argument placed in this section strongly affirms not only the certainty of Christ's resurrection but also Christ's resurrection as the guarantee of the future events, especially the certainty of the resurrection of the dead. Paul makes the resurrection of Christ as an absolute necessity for the resurrection of all the dead in Christ. After the parallel explanation of the death and life, respectively through Adam and Christ, Paul says, *it* will take place (Paul's main argument, i.e., the resurrection of the dead) in his own order. Verse 24c-28 explains about the order of the events that need to take place right before Christ hand over the kingdom to his father. Paul notes that death came through Adam but life through Christ. He reveals the resurrection in two stages: first Christ, next those who belong to him. Then comes the end, when Christ will deliver the kingdom to God the Father. All his enemies will be destroyed, including death. When the Son has delivered everything to the Father, then he himself is subject to God so that God maybe all in all.

In verses 30-34, Paul strongly says, it is the hope of the future resurrection that strengthens me to put myself in danger in every hour and every day. Paul was happy to put his life in danger for the sake of the gospel because he knew that though he loses his life in this world, it will be resurrected at the coming of Christ. The hope Paul had was no human hope but divine. In verse 32, Paul says, *if with merely human hope, I fought with wild animals at Ephesus, what would I have gained by it?* The concluding clause in this verse is noticeable. Paul's question, *what would I have gained by it* shows that if there is no resurrection he has played a foolish game with his own life. Thus, Paul exhorts the Corinthian that without resurrection their earthly struggles are meaningless.

With a number of examples taken from the natural world in verses 35-58, Paul explains the means and the manner of the resurrection from the dead. He writes about seeds and plants; the flesh of animals, birds, and fish; the splendor of the sun, moon, and stars. He teaches that the dead will rise with the bodies they had on earth, except that they are raised imperishable in glory as spiritual beings. Paul reveals that as Adam passed on his earthly body to his descendants, so Christ is passing on his heavenly body to believers. Paul declares that at the return of Christ, the transformation of the believers will occur in a flash with the sounding of the last trumpet. Then the dead come back to life and those who are in Christ will be changed. They will be imperishable and immortal. Paul taunts death by quoting from the prophecies of Isaiah and Hosea and expresses thanks to God for the victory through Jesus Christ. He exhorts the readers not to doubt on the post-mortal existence because without resurrection it is not possible for the dead to have a glorious, imperishable body to enter into the kingdom of God.

2.2.7 Paul's Final Words to the Corinthians (16:1-24)

After responding to the matters addressed to him by way of report (from Chloe) and by letter (from the Corinthian believers), Paul now responds to the question of collection for the suffering saints in Jerusalem. Though there is no evidence with regards to its source, presumably it was asked by some members of the church, to know their role in contributing for their poorer brethren in Jerusalem. However, unlike other chapters of this epistle, Paul deals with this query in just four verses (vv. 1-4).

In the remaining part of this chapter, Paul expresses his plan concerning his next visit to Corinth (vv.5-9); his concern for his fellow workers (vv. 10-

12); and his concern for the Corinthians in terms of their spiritual maturity (vv.13-18).

2.2.7.1 Collection for the Poor Saints in Jerusalem (vv. 1-4)

The current section gives few concrete instructions with regards to the collection for the saints. It seems that the Corinthian believers had planned to collect it, not because Paul had asked them to do so, for if they were requested by Paul, he would have given them more information than what is described in verses 1-4. Therefore, it is assumed that the collection of money was yet another query addressed to Paul by the Corinthian believers. Thus Paul advises them how to go about it, and how to send it to the suffering saints in Jerusalem.

2.2.7.1.1 "Believers Must Contribute to the need of the Suffering Saints in its Right Manner"

Paul starts this section with yet another (fifth) Περὶ δὲ "Now concerning," which suggests that Paul is responding to their letter. Therefore, the whole phrase "Now concerning the collection for the saints," implies a new topic. This is possibly the first of three (2 Cor. 8:13, 9:9; Rom.15:26) instances in Paul's letters where he mentions about the collection for the poor among the saints in Jerusalem. Though the destination for the collection is not mentioned in the first phrase (v.1a), the Corinthians knew for whom it was intended (v.3). This may be the reason for the minute information about the collection and its purpose given in this section unlike the other two sections mentioned above.

The Greek word used to describe *collection* in this verse is λογείας (*logeias*), which literally means, the collection of money. In other epistles while Paul talks about collection, he uses this term in terms of its theological content such as, fellowship, service, grace, blessing, and divine service etc. But here the word λογείας or λογεῖαι in verse 1 and 2 purely means, financial contribution. Even in Papyri this word is used to convey the meaning of "financial contribution."[152] It also occurs in texts mentioning collections for sacred purposes.[153] Thus, it is clear that Paul is giving instructions for the actual collection of money. The second part of verse 1 gives the indication with regards to the manner of collection.

In verse 1a Paul says to the Corinthians that, *you should follow the directions I gave to the churches of Galatia*. Paul gives them this instruction since he had recently come through Galatia on his way to Ephesus (Acts 18:23). According to the book of Acts, Paul evangelized the territories of Galatia during his second missionary journey (16:6) and passed through the same territory once again during his third missionary journey to Ephesus (18:23). Probably, during this time, he had informed them of the collection, and how they could best go about laying it aside and repeats the same counsel to the Corinthians on account of their query.

Verse 2 describes the instruction Paul had given to the churches of Galatia, which the Corinthians are to follow as well. The phrase *on the first day of every week* literally means, *during one each Sabbath each person*. Probably denotes during each Sabbath everyone is expected to set apart a portion of their income. Thiselton comments that the phrase κατὰ μίαν σαββάτου (*kata mian sabbatou* – during every Sabbath) provides an early reference to Sunday as the day of worship.[154]

However, the word σαββάτου is employed in the New Testament to denote the seventh day as the Sabbath day. At the same time the singular form σαββάτου is also used in the New Testament (νηστεύω δὶς τοῦ σαββάτου, *nēsteuō dis tou sabbatou* – I fast twice a week [Lk. 18:12]) to mean *a week* or *seven days*, thus the meaning will be, *once in every seven days*. However, in Christian tradition, the 'first day of the week' mentioned in verse 2 is considered to be, Sunday.

Fee suggests that, traditionally this has been one of the three[155] New Testament texts that have been used to support Christians' use of Sunday, rather than the Jewish Sabbath, as their day of worship.[156] On this day, the first century Christians used to gather for worship, which included the celebration of the Lord's Table (Acts 20:7). Therefore, Paul opportunely informs them it is also the proper time to remember the poor among the saints in Jerusalem.

Paul is very clear about each person's contribution towards the share of this ministry, the contribution for the suffering saints. In verse 2b Paul says, each of you is to put aside and save whatever extra you earn. The literal translation of the verse is, let each one of you put for himself, storing up whatever one gains. By employing the pronoun ἑαυτῷ (*hēautō* - for himself) along with ἕκαστος (*hekastos* - each one) and the verb τιθέτω (*tithetō* - to place), accelerates Paul's emphasis of individual participation in the contribution for the saints, rather than the giving of a fixed amount from each family. Thus, Paul does not mean them to give a tithe or a proportionate giving, but to keep aside whatever they earn extra, week after week, as per their ability. For, though they may put aside only a little amount each week, such a step will ensure a greater gift than a single collection by the time of Paul's arrival.

Foreseeing a sizable gift from the Corinthian congregation Paul says, when I arrive, I will send, anyone whom you approve, with letters, to take your gift to Jerusalem. Paul advises them not only to collect the money but also to choose trustworthy members of the congregation to carry the letters of recommendation along with the gift collected for the saints in Jerusalem. The phrase τὴν χάριν ὑμῶν (*tēn charin humōn* – your gift) literally means, *your favor or benefaction,* which is a rare use of χάρις found only in three other instances in Pauline corpus (2 Cor. 8:4, 6-7, 18). He also assures them that he will write for them a commendatory ἐπιστολῶν (*epistolōn* – letters), because it was customary in the ancient world to carry a letter of commendation by persons assigned for any delegation.

In verse 4, Paul gives the Corinthians another assurance that if it is worthwhile, or they wish, he himself will go along with the representatives of the church. Paul says they will accompany me. Employing the phrase σὺν ἐμοὶ πορεύσονται (*sun emoi poreusontai* – they will accompany me), literally mean, *they will go/proceed with me*, Paul thus mean that as an apostle/a leader I will lead them to Jerusalem along with the offering collected for the suffering saints.

Thus, Paul explains the role of every Christian contributing to the need for suffering saints, and the proper method of collection for such a noble purpose. The inventiveness Paul demonstrated in this regard, also expresses how a leader must exercise his responsibility in meeting the financial needs of believers. Being aware of the pathetic situation and the financial need of the poor saints in Jerusalem, in spite of his busy missionary journeys, Paul as an effective leader, exercised his responsibilities appropriately.

2.2.7.2 Itinerary of Paul (vv. 5-9)

From verse 5 on, Paul moves from responding to their questions to giving advice to the Corinthian believers. So far in this epistle, Paul was correcting the Corinthians and giving various exhortations which they needed to follow in their socio-political and religious life as they awaited a glorious eschatological living. Now, through verses 5-18, using his own life examples, Paul advices them about proper exercise of the responsibilities of a Christian leader in terms of spending his/her time with their people, care and concern for their fellow-workers, and spiritual maturity of their people/followers.

First of all, Paul discusses regarding the proper exercise of a leaders' responsibility in spending his time with his people (vv.5-9).

2.2.7.2.1 "A Christian Leader Must Properly Exercise his Responsibility by Spending Time with his People"

After his instructions regarding the collection of money in the previous section, Paul now proceeds to inform the Corinthians about his travel plans in verses 5-9. Paul had already mentioned about his forthcoming visit to Corinth in 4:19; 11:34 and 14:6. However, in this section, Paul particularly mentions about the route he plans to take, and his desire to be with them preferably for a longer time, than just passing through.

In verse 5a, Paul begins to outline his itinerary by telling the Corinthians that he is taking the route through Macedonia. He says, "I shall come to you after I go through Macedonia." His plan was apparently to spend late spring and summer with them in Corinth. Lucan account also gives the same version that Paul planned to travel via Macedonia to Corinth, and from there to Jerusalem (Acts 19:21). According to Acts 20:1-3a, Paul did indeed visit the churches in Macedonia and eventually arrived in Corinth where he stayed for *three months*. The time spent there was undoubtedly during the winter months when sea travel was impossible. However, as Paul mentions his plan Μακεδονίαν γὰρ διέρχομαι (*Makedovian gar dierchomai* – for I will be going through Macedonia), emphasizes both, his desire and the degree of delay it will take.

Verses 6 and 7 stresses Paul's strong desire to spend considerable time with them in Corinth. Verse 6a says, *and perhaps I will stay with you or even spend the winter*. By this Paul indirectly says that the Corinthian community is important to him. On the other hand, the reason for his desire to have a long stay with them is probably to resolve the interrupted relationship between him and them. Verse 7 starts with an explanatory clause γὰρ (*gar* - for). It says, "*For I do not wish to see you now just in passing; for I hope to remain with you for some time, if the Lord permits*.

Paul promises to come to Corinth after he passes through Macedonia, the Roman province which included Philippi, Thessalonica, and Berea. The term διέλθω (*dieltho*- "pass through") used in v.5 implies, that he intended to spend a longer period of time with them, than being there overnight and proceeding on. What Paul means is that, he is on a tour of supervision through various churches. Thus, when Paul makes this statement he emphasizes his desire to visit these churches and informs the Corinthians that "very soon" he will visit them. He wants to make them aware of his visit to them. As he says, in near future 'I will surely visit you'. But this time as he visits, he wants to spend more time with the believers at Corinth.

In v. 6 Paul says, "*And perhaps I shall stay with you, or even spend the winter, that you may send me on my way wherever I may go*." This verse shows the purpose of Paul's eagerness to spent considerable time with them. The term *perhaps* seems like uncertainty about the verb *stay*. However, at this point, it does not reflect the uncertainty about his future plan, but as a polite desire which Paul expresses to the Corinthians concerning his future visit. The emerging problems at Corinth also dictate that the reason for his long stay is intended to help them to correct their wrong practices. Altogether, Paul's expression in verse 7, *"For I do not wish to see you now just in passing; for I hope to remain with you for some time if the Lord permits"* expresses his true desire to spend more time with them. Thus, Paul sets forth an example that, as an effective leader, one must find time to spend with one's own people.

2.2.7.3 Concern for fellow Workers (vv. 10-12)

Paul continues his concluding remarks by requesting the Corinthians to express their love and concern for him, by taking good care of Timothy, his fellow worker who may visit them. Paul also informs them about the arrival of Apollos in an opportune time. Fitzmyer comments Paul here adopts the style of *epistolē systatikē* (letter of recommendation). Certainly, it is true, for, before their arrival, Paul sends this letter to the Corinthians so that they will make all the needed arrangements for Timothy and Apollos. Thus, this following section presents Paul's concern for his fellow-workers and serves as an appropriate example to be followed by all Christian leaders.

2.2.7.3.1 "A Christian Leader Must Properly Exercise his Responsibility by having Concern for his Fellow-Workers"

In these three verses, Paul is talking about two of his fellow-workers, Timothy and Apollos. Regarding Timothy, Paul had mentioned in 4:17 that he has already sent Timothy to Corinth. However, the phrase Ἐὰν δὲ ἔλθῃ *"if he comes,"* in 16:10 seems like indefinite, that even Paul is not sure about Timothy's coming to them. Nevertheless, the indefinite construction here does not refer to the uncertainty of Timothy's arrival *per se*, but, refers to the specific time of his arrival.

After mentioning about Timothy's visit to them, Paul says, *see that he is with you without cause to be afraid; for he is doing the Lord's work, as I also am.* This reflects Paul's deep concern for Timothy and how he should be treated in Corinth. The special concern which Paul had for Timothy may be because of what was said in chapter 1:12. There we see the division in the church where people claimed, I belong to Paul, I belong to Apollos, I belong to Cephas, and I belong to Christ. It seems that since Paul mentions regarding the visit of Apollos (16:12), they may prefer to welcome Apollos, than Timothy. Hence Paul says that they have to treat Timothy, just as they would treat him, for Timothy also is doing the work of the Lord. Furthermore, in verse 11, Paul adds, "no one should treat him with contempt". All these show Paul's concern for his spiritual son, Timothy.

Secondly, in verse 12, Paul talks about Apollos. Though in verses 5-20 Paul gives his personal exhortation to the Corinthians, verse 12a displays the sixth and the final use of Περὶ δὲ "Now concerning," in this book. Like in its earlier occurrence, the phrase Περὶ Δε gives the notion that Paul is responding to the questions asked by the Corinthians. It is assumed that the Corinthians have requested Paul to ask Apollos to return and minister among them. However, verse 12b displays Paul's personal request and encouragement to Apollos to visit the Corinthians.

Apollos was an eloquent preacher and an effective leader to them, and many in Corinth were anticipating his visit to them. This may also be the reason why Paul requests Apollos to visit Corinth. However, Paul's attitude towards Apollos is well displayed in verse 12b. In verse 12b Paul says, *I encouraged him greatly to come to you with the brethren; and it was not at all his desire to come now, but he will come when he has opportunity.* Though there was division in the church in the name of Paul, Apollos, Cephas, and Christ, Paul himself did not have any problem with Apollos. For Paul, though Apollos is an eloquent preacher and an effective leader, he is like Timothy, who is doing the ministry of God, just as he is. Thus, Paul commands the Corinthians to take good care of both of them when they reach Corinth.

2.2.7.4 Concern for the Spiritual Maturity of Corinthians [vv. 13-18 (19-20)]

After giving instructions about Timothy's coming and the news about Apollos' delay, Paul now expresses his concern for the spiritual maturity of the Corinthian believers. This section is also known as the general hortatory words of Paul to the Corinthians. However, the transition to this paragraph is abrupt, and the paragraph mixes both exhortations (vv. 13–14, 15b–16, 18b) and information about Corinthians who have met Paul in Ephesus (vv. 15a, 17–18a).

2.2.7.4.1 "A Christian Leader Must Properly Exercise his Responsibility by being Concerned for the Spiritual Maturity of His People"

Paul begins this section by giving them exhortations to become mature in their spiritual life (vv.13-14). Paul says, "*Be on the alert, stand firm in the faith, act like men, be strong. Let all that you do be done in love.*' These five exhortations are all in the present tense imperatives demanding continuous action from their side. First of all, the Corinthians are urged to "be watchful" or "alert." In the New Testament, these words are mostly used in connection to the eschatological context, urging watchfulness in connection to the Lords coming. Throughout the letter, Paul reminds the Corinthians of the coming eschatological judgment, which should shape how they live their lives. Thus, it gives us the idea that, this is a call for them to look intently for the coming of the Lord, and to conduct themselves in a way appropriate to that hope.

It is also applicable to the second imperative, "stand firm in the faith" which is considered to be the modified version of the expression in 15:1,58 wherein Paul mention about the Gospel which they have received and in which they are standing. Thus, it is understood as, Paul encouraging them to abide in the tradition which Paulhas passed on to them. The 3rd and 4th imperatives (*act like men, be strong*) encourages them to be courageous. While all the aforementioned imperatives have to do with their faithfulness in terms of the gospel they received, the final one is to do with their relationships to one another, for Paul says, "Let all that you do be done, in love."

In verses 15-18, Paul mentions *the characteristics of spiritual maturity***.** Paul gives five characteristics of spiritual maturity such as – *service, submission, friendship, hospitality,* and *affection.* In verse 15, Paul mentions about Stephan as and his family who have submitted themselves to serve the saints. Stephan as and his family were Paul's first converts in Achaia. They had given themselves selflessly to serving the Corinthians. So in verse 16, Paul's main concern is that the Corinthians should give proper recognition to Stephan as and his household, as one of the main problems the Corinthians had was, submitting themselves to authority. Thus, Paul says, submit to them as they labor for the Lord. In verse 17, Paul mentions about Fortunatus and Achaicus who helped him financially.

About hospitality, Paul says, Aquila and Priscilla opened up their home and hosted a church. In the New Testament, we see this couple's name mentioned in connection with three cities– Corinth, Ephesus, and Rome. And in all three places, they had a church in their home. Finally, Paul talks about affection in Christ. He says to the Corinth church, greet one another with the holy kiss (v.20) which expresses a kind of affection, unity, and oneness among them.

All the imperatives mentioned in this section are essential aspects of growing in maturity in the Lord, and in our relationships with God's people. Thus Paul underlies his concern for the spiritual maturity of his people and exhorts them to express these characteristics of spiritual maturity in their Christian life.

Summary

Even at the closing of the body of the letter, Paul was very particular in exercising his apostolic authority wisely in expressing his concern towards the suffering saints in Jerusalem, to his fellow-workers and to the Congregation in Corinth. In regards to the suffering saints in Corinth Paul instructs the Corinthians believers to do as he has commanded to the Galatians. Paul charges them to set aside money regularly on the first day of the week so that when he arrives in Corinth no collections will have to be made. He will write letters of introduction for the men who will carry the gift to Jerusalem, and he himself may accompany them if it is worthwhile. Before mentioning about his concern towards his co-workers, Paul reveals his travel plans to the Corinthians. He takes the opportunity to inform them about his forthcoming visit to Corinth and his wish to stay with them for a long time. However, Paul also mentions that the proposed visit will take place after a while since he got an opportunity for a fruitful evangelistic work at Ephesus. After giving his plan for the visit Paul informs them about the soon arrival of Timothy in Corinth, and Paul asks the Corinthians to receive him warmly because of his work. He advises the readers to send Timothy on his way. Paul also conveys them the unwillingness of Apollos, who was invited to visit Corinth, however, he gives them the hope that Apollos will visit them in the opportune time. Paul ends the section with his concern for the spiritual maturity of the Corinthians. He exhorts them to be alert, stand firm in their faith, be courageous, be strong and to do everything in love. Finally he exhort them to reflect the characteristics of the true spiritual maturity i.e., to submit themselves to all leaders who labored among them for the sake of Christ.

Endnotes

1. Dictionary of Paul and His Epistles.
2. The term *parakaleō* is used 6 times in 1 Corinthians (1:10; 4:13; 4:16; 14:31; 16:12; 16:15). The term *parakaleō* is the combination of two Greek words, para = beside + kaleo = to call- to call to one's side. It also means to do a good thing or for someone such as to summon, encourage or comfort them; or it may be pleading with someone for their benefit or our own, to call near, i.e., invite; beseech, call for, comfort, desire, exhort, to encourage, instruct, teach, etc.
3. Anthony C. Thiselton, The First Epistle to the Corinthians: *NIGTC* (Michigan: William B. Eerdmans Publishing Company, 2000), 184.
4. Joseph A. Fitzmyer, *I Corinthians, A New Translation with Introduction and Commentary* (Landon: Yale University Press, 2008), 156.
5. A particular way or method of doing something.
6. Leon Morries, I Corinthians, *TNTC* (Grand Rapids: William B. Eerdmans Publishing Company, 1985), 132.
7. Both the verbs are in aorist indicative active. It shows the action done in the past with reference to the time of speaking.
8. David E. Garland, I Corinthians, *BECNT* (Michigan: Baker Aademic, 2003), 111-112.
9. Richard A. Horsley, I Corinthians, *ANTC* (Nashville: Abingdon Press, 1998), 64.
10. Four kinds of questions are common in Greek: 1) Ordinary Question, 2) Hesitant questions, 3) Question expecting the answer 'No', 4) Question expecting the answer 'Yes.' W. Wenham, *The Elements of New Testament Gree*k (Cambridge: University Press, 1965), 75.
11. Jouette M. Bassler, "Expository Article on I Corinthians 4:1-5," *Interpretation*, Vol. XLIV (April 1990), 181.
12. Horsley, *ANTC*, 71.
13. Mac Arthuer, *I Corinthians* (Chicago: Moody Press, 1984), 137.
14. Refer to footnote 36.
15. Kistemaker, *BNTC,* 180.
16. Fitzmyer, *First Corinthians*, 254.
17. Garland, *BECNT*, 222.
18 Fitzmyr, *I Corinthians*, 263.
19. Bruce, *I Corinthians*, 62.
20. Garland, *BECNT*, 229.
21. Kistemaker, *First Epistle to the Corinthians*, 133.
22. The dative substantive indicate the person interested in the verbal action.
23. Fitzmyer, *1 Corinthians*, 260.
24. Anthony C. Thiselton, The First Epistle to the Corinthians, *NIGTC* (Michigan: Eerdmans, 2000), 475.
25. Some translations like NEB, NRSV, and NIV do not consider the last clause part of the Corinthian slogan but many scholars do. For example, Thiselton, Hays, Barrett and Bruce.
26. Fee, *I Corinthians*, 275.
27. Fitzmyer, *I Corinthians*, 280.

28. Thiselton, *NIGTC*, 508.
29. Fitzmyer, *I Corinthians*, 293.
30. Kistemaker, *BNTC*, 225.
31. Fee, *NICNT*, 302.
32. John F. MacArthur, *I Corinthians* (Chicago: Moody Press, 1984), 114.
33. As cited in Thiselton, *NIGTC*, 552.
34. MacArthur, *I Corinthians*, 115.
35. Thiselton, *NIGTC,* 551.
36. MacArthur, *I Corinthians*, 115.
37. Kistemaker, *BNTC*, 232.
38. Fee, *The First Epistle to the Corinthians*, 322.
39. MacArthur, *I Corinthians*, 178.
40. Fitzmyer, *I Corinthians*, 314.
41. Elliott, J. K. "Paul's teaching on Marriage in I CorinthiansL Some Problems Considered," *NTS* 19 (1972-73) 219; Hurley, R., "To Marry or Not to Marry: The Interpretation of I Cor 7:36-38," *EstBib* 58 (2000) 16; Ford, J.M., "Levirate Marriage in St. Paul (I Cor.vii)," *NTS* 10 (1963-64) 362 as cited in Fitzmyer, *First Corinthians*, 314.
42. Carson, *NBC*, 18.
43. Kistemaker, *BNTC*, 238.
44. Kistemaker, *BNTC*, 251.
45. Robertson, A. and A. Plummer, *A Critical and Exegetical Commentary on the First Epistle of St. Paul to the Corinthians* (Edinburgh: Clark, 1914), 242.
46. Conzelmann, H. *I Corinthians* (Philadelphia: Fortress, 1975), 177-178.
47. Barrett, C. K. The First Epistles to the Corinthians. *HNTC* (New York: Harper & Row, 1968), 242.
48. Peter D. Gooch, *Dangerous Food; I Corinthians 8-10 in its Context* (Canada: Wilfrid Laurier University, 1954), 38-40.
49. Gooch, Dangerous food, 37; Garland, I Corinthians, *BECNT*, 348.
50. Gooch, *Dangerous Food*, 43.
51. MacArthuer, *I Corinthians*, 190.
52. MacArthuer, *I Corinthians*, 190.
53. Fitzmyer, *I Corinthians*, 338.
54. Carson, *NBC,* 20.
55. Fitzmyer, *I Corinthians*, 345.
56. Οὐκ is used before a word stats with smooth breathingand Οὐχὶ is used before a word starts with rough breathing. J. W. Wenham, *The Elements of New Testament Greek* (Cambridge: University Press, 1965), 200.
57. Leon Morris, The First Epistle of Paul to the Corinthians: An Introduction and Commentary, *TNTC*, 2d ed. (Grand Rapids: Eerdmans Publishing Co, 1985), 130.
58. John C. Hurd, *The Origin of 1 Corinthians* (Macon: Mercer University Press, 1983), 109.
59. Fitzmyer, *I Corinthians*, 358.
60. Kistemaker, *BNTC,* 292.
61. Kistemaker, *BNTC*, 325.
62. Fitzmyer, *I Corinthians*, 378; Kistemaker, *BNTC*, 327.
63. Fitzmyer, *I Corinthians*, 386.
64. Fee, *NICNT*, 464.
65. Fitzmayer, *First Corinthians*, 389.

66. Fitzmyer, *First Corinthians*, 398.
67. Fitzmyer, *First Corinthians*, 400.
68. The word parado,seij, *paradoseis* is a technical term used in the Jewish culture for the oral transmission of religious instruction. B. Gerhardsson, Memory and Manuscript: Oral Tradition and Written Transmission in Rabbinic Judaism and Early Christianity (Michigan: WB. Eerdmans Publishing, 1961), 290.
69. Fee, *NICNT*, 503.
70. Kistemaker, *BNTC*, 366.
71. Jerome Murphy O'Connor, "The First Letter to the Corinthians," *The New Jerome Biblical Commentary* I. Edited by Raymond E. Brown, Joseph A. Fitzmyer and Ronald E. Murphy. (Bangalore: Theological Publication in India, 2002), 809.
72. B. W. Winter, After Paul Left Corinth: *The Influence of Secular Ethics and Social Change* (Grand Rapids: Eerdmans, 2001), 127.
73. Fitzmyer, *First Corinthians*, 413.
74. Kistemaker, *BNTC*, 370.
75. Morna D. Hooker, "Authority on Her Head: An Examination of I Cor. XI.10," *NTS* 10 (1963–64): 415–16, as cited in Kistemaker, *BNTC*, 376.
76. James B. Hurley, "Did Paul Require Veils or the Silence of Women? A Consideration of 1 Cor. 11:2–16 and 1 Cor. 14:33b–36, "*WTJ* 35 (1973): 193–204, as cited in Kistemaker, BNTC, 377.
77. A. Robertson and A. Plummer, *A Critical and Exegetical Commentary on the First Epistle of St. Paul to the Corinthians* (New York: Scribner's Sons, 1975), 232.
78. P. Rose "Power on the Head," *ExpTim 23* (1911-12): 183-84.
79. Fitzmyer, *First Corinthians*, 417.
80. Fitzmyer, *First Corinthians*, 418.
81. Fitzmyer, *First Corinthians*, 418.
82. R. F. Collins, "Reflections on I Corinthians as a Hellenistic Letter," The Corinthian Correspondance (BETL: Bieringer,_____), 40; O'Connor, "Sex and Logic in I Corinthians 11:2-16," *CBQ* 50 (1988), 497; Garland, I Corinthians, *BECNT*, 60; R. B. Hays, *First Corinthians* (Louisville: John Knox, 1997), 89.
83. Joseph A. Fitzmyer, "A Feature of Qumran Angelology and the Angels of I Cor. XI.10," *NTS* 4 (1957–58): 48–58.
84. Barrett, C. K. *A Commentary on the First Epistle to the Corinthians*. Harper's New Testament Commentaries series (New York and Evanston: Harper and Row, 1968), 256.
85. Kistemaker, *BNTC*, 381-82.
86. Fee, *NICNT*, 561.
87. Thiselton, *The First Epistle to the Corinthians*, 517.
88. Thiselton, *The First Epistle to the Corinthians*, 517.
89. Fitzmyer, *First Corinthians*, 447.
90. Fitzmyer, *First Corinthians*, 476.
91. Fee, *NICNT*, 613.
92. Kistemaker, *BNTC*, 439.
93. Fitzmyer, *First Corinthians*, 488.
94. Fitzmyer, *First Corinthians*, 492.
95. Kistemaker, *BNTC*, 458.
96. Fee, The First Epistle to the Corinthians, *NICNT*, 718. Mark I.Wegener, "The rhetorical strategy of 1 Corinthians 15," *Currents in Theology and Mission* 31/6 (2004): 438.

97. Thiselton, The First Epistle to the Corinthians, *NIGTC*, 1214.
98. Thiselton, *The First Epistle*, 1214; Wegener, "The rhetorical strategy of 1 Corinthians 15," 447.
99. Fee, *The First Epistle to the*, 713.
100. Garland, 1 Corinthians, *BECNT*, 697.
101. The force of the perfect passive ἐγήγερται is that Christ was raised and continues to live, i.e., the present state on the basis of past event or the present reality of the historic fact. Thiselton, *The First Epistle to the Corinthians*, 1216; W. Harold Mare, *I Corinthians* (Michigan: Zondervan, 1976), 283.
102. Thiselton, *The First Epistle to the Corinthians*, 680.
103. Garland, *1 Corinthians*, 698.
104. The Greek word is mine.
105. Fee, *The First Epistle to the*, 740.
106. Margaret M. Mitchell, *Paul and the Rhetoric of Reconciliation: An Exegetical Investigation of the Language and Composition of 1 Corinthians* (Louisville: Westminster John Knox Press, 1993), 176-177.
107. Garland, *1 Corinthians*, 698.
108. Fee, *The First Epistle to the Corinthians*, 741.
109. Fee, *The First Epistle to the Corinthians*, 715.
110. Fee, *The First Epistle to the Corinthians*, 715.
111. Gnosticism emphasized the dualism between spirit (God, whichis good) and matter (material things, which are evil).
112. Ray C. Stedman, *Letters to a Troubled Church: First and the Second Corinthians* (Michigan: Discovery House, 2007), 170.
113. Fee, *The First Epistle to the Corinthians*, 715.
114. Kistemaker, First Epistle to the Corinthians, *BNTC*, 540.
115. Fee, *The First Epistle to the Corinthians*, 715.
116. Kistemaker, *First Epistle to the Corinthians*, 540.
117. Thiselton, *The First Epistle to the Corinthians*, 1172-1173.
118. Garland, *1 Corinthians*, 698.
119. Garland, *1 Corinthians*, 678.
120. Wilson, J. H., "The Corinthians Who Say There Is No Resurrection of the Dead," *ZNW* 59 (1968): 94.
121. Thiselton, *The First Epistle to the Corinthians*, 1218.
122. Richard A. Horsley, 1 Corinthians, *ANTC* (Nashville: Abingdon Press, 1998), 197.
123. Kistemaker, *First Epistle to the Corinthians*, 541.
124. Kistemaker, *First Epistle to the Corinthians*, 541.
125. Fee, *The First Epistle to the Corinthians*, 741.
126. A syllogism (Greek: συλλογισμός- "conclusion," "inference") is a kind of logical argument in which one proposition (the conclusion) is inferred from two or more others (the premises) of a certain form. A categorical syllogism consists of three parts: the major premise, the minor premise and the conclusion.
127. William F. Orr and James Arthur Walther, *I Corinthians* (Garden City: Doubleday and Company, INC., 1976), 325-326.
128. The major premise presents general categories, general alternatives or general conditions. Thus it is known as a statement of a general or universal nature.
129. The minor premise represents an instance of what is presented in the major premise.
130. It is the inevitable result of accepting the major and minor premise.

131. Jerome Murphy. O'Connor, "The First Letter to the Corinthians," *The New Jerome Biblical Commentary* (ed. Raymond E. Brown, Joseph A. Fitzmyer and Roland E. Murphy; Bangalore: Theological Publications in India, 2002), 812.
132. Thiselton, *The First Epistle to the Corinthians*, 1218.
133. Kistemaker, *First Epistle to the Corinthians*, 541.
134. Fee, *The First Epistle to the Corinthians*, 742.
135. Here "Christ" has the article; perhaps it is anaphoric (= the Christ of whom we are speaking). More likely the title is always implied in the name. Hence "Christ the Messiah."
136. Fee, *The First Epistle to the Corinthians*, 742.
137. Kistemaker, *First Epistle to the*, 543; Orr, *I Corinthians*, 324; Fee, *The First Epistle to the*, 742.
138. Kistemaker, *First Epistle to the Corinthians*, 543
139. Fee, *The First Epistle to the Corinthians*, 742.
140. Fee, *The First Epistle to the Corinthians*, 742.
141. Orr, *I Corinthians*, 324.
142. O'Connor, "The First Letter, 812.
143. Kistemaker, *First Epistle to the*, 543.
144. Thiselton, *The First Epistle to the Corinthians*, 1219-1220.
145. Thiselton, *The First Epistle to the Corinthians*, 1220.
146. Kistemaker, *First Epistle to the Corinthians*, 544.
147. Kistemaker, *First Epistle to the Corinthians*, 544.
148. Wolfhart Pannenberg, *Jesus: God and Man* (translated by Duane Priebe and Lewis L. Wilkins; Philadelphia: Westminster Press, 1968), 74.
149. Fee, *The First Epistle to the Corinthians*, 744.
150. Kistemaker, *BNTC*, 549.
151. Fitzmyer, *First Corinthiasn*, 573.
152. TDNT, 4: 282-83.
153. Fitzmyer, *First Corinthians*, 613.
154. *Thiselton, The First Epistles to the Corinthians*, 753.
155. The other two are Acts 20:7 and Rev. 1:10. Fee, *NICNT*, 813.
156. Fee, *NICNT*, 813.

Chapter 3

THE CLOSING

The Peace Benediction, Hortatory Section, Greetings, Autograph, and the Grace Benediction

3. The Closing (16:19-24)

The closing of Pauline letters are usually signaled by the eschatological conclusion (Rom.11:25-36; I Thess. 3:11-13). Paul has also used the typical closing greetings of Hellenistic letters in order to link the congregations with his own traveling ministry (Rom 16:3–16, 21–23; 2 Cor. 13:12–13; Col 4:10–17). However, he did not include the customary health wish or Greek word of farewell, instead, a benediction (1 Cor. 16:23; Gal 6:16, 18; Eph. 6:23–24; 2 Thess. 3:16, 18); or doxology (Rom.16:25–27; Phil 4:20; Heb. 13:20–21). The final benediction, which brings the letter to a definitive conclusion, often gives expression to Paul's strong desire (that the grace of the Lord Jesus may be with them, 1 Cor. 16:24) and strikes a note of confidence.Other closing conventions Paul used includes references to his writing a phrase or two in his own hand (1 Cor. 16:21; Gal 6:11; Col 4:18; 2 Thess. 3:17), his use of a secretary (Tertius, Rom 16:22), and a form of greeting one another (a holy kiss, Rom 16:16) etc.

However, technically there are five main elements that consistently appears in the Pauline letter closings such as: the peace benediction, hortatory section, greetings, autograph, and the grace benediction. All these elements, though not seen in all of his epistles, serves the larger purpose of the letter as a whole.

3.1 The Peace Benediction

The peace benediction is referred to by a number of different titles such as: prayer wish,[1] homiletic benediction,[2] and the benedictory prayer.[3] Such kinds of benedictions were very common in the Semitic and the Greco-Roman letter writings. Both, the peace wish of the Semitic letters and the health wish of Greco-Roman letters were considered as the closing of the whole letter. Though J. L White do not agree with this fact,[4] a strong evidence to this is seen in the deliberate inclusion that is formed with the opening salutation of the Pauline letter, *grace to you and peace*, which appears at the beginning of the letter that is echoed in a chiastic fashion at its closing, first by the peace benediction which is followed by the grace benediction. This proves that the chiastic repetition of the grace and peace wish in the opening and closing sections demonstrate its close connection not only to the body of the letter but to the letter as a whole.

3.1.1 Basic Elements of Peace Benediction

Though we do not have a peace benediction in I Corinthians, it is important to know its basic elements in various Pauline letters. The peace benediction is seen only in six of Pauline letters, but seven occurrences, such as Romans (15:33, 16:20); 2 Corinthians (13:11); Galatians (6:16); Philippians (4:9); 1 Thessalonians (5:23); and 2 Thessalonians (3:16). All these occurrences are marked with a consistent pattern that involves four basic elements.

First of all, these peace benedictions start with the *introductory elements* that consist either the adversative particle δὲ when a peace benediction occupies the first position in a letter closing (Rom. 15:33; 1 Thess. 5:23; 2 Thess. 3:16; Rom 16:20a), or the conjunction και when it is preceded in the closing by other epistolary elements (2 Cor. 13:11b; Gal. 6:16; Phil. 4:9b).[5]

Next, there will be a *divine source* of wish, i.e., a wish that has God as its source, in contrast to the grace benediction. In most occasions, the divine source is the Lord Jesus Christ. This is a chiastic expression that naturally follows from the salutation in the opening of the letter.[6]

Next, the content or the wish of the peace benediction is complicated in some instance because of its use of *to be* verbs which is either used specifically or is indirectly implied. In the former case, the content of the wish is taken from the qualifying genitive phrase, thus Paul's statement, *may the God of peace be with you* is equivalent to saying *may the God of peace give you peace*. In fact, the peace benediction of 2 Thess. 3:16 states this wish explicitly: *May the Lord of peace himself give you peace*. In the latter case, the content of the wish still includes peace (since the source is similarly "the God of peace"), but also includes an additional wish expressed by the transitive verb.[7]

Finally, the section is marked with the inclusion of the recipient of the peace benediction. The recipients are frequently introduced with the preposition μετά (*meta* - with) and followed by the personal pronoun in the second person plural ὑμῶν (*humon* – you).[8] Though there is a slight change in some of the peace benediction in this regard, the identity of the recipient is always indicated by the second person plural form.

3.2 Hortatory Section

The word *hortatory* is defined as, a strong plea or request of a person so as to take a particular action by the addressee. The word has its root in the Latin word *hortatorius,* which means encouraging or cheering, from *hortatus*, past participle of *hortari*, means to exhort, encourage, urge, incite, or instigate. Both, in the writings of the antiquity and in the Pauline corpus, such passage represents the attempt of the writer to have the addressee do something or act in a certain way. In other words, a hortatory exposition is a text, whose purpose is to persuade the readers that something should, or should not be the case, or be done. However, comparing to the other four epistolary elements, the hortatory passages found in the closing of the Pauline writing divulges that these final exhortations are neither organized nor tightly structured.

3.2.1 Basic Elements of Hortatory Section

There are two main elements that are very common to the hortatory passages of the Pauline letters. The first element is the use of the word Λοιπόν (*Loipon*–finally), which is a less common means by which the hortatory sections are introduced in Paul's letters (2 Cor. 13:11; Gal. 6:17; Phil. 4:8). The section is also signaled by a command (use of imperative mood) which is obviously seen in the hortatory materials. In the absence of an imperative mood, a verb of entreaty or adjuration expresses the same mood such as Παρακαλῶ [*Parakalō*-to exhort, urge (Rom.16:17; I Cor.16:15); 'Ενορκίζω (*Enorkizo* - to charge, to adjure) (1Thess. 5:27)].

The second element which is mostly seen as part of Pauline hortatory section is the vocative expression of the word ἀδελφός (*adelphos* - brother). The word occurs frequently in Pauline hortatory in its vocative case ἀδελφóI [*adelphos* – brothers, lit. O brothers (Rom.16:17-18:19b; 2 Cor. 13:11a; Gal. 6:17; Phil. 4:8-9a; 1 Thess. 5:25-27; Phil. 20)]. The same expression was also very common in ancient Greek letters.

The hortatory section in 1 Corinthians is also gesticulated by the vocative case ἀδελφόι. Traditionally, 1 Corinthians 16:13-22 is considered as the hortatory section. However, in this author's observation, verses 19-22 falls under two other sections of Pauline conclusion (vv.19-21: greetings; vv.21-22: autograph). Since verses 13-18 is brought under the main heading to prove how a Christian leader must properly exercise his responsibilities with regards to his concern for the spiritual maturity of his congregation (cfr. 2.2.7.4.1), verses 13-18 is not included under the closing section.

However, in verse 15 with the vocative case ἀδελφοι Paul exhorts the Corinthians to honor the household of Stephanas and others like him who labored in their midst. This hortatory element is used here probably because a cardinal issue with the Corinthians was their disrespect for spiritual leaders who worked diligently among them to advance the cause of Christ.

3.3 Greetings

This section in Pauline letters is meant to convey the closing greetings to the recipients. It mostly includes an occasional command that they greet each other with a "holy kiss", a cultural norm. Through such closing Paul vividly reflects the epistolary practice of his day, as such greetings were a common feature of Hellenistic and Semitic letters. However, Paul did not blindly follow the Hellenistic and Semitic writers rather customized it in such a way that helped him to express his and his fellow-workers intimate affection to the readers. Thus, Weima comments that the primary function of Paul's closing greetings was that of expressing 'philophronesis,' which means, the friendly relations that existed between Paul and his letter's recipients.[9] Such kind of expression was very important for Paul, because being a busy evangelist, missionary, and church planter, among other things, it was impossible for Paul to be with, or visit his congregations, as he wants. Hence, the greetings served as a means to convey his affection and spiritual presence with his readers.

It is also interesting to look into the different kinds of greetings in Pauline letters. Weima classifies Pauline greetings under four titles, such as-first person type greetings, second person type greetings, third person type greetings, and cultural greetings.[10]

3.3.1 Different Types and Elements of Pauline Greetings

3.3.1.1 First Person Greetings

First person type of Paul's greeting is found only in his letter to the Romans, where his secretary, Tertius personally greets the readers. Therefore, such kind of Paul's direct greeting (ἀσπάζομαι, *aspazomai* - I greet) is not found in Pauline writings. Even such kind of greetings was not commonly used in Hellenistic letters. It is assumed that because of the personal greetings in the opening salutation of his letters, Paul avoided it in the closing.

3.3.1.2 Second Person Greetings

In this category, the addressee become the agent of the sender of the letter as they play the role of establishing and maintain communication with a third party. Such occurrences in Pauline letter suggest that the people being specifically greeted were not part of the congregation to which the letter is primarily addressed. Thus, as Mullins states, such kinds of greeting employed by Paul posturizes his close relation and confidence in his recipients that they will act on behalf of him.[11] This form of greetings are the most frequent type of greetings, seen twenty times in the letters of Paul.

3.3.1.3 Third Person Greetings (vv. 19-20a)

In this category, Paul passes the greetings of others who are with him to his addressees. This kind of greetings' form is given either in the singular or the plural of the present indicative, depending on the number of those sending greetings. In this regard, Paul plays the role of an agent expressing greetings on behalf of specific individuals (1 Cor. 16:19b; Rom. 16:21, 23; Phlm. 23); or well-defined groups (1 Cor. 16:19a; Phil. 4:22); or of a general group (1 Cor. 16:20; 2 Cor. 13:12b; Phil. 4:21); on behalf of all saints (2 Cor.13:12b); or on behalf of all churches of Christ (Rom. 16:16b). All the above-mentioned category of greetings commonly follows the basic elements of the Greco-Roman letters such as, the greeting verb, the giver of the greetings, and the recipients of the greetings.

The best example of such greeting which includes the verb, sender, and the recipient, is seen in 1 Corinthians 16:19-20. *The verb* employed in this section is ἀσπάζομαι (*aspazomai* – lit. he, she, or it greets) that occurs four times in this section (19a and b; 20a and b).

With regards to *the sender*, verses 19 and 20 gives three specifications such as (a) all the churches of Asia, (b) Aquila and Priscilla, and the church that meets in their house, and (c) all the brothers present with Paul at the time of writing this letter. The greeting from all the churches of a province occurs only here in Paul's extant letters. Though it is difficult to specify the number of churches and who are they, possibly these churches may have been established through the ministry of Paul during his missionary journeys.

The greeting from Aquila and Pricilla probably reflects a twofold reality. First, these were former Corinthians (Acts 18:2-3), who now join Paul in warmly greeting old friends. Secondly, this is most likely the house church in Ephesus to which Paul himself is attached. Hence, the greeting comes not only from their friends but from the church as well. Like in the first case (the churches of Asia), one cannot be sure whether "all the brothers" in v. 20a is a redundant generalizing, or whether, more likely, it refers to Paul's various fellow-workers and traveling companions. However, Paul conveys everyone's greetings to the Corinthians as he sends this letter.

With regards to *the recipients*, only once the personal pronoun is used to emphasize the recipients of these greetings. In verse 19b Paul says, ἀσπάζεταιὑμᾶςἐνκυρίῳ (*aspazetaihumasen kuriō* - greet **you** in the Lord). Though the name of the recipient is not mentioned specifically, it is implied that Paul writes this letter to the Corinthian congregation.

3.3.1.4 Greetings with Holy Kiss (v. 20b)

Paul's command to greet one another with a 'holy kiss' is a distinct type of greeting identified only in four of his writings (Rom. 16:16; 1 Cor. 16:20;

2 Cor. 13:12; 1 Thess. 5:26). Such practice as part of greeting was widespread in the countries of the East, especially in East Asian countries. Throughout the Old Testament and in Inter-Testamental literature we see examples of such practice of Jews greeting one another with a kiss. This practice was very common in Palestine even during the time of Jesus (Mk.14:45; Lk. 7:45; 15:20), and in Paul's time (Acts 20:37). Though it is not emphasized much in all the New Testament books, Paul in his writings explicitly refers to this greeting as a *holy* kiss. By employing the term *holy,* Paul distinguishes the kiss between believers and those outside the faith. For people outside the faith, a kiss was just an expression of friendship and goodwill; but among the believers it had a deeper meaning, showing unity and belongingness as part of the body of Christ. Thus in verse 20b, while Paul commands the Corinthians to greet each other with the holy kiss, it is more than just an exhortation. It is a strong command to all the believers to maintain unity among themselves, as they are the members of the body of Christ.

3.4 Autograph (21a)

In v.21a Paul says, Ο ἀσπασμὸςτῇ ἐμῇ χειρὶ Παύλου (*ho aepasmostēmē cheri Paulou* – I Paul, write this greeting **with my own hand**. This distinct formula of greeting is seen also in 2 Thess. 3:17; Col. 4:18; Gal 6:11; and Phlm.19. It was a common feature used in all the ancient letters. Though the content of the letter was mostly dictated, the closing part was written by the sender himself. The phrase τῇ ἐμῇ χειρὶ (*tēemē cheri* - with my own hand) in v.21 implies that Paul till this part of his letter was using an amanuensis (a secretary), but now, writes his personal greetings with his own hands.

3.5 The Grace Benediction (v. 23)

In Paul's day, the secular letters naturally ended with the *farewell wish,* expressed either with words like, *be strong* (also seen in Acts 15:29- ἔρρωσθε) or, *prosper* (ευ'τύχει). This kind of expression indicated the absolute closing of a letter. However, in Pauline letters, it is replaced by the Christian grace benediction i.e., the grace of the Lord Jesus be with you. This is the most common epistolary convention found at the end of Paul's letters.

3.5.1 The Elements of Grace Benediction

The grace benediction commonly consisted of three basic elements–the wish, the divine source, and the recipient.

The wish of the grace benediction is grace. Paul's grace benedictions are a call to God to give his recipients the gift of grace, in contrast to the secular farewell that expresses the desire that the readers would have physical strength or success. In some instances, the wish forms an inverted or chiastic inclusion with the greeting of the letter opening, *Grace to you and peace.*[12]

The divine source in the grace benediction is expressed by means of genitive phrase τοῦ κυρίου'Ιησοῦ (*toukuriouYe¯sou meth humon* – Lit. of the Lord Jesus). Although Paul usually refers to God as the source of grace, most often, in the closing, Christ is depicted as the source of grace.

The recipients of the wish or the benediction normally signaled by the prepositional phrase μεθ'ὑμῶν (*meth humon* – with you). However, the mood of this benediction varies from letter to letter. It also occurs in many other ways, such as, the grace of our Lord Jesus Christ *is* with you (indicative mood); the grace of our Lord Jesus Christ *be* with you (imperative mood); and, *may* the grace of our Lord Jesus Christ be with you (optative mood) which is most commonly used by Paul (Rom.15:5-6; 15:13; 1 Thess. 3:11; 3:12-13; 2 Thess. 2:16-17; 3:5; 3:16 etc.).[13] Since in most occasions the optative mood is employed in the grace benediction, it is clear that it is Paul himself who is conveying a wish or a prayer to Christ to send his grace into the hearts and lives of his readers.

Summary

1 Corinthians ends with greetings that included various elements of an epistolary closing. The section consisted of greetings from three groups-from churches in the province of Asia, from Aquila and Priscilla along with their house church, and from all believers. At the end, Paul gave his greetings written by his own hands.

However, the detailed analysis of this closing section demonstrated that this is not just a literary construct like the closing of the Greco-Roman letters, but a very significant part of Pauline letters. We saw that in most of his letters there were five main elements (peace benediction, hortatory section, greetings, autograph, and grace benediction). All these elements served the larger purpose of his letters.

We also observed that Paul generally shaped and adapted his letter endings in such a way as to relate this final section directly to the major concerns of the letter as a whole. Consequently, it demonstrated great explanatory value, providing important clues for understanding the key issues and themes addressed in the content, as well as enlightening us about the readers and their *sitz-im-leben*. Thus, Pauline letter closings play an important role in any investigatory explanation of his letters.

Endnotes

1. G.P. Wiles, *Paul's Intercessory Prayers* (Cambridge: Cambridge University Press, 1974), 63–68.
2. R. Jewett, "The Form and Function of the Homiletic Benediction," *ATR* 51 (1969): 18–34.
3. G. Fee, *God's Empowering Presence: The Holy Spirit in the Letters of Paul* (Peabody: Hendrickson,1994), 63.

4. According to him, the peace benediction of Pauline letters are the formal closure of the letter body than the letter as a whole. J.L. White, "Ancient Greek Letters," in D. E. Aune (ed.), *Greco-Roman Literature and the New Testament* (Atlanta: Scholars Press, 1988), 97.
5. Jeffrey A. D Weima. *Sincerely, Paul: The Significance of the Pauline Letter Closing* (Grand Rapids: Calvin Theological Seminary, 2010), 311.
6. Weima. *Sincerely Paul*, 311.
7. Weima. *Sincerely Paul,* 313.
8. Weima. *Sincerely Paul,* 313.
9. Weima, *Neglectd Endings: The Significance of the Pauline Letter Closing* (Sheffield: Academic Press, 1994), 115.
10. Weima. *Sincerely Paul,* 325-332; Weima, *Neglectd Endings,* 107-109.
11. David Philip Mullins, *Greetings from Below* (Louisville: Sarabande Books, 2010), 425-426.
12. Weima. *Sincerely Paul,* 341.
13. Weima. *Sincerely Paul,* 343.

Conclusion

The church to which this letter was addressed was located in the midst of a very corrupt city and culture. The immorality of the city was such that, throughout the Mediterranean world the term *Corinthian girl* was considered a synonym for a promiscuous woman. In such a city, Paul established the church with few members. Gradually, the congregation grew in number and was blessed with different kinds of spiritual gifts.

However, the church started to collapse in its spiritual life because of internal and external issues such as pride, immorality, and emphasis on social status. Their divisions, lack of church discipline, lawsuits, the wrong exercise of Christian liberty, misbehavior during Lord's Supper, and overemphasis on the gift of speaking in tongues etc. turned one of the most spiritually blessed church, into a most troubled church of first century Christianity.

Paul began his letter by addressing them as the church of God who are sanctified in Christ Jesus and called to be saints/holy. The first nine verses of the book are saturated with reasons for hope. In spite of the willful sins they committed, Paul did not question their conversion experience but affirmed the present and future benefits of their call and commitment, and systematically corrected them for their wrongdoings (1:10-16:18).

Though Paul corrected them with harsh words and sharp sarcasm, he clarifies that he does not mean to shame or denigrate them, but admonish them as beloved children. As a good leader and the spiritual father of the Corinthians, Paul's desire was to see them becoming true imitators of Jesus, just as him. Though Paul gave specific arguments in each section, the pinnacle of his argument is seen in chapter 13, where he emphasizes **the importance of love, over and above everything else**.

The myriad problems the church at Corinth faced is not foreign to the present churches. These irregularities are clearly seen even in today's churches, both in its social and religious domains. Thus, the advice Paul gave to the church at Corinth is equally applicable for all churches in all times. Hence, one cannot undermine this letter whose efficacy is limited only to the believers of the first century Christianity.

Consequently, the significance of I Corinthians remains the same; for as long as the church exists, it is imperative for all Christians to learn lessons from this letter of Paul to the Corinthian, to view the church as the body of Christ, and to remain in the love of God and to grow in unity and strength.

May the church remain holy and blameless… *Soli Deo Gloria!*